THE ESSENTIAL
WEIMARANER

Patsy Hollings

RINGPRESS

Published by Ringpress Books Ltd,
POBox 8, Lydney, Gloucestershire GL15 6YD

Discounts available for bulk orders
Contact the Special Sales Manager at
the above address. Telephone 01594 563800

First Published 1996
© 1996 RINGPRESS BOOKS
AND PATSY HOLLINGS

ISBN 1 86054 091 0

Printed and bound in Singapore
by Kyodo Printing Co

CONTENTS

4

Acknowledgements

While I have indeed written this book, it must be said that Stephen, my husband, and I work as a team and therefore he has contributed equally, both through knowledge gained and support.

Thanks must also go to all who sent photos and information which both enthralled and fascinated me and will, hopefully, do the same for the readers. Thank you to Keith Allison for the wonderful photography work and to Val Grant for her dedication, time and effort in deciphering my writing and transferring it to legible print via the computer.

Thanks must also go to Ines Dawes for contributions on Germany, and to Fern Sweet for her excellent line drawings.

Title page photograph (pictured left to right): Aust. Ch. Besko Silver Rose, Aust. Ch. Besko Silver Baron, and Aust. Ch. Besko Yartune.

PREFACE

This versatile 'Jack of All Trades' breed suits many owners' needs, either for work, as a show dog, or as a welcome additional family 'member' who will integrate into the lifestyle of many families with great success. The dedication of breeders of note, be they past, present or consistently there, have produced a breed to be proud of, through soundness in construction, temperament and versatility. Over the years this breed has steadily improved, with many facets of the dog's ability being jealously preserved.

It was said to me by Di Arrowsmith that "Weimaraners are retrievers who point as opposed to GSP, Vizsla and GWP, who are pointers that retrieve." This statement has proved true for me and describes where the Weimaraner differs so much from the other HPR breeds when working. The Weimaraner's thinking also differs from the breeds associated with obedience. This is an intelligent dog but also a questioning one who will only respond positively to a command if there is respect between the dog and the handler and the exercise set is of worth. If asked repetitively to perform a command that serves no useful purpose, the Weimaraner will look down that aristocratic nose and defy you. This is a quick-thinking dog who responds to intelligent clear rules and who, given respect, will return that respect twofold.

Chapter One

THE DEVELOPMENT OF THE WEIMARANER

The Weimaraner was first recognised as a pure breed and entered into the German Stud Book in 1896. Yet, this was not the real beginning of a breed that is equally valued for its looks and its working ability. In fact, much of the Weimaraner's history is shrouded in mystery. We do know that Grand Prince Karl August, born in 1757 and head of the court of Weimar, fancied the breed, and members of his court were allowed to own and hunt with it. The Grand Duke lived in Weimar, now an industrial town, in the district of Erfurt in Germany. He first encountered the breed while hunting on the estate of Prince Esterhazy e Aversperg in Bohemia and recognised how the attributes of the Weimaraner would lend themselves perfectly to his environment and needs.

The forests around Weimar were rich in game such as wild boar, wildcat and deer, and this powerful, courageous, athletic breed, with an inherent protective instinct, provided the perfect aid to the Grand Duke's hunting activities. He wielded great power and therefore dictated who could have the breed for hunting purposes. Carefully protected, the Weimaraner was not allowed to be owned as a pet. The Duke primarily developed the breed for his family and high ranking members of his court and nobility. Breeding programmes were secret and any records pertaining to the breed were closely guarded, and appear to have been either destroyed or lost, which is why speculation abounds regarding the ancestry of the breed. The name Weimaraner was obviously taken from the Duke's home of Weimar and he is the person who bred and developed the breed in any numbers. Although it does appear to be a very old breed it is not known exactly how old, but there is a dog bearing an uncanny resemblance to the Weimaraner featured in a painting at the side of the young Prince Rupprecht von Pfalz by Van Dyck (circa 1631).

The St Hubertus Branchen, named after the monks at the monastery of St Hubert in the Ardennes, is often thought to be the most likely ancestor. These were heavily-built dogs, long in body and of medium height with excellent noses for hunting, coupled with power and hunting ability. They were black, with red or fawn marks over their eyes and similar markings on the legs, with only occasionally a small white mark on the chest. Looking at the description it is easy to see why they are thought to be the most likely ancestors of the Weimaraner. It is proven that two black animals can produce a grey one, leading us back to this breed again. Another point is that occasionally puppies today can be produced with the ginger marking over the eyes and on the legs.

Interestingly, the St Hubertus Branchen was thought to have originally been sent to France by the monks of Morgan Abbey in England, then on to Germany. The Branchen is thought by Professor Lutz Heck, a former director of the Berlin Zoo, to be the oldest breed of hunting dog and the one from which all hunting dogs descend. In 1940 Professor Ferlinger explained that 'Branchen' as a word could be traced back to the Bishop Brancie who lived in the 7th century. He was a renowned hunter and used such dogs on his hunt. All these facts convince me that the

The Weimaraner still retains the instinct and power to retrieve game such as fox, as demonstrated by Steve Riley's Savril Lucky Strike.

Weimaraner was originally a mutation within the Branchen hound. The grey mutations were then paired to produce the Weimaraner.

Given the dog's excellent scenting abilities and inclination to ground-scent rather than air-scent, this leads me to think there are probably hound origins within the breed – and, for example, the Bloodhound is thought to have the Branchen in his forefathers. It is also thought that all 'Vorstenhunde' (German name for Pointers) had the Branchen in their ancestry.

RECOGNITION OF THE WEIMARANER

1887 was the year the Weimaraner Club of Germany was formed, following the long struggle to have the breed recognised. It was another Karl, the celebrated dog expert of the time, Karl Brandt, who finally convinced the Delegate Commission that this lovely grey dog, who caught his interest, should be included in the Stud Book. Interestingly, Karl Brandt said "Even if the Weimaraner were painted a brown colour, one could instantly recognise him as a Weimaraner" – a statement with which I am in total agreement. The Club had its headquarters in Thuringia, and was formed by shooting men who drew up their own standard.

The official standard of the breed was not completed and accepted until 1935 and was drawn up by both The Weimaraner Club of Germany and the Weimaraner Club of Austria. It was Prince Hans von Ratibor who introduced the breed into Austria with his good friend, Otto von Stockmayer. In 1913, Prince Hans von Ratibor became the President of the Austrian Club.

In Germany, Major Robert aus der Herber nurtured the breed and regularly shot over Weimaraners from 1915. Such was his devotion to the breed that he gained the nickname 'Father of the Weimaraner'. He was the author of a reputedly splendid book of the breed, unfortunately unobtainable now. He became President of the German Club in 1921. His affix was aus der Wulssriede. D. Paul Kleeman, an authority on the German Shorthaired Pointer and President of the Berlin Stud Club for many years, also had the interests of the Weimaraner at heart. As with many German breeds, it is the practice of the Breed Warden to enforce restrictions on breeding Weimaraners, and even today restrictions are set.

A GREAT DOG MAN

Another great German dog man was Heinz Reuper. Born on June 27 1923 he had a great interest in hunting his dogs and although he had other hunting breeds, his greatest love, in dogs, was the Weimaraner. In fact he is recognised in Germany as the top field trial judge ever, yet such was the man that he would be there for all, helping novice and experienced handler alike, freely giving of his time. His first Weimaraner was a dog called 'Flanko', whom he carried home on his motorbike in an old cigar box, before World War II. After the war he would go hunting with this Weimaraner and his other hunting dog. Because, of course, at this time, no guns were allowed in Germany, the dog would hunt foxes and take the fox around the throat and kill the animal this way, showing the strength and bravery of the Weimaraner.

Heinz Reuper's first bitch, Kora, was bought from a well-known breeder, Frank Heduter. Being short of money at this time, the deal consisted of two bitches – the other being Otti vom Elchwinkel – in exchange for 12 ducklings, one bag of maize and the money Heinz had in his pocket at that moment. Otti

Heinz Reuper played a great part in the development of the Weimaraner in Germany.

was the bitch who started the 'vom Zehnthof' line, bearing Heinz Reuper's first Weimaraner litter. Incidentally, in forty years in the breed, thirty litters were produced with the vom Zehnthof affix. This bitch had a wonderful nose and was called 'a phenomenon' by the field trial judges, never failing to pick up scent, whatever the conditions. She achieved the highest marks ever and became the top-winning hunting Weimaraner of all time. In fact Heinz preferred bitches and all his Weimaraners gained 'Meister Prufung' (Master Hunting Certificate), a great accolade to this great man, who had such an affinity with nature and animals. He was often called out to locate lost animals and, day or night, in any appalling weather conditions he would go, never giving up until all avenues were fully explored. On the rare occasions that an animal was not found he was devastated, thinking someone else perhaps could have done better, while everyone realised this would not have been the case. In fact the hunting fraternity nicknamed him 'The Wizard of Hunting'. I never met Heinz. My information on him, and the present day Weimaraner 'goings on' in Germany, came to me courtesy of Ines Dawes (affix Aquila),who had the pleasure of meeting and talking to this great man. His motto 'For the sake of the breed only breed the very best, do not breed from something that is just good enough' is something I identify with, as we should not kid ourselves into breeding for the wrong reasons, with the wrong animals. We, at Gunalt, have always maintained that the faults you start with are always in there, capable of coming out when least expected. To give some measure of the esteem in which this man, who died on March 20 1995, was held by his peers, 385 dog folk were present to pay their last respects at his funeral, in addition to all his family and friends, and instead of flowers, the family asked for donations to a centre for the early detection of cancer. These topped four and a half thousand deutchmarks.

*Kevin Bingham
with Nl Lux
Germ (UDH)
European Ch.
Zilverein Captain
Lad, bred by Jim
and Karen
Gibson, Ireland.*

GERMANY TODAY

As stated earlier, The Weimaraner Club of Germany was recognised following a long struggle. Today the Club consists of seven members of the committee, two chairmen, and various secretaries, e.g. social, field trial and breed control. There are also nine local district chairmen who look after the nine districts of Germany and are there to help Weimaraner owners and answer queries etc. Every dog registered with the Club in Germany has to be hip scored and have a hunting certificate before being bred from, and to this end the Club donates £12 back to each owner to help and encourage this responsible attitude.

With up to 50 per cent of all Weimaraners bred not going to hunting homes, the Weimaraner Club try to discourage members from showing their stock, in the vain hope of stopping the breed becoming popular as pets and show dogs. In Germany there is a feeling that if showing is accepted unabated, there is a danger of the Weimaraner developing into two 'types', another reason for dissuading breeders from selling stock for the ring. In England, Weimaraners are among the top six most popular gundog, yet I feel strongly that the beautiful, sound dogs we show still have a strong instinct to work if that be the owner's forte. Certainly, our own Portman, who is the only male to win BIS at a general Championship Show, is regularly taken out during the shooting season.

In Germany, puppies sold through the Club go for a fixed price and members are careful to place puppies in working homes. This has the effect of having backstreet breeders charging exorbitant prices for puppies. The fee, as in the UK, is paid at the time of service, and is non-returnable if the bitch misses. However, if a litter of over six occurs, for each puppy over that number an extra fee is paid to the owner of the stud. 1994 saw 35 litters registered in Germany of shorthaired Weimaraners and 7 litters of longhaired. The longs are becoming popular and there is talk of a Club especially for the longhaired Weimaraner variety.

The docking of Weimaraner puppies' tails, about which such a fuss is made in the UK, is not an issue in Germany where it is performed quite matter of factly. This is strange, considering that the argument is focused on 'cosmetic reasons' for docking by the anti-docking brigade, yet Germany has little time for showing and promoting the breed on its beauty. In Germany it is not deemed necessary to remove dewclaws unless it is thought the animal may at sometime be exported to a country where snow is heavy. The dewclaws would then be removed as they could become very sore in such conditions. Incidentally, before the Second World War the death rate of baby puppies was very high in Germany, many dying before five weeks of age. Inoculations were not administered as they are now, but nevertheless there was an obvious weakness in the breed at this time.

There have been rumours that Germany condones 'cat fighting' by the German breeders of Weimaraners. Many years ago some Weimaraners – and other breeds also – were 'toughened up' by a few breeders through baiting the dog with wild cat and, indeed, foxes. This was because, if a Weimaraner was asked to track wild boar, which is a massive and extremely dangerous animal, the dog must respect that danger and be able to deal with it, otherwise both dog and handler could be in mortal danger. This practice is now outlawed, and, I repeat, was never widely practised.

DEVELOPMENT IN THE USA
It was Howard Knight of Rhode Island who was instrumental in introducing the Weimaraner to the USA. He first met the German, Fritz Grossman, in 1928 and they found that they both enjoyed field sports enormously. Fritz Grossman was invited to join Howard Knight out hunting. It was through the ensuing friendship that Knight learned of the Weimaraner. He subsequently became the first American to become a member of the German Weimaraner Club. This was in 1929, following Fritz Grossman's repeated applications to the Club.

In this same year the dog, Cosack von Kiebitztein, and the bitch, Lotte von Bangstede, were imported into the USA by Knight. However, unbeknown to him, the pair were sterile, following ultra-violet ray treatment before leaving Germany. Grossman, who had selected this three-year-old pair, was also unaware of this fact. However, they were retained by Knight and he worked them regularly, in the course of which he continued to discover what a wonderful hunting breed this is. He later imported a number of puppies but all but one, a dog named Mars aus der Wulfsmeide, died.

Howard Knight then received a gift from Major Herber who, to show good faith in the breed, send a bitch, Dorle v Schwarzen Kamp. He also supervised the arrangements involved in sending an in-whelp bitch, Aura von Gailberg. Knight was a man of strong character who never sold any puppies, but gave them to very close friends with the stipulation that the dogs should never be cross bred and that, if any puppies produced were mismarked in any way, or had too much white, then these whelps had to be put to sleep. He was also against line breeding. In fact he only favoured hunting with his Weimaraners. But then he gave up hunting and agreed to let Mr and Mrs Horn of the Grafmar Kennels have his Weimaraners, on the condition that they acted with responsibility towards the breed and that, at some time, he could have a puppy back.

US RECOGNITION OF WEIMARANERS
The breed was recognised by the American Kennel Club in 1942 and the Weimaraner Club of America was formed in Boston in February, 1943. The President of the Club was Howard Knight. A committee was appointed and a constitution for breeding, keeping and registering the breed was drawn up, although only the Horns were breeding Weimaraners at this time.

The Weimaraners they had acquired from Howard Knight were the bitches Adda von Schwarzen

Kamp and Dorle von Schwarzen Kamp, who were litter sisters, Avra von Gailberg and the male, Mars aus der Wulfsriede. It is from these four that the Weimaraner was started in America. The Horns produced their first Weimaraner litter in 1939, Mars ex Adda. This mating was repeated in 1942. A dog from the first mating, Grafmar's Silver Knight ultimately sired six Champions; Grafmar's Ador, from the repeat sired 16 Champions – so both of them proved what good stock was originally imported into the USA. Avra von Gailberg excelled in Obedience work and became the first Weimaraner to gain her Obedience title in the US. She had four litters, three by Grafmar's Silver Knight, and many progeny from this coupling gained Obedience titles. A daughter from this pair, Grafmar's Silver Dusk CDX, went on to produce the first Group winning Weimaraner in the USA, Ch. Forever Silver Dawn. This bitch also won BOB at the Great Westminster Show in 1946 and 1949.

POST-WAR WEIMARANERS IN THE US
Following the war, an influx of Weimaraners came to the US because of many American soldiers bringing them home – so much so that the German Club decided to limit foreign sales. Obviously these ancestors of the present-day American Weimaraner contributed much to the current quality of the dogs. In fact the imported Ch. Dido v Lechsteinhof was such a magnificent hunting dog that the phrase 'you can't win big in the field unless Dido is in the pedigree' is often used even now. Out of all the imports, dogs from the Harrasburg kennel provided the most outstanding lines, particularly Alto v.d. Harrasburg who, through his winning progeny, can be found behind most quality Weimaraners in the US. Through the years the number of imports declined but in the early 1960s the bitch, Bella v.d. Reiteralm CD BROM was brought in and she, when mated back to descendants of Alto, cemented the good foundations of the breed.

During the 1950s the breed was used in many advertisements. Articles were written depicting the great attributes and intelligence of the Weimaraner, culminating in the dog becoming the ultimate status symbol to own. This, in turn, led to indiscriminate breeding by folk out to make a quick buck, with no in-depth knowledge of the breed. Registrations of the Weimaraner with the American Kennel Club peaked in 1957 with 10,011 of them registered. During this time the Weimaraner was termed 'The Wonder Dog'. President Dwight Eisenhower and film stars Grace Kelly and Roy Rogers were among those who owned this elegant 'grey ghost' with the beautiful silver coat.

Due to gross exaggerations about the breed written in various publications, many new owners had a rude awakening after purchasing their Weimaraner. Great intelligence, yes, but as owners of the breed know, the Weimaraner takes advantage of the uninitiated. Consequently sales dropped and the breed's registration figures reduced slowly over the years, until in the late 1980s a more realistic three to four thousand Weimaraners were registered with the AKC. As the breed stabilised in numbers, so did it in quality. In 1985 the Weimaraner Club of America's President, Tom Wilson, noted that for every 16 Weimaraners registered with the AKC, one gained the title of Champion, compared with, for example, Poodles of the same year, where one title was gained for every 486 dogs registered. I know that the US imports in the UK have contributed much to the breed and we must be grateful for the enthusiasm and dedication of the American breeders.

DEVELOPMENT IN THE UK
It was 1947 or 1948 when Lt. Colonel Eric Richardson first met Major R.H. Petty. The two men, who were serving in the British Army in Germany, shared an interest in guns, shooting and gundogs. Major Petty had been down to the American Zone where he had seen Weimaraners belonging to two American Air Force Officers.

Delighted by the dogs, he set out to obtain one or two Weimaraners for himself. So strong was his desire, that he even talked of crossing the border into East Germany himself, which would be extremely dangerous. However, he managed to contact a German Forstmuster, who had crossed from the Eastern Zone, bringing with him a couple of Weimaraners. An authority on the breed, he negotiated through friends he had left in the Eastern Zone, to smuggle some Weimaraners over the border for payment, or for commodities which were in short supply in the East, primarily coffee beans, and so Major Petty achieved his ambition to own Weimaraners, a fact of which I am truly grateful, otherwise none of us would have encountered this remarkable breed!

His first Weimaraner, a bitch, reputably a beautiful animal, was Cobra von Boberstrand, which Major Petty imported into England where she lived a long life. Accompanying Cobra was a dog, Bando von Fohr. In March 1952 this pair went into quarantine in England and into the history books as the first Weimaraners to arrive in the UK. Major Petty imported six more into the country, only three of which he considered good enough to register with the Kennel Club. Major Richardson brought five Weimaraners over, only two of which were registered with the Kennel Club. Mrs Olga Mallett also imported a dog, Arco von der Kolfuster Heide and an in-whelp bitch, Babette von der Katzbach. These nine Weimaraners registered with the Kennel Club form the foundation of Weimaraners in the UK. Through the years, we have had other imported stock, primarily from the United States of America, which have improved the quality of stock, both in conformation and temperament.

Lt. Col. Eric Richardson bred under the Monksway affix but he was never as committed to the breed as was his good friend Major Petty, who took on some of the Monksway stock when Richardson was posted to Hong Kong. Major and Mrs Petty's affix Strawbridge produced the first Champion in the breed, Ch. Strawbridge Oliver, who was out of the imported Cobra by Ipley Apollo and was owned by Mr G. Webb. The Pettys bred two more Show Champions, Strawbridge Czarina for owner Mrs F. Bainbridge and Strawbridge Yuri for owner Mrs S.M. Roberts. When The Weimaraner Club of Great Britain was formed in 1953, Major Petty became the first secretary. He was instrumental in translating the German Standard of the breed. Mrs Olga Mallett bred under the affix of Ipley. Her imported bitch, Babette von der Katzbach, produced Ipley Apollo, a significant sire. As well as Ch. Strawbridge Oliver, his progeny include Strawbridge Duke, Strawbridge Venessa and Manana Athene and Manana Adonis, names which can be found in the pedigrees of the top kennels and top producers. Mrs Mallett only bred two litters, and Major Petty took on her Weimaraners when she returned to her native Canada.

Another kennel stemming from Major Petty's stock was Mr and Mrs Causeley's Sandrock, based on the top winner Strawbridge Carol, whelped in July . At Crufts she was awarded Best Bitch in the breed for four consecutive years – 1955 to 1958. She obviously would have been a Show Champion if Challenge Certificates had been on offer at this time. The breed was only granted Championship status by the Kennel Club in 1960. Carol had four litters, one by Sandrock Admiral, whose daughter, Sh. Ch. Wolfox Silverglance, bred by Mrs Barbara Douglas Redding, became the first Show Champion. She bred another Show Champion by this dog Admiral – Sh. Ch. Ace of Acomb. Admiral also sired Sh. Ch. Cabaret Cartford Platinum and Mrs Joan Matuszewska's first homebred Show Champion, Monroe's Dynamic, who, incidentally, was the first Weimaraner to win a Best in Show, in 1964.

EARLY UK AFFIXES

Admiral and Ace of Acomb were owned by Dr Alex Mucklow, who favoured dogs. However, she did have a bitch, Coninvale Greta of Acombdole (Dr Mucklow's affix), who was by her Sh. Ch. Ace of Acomb, bred by Mrs Johnson, as was another dog belonging to Dr Mucklow, Sh. Ch.

Sh. Ch. Ballina
Of Merse-side.

Coninvale Paul of Acombdole. Through Coninvale Greta of Acombdole, Dr Mucklow bred Acombdole Athene, who in turn produced Sh. Ch. Oneva Trenodia, bred by Mr and Mrs Bright. Mrs Maddock's foundation bitch, Strawbridge Ermegard, although not remembered for her beauty, nevertheless was behind many great dogs of today. Manana, the Maddock's affix, did not directly produce any Champions or Show Champions; but look back into your pedigree far enough and Manana-bred stock often appear. The most famous was that illustrious breeder Joan Matuszewska's foundation bitch, Manana Athene (dam of Silverglance and Ace of Acomb), who also started the Wolfox affix of Mrs Douglas-Redding. Besides these Show Champions, this affix produced Sh. Ch. Wolfox Bittersweet, Sh. Ch. Wolfox Nyria, Sh. Ch. Wolfox Moonsdale Whisper and Sh. Ch. Wolfox Lycidas. Mr and Mrs G. Webb were the holders of the Theocsbury affix. They bred Ch. Theocsbury Abbie and litter brother Sh. Ch. Theocsbury Archduke, who both went on to produce Champion offspring, the most famous being Abbie's daughter, Sh. Ch. Hansom Syhill Odette who is behind the Hansom and the subsequent Gunalt and Denmo lines.

Interestingly, Archduke was the sire of Arlebroc Abbot, the sire of that long-time recorder holder of CCs in bitch, Sh. Ch. Ballina of Merse-side, owned by Mrs Elizabeth Hackett and bred by Mr Thirlwell. In 1976, the time when we came into the breed, it was hard for Weimaraners to be taken seriously by non-breed judges; this 'new continental gundog' was treated with caution, as many did not understand the Standard of the breed. The long body and amber eyes alone were so different to the normal, shorter body and dark appealing eye and expression associated with gundogs. Also the breed did not have the overall soundness seen in today's Weimaraner. Therefore, for Ballina to achieve so many top awards at all-breed open shows says much for her quality. Although the record for Challenge Certificates was broken in 1995 by Sh. Ch. Ansona Purdy, Ballina will, rightly, be remembered as a great.

Mr and Mrs Farquhar held the Andelyb's affix. The most famous bitch bearing this affix was Ch. Andelyb's Balch, who produced Sh. Ch. Waidman Gunnar for Louise Petrie-Hay and Sh. Ch. Monroe's O'Netti and Sh. Ch. Monroe's Nadine for Joan Matuszewska. O'Netti was owned by Nev Newton (Nevedith). Nadine was owned by Dorothy Chapman, Heronshaw, whose Sh. Ch. Heronshaw Silver Fortune was a son of Nadine who, in turn, went on to sire puppies for his owner, Fiona Dow, under the Vimana affix. Our foundation bitch Vimana Viveca of Gunalt was by this dog. Mrs Chapman also bred Hubball's Sh. Ch. Heronshaw Silver Sunday of Wightwick.

Sieglinde Smith started her 'Czersieger' line with Heronshaw Silver Solveig. Solveig's most famous son was Hill's Sh. Ch. Czersieger Clever Clown. Tina Morris began the Kalimores with a

Solveig daughter and Ines Dawes' first Weimaraner was a son of this bitch. Louise Petrie-Hay, Waidman affix, is a field trial judge and this is where her main interest lies. She bred Waidman Giselle who won two Challenge Certificates and started the Gunmetal Weimaraners. Waidman Jemima started the line in Weimaraners of the Gray's Abbeystag, which produced the lovely dog Sh. Ch. Abbeystag Oceanmist which is behind many good Weimaraners of today.

John Taylor, Hepton, is very well-known in English Setters but also bred Weimaraners and judges the breed. From his Cartford Silver Sand, he went on to produce Hepton Queen. She was mated to the great Ch. Ragstone Remus to produce Sh. Ch. Knowdale Annabella for John's cousin, Geoff Taylor. Interestingly, it was John Taylor who was the breed judge of the day when Dick Finch's Sh. Ch. Hansom Hobby Hawk won the Gundog Group and Best Bitch in Show at Birmingham Championship Show. This was the first time a Weimaraner had won Best in Group at Championship Show level. The year was 1974. Rangatira is the affix of farmers Chris and Grace Brown. They bred John Lock's elegant Sh. Ch. Rangatira Deerstalker and also owned Sh. Ch. Warehead Marion of Rangatira. Their first Weimaraner came from Jackie Atkinson, Grinshill, who, although not very active on the show scene, has always been an asset to the breed with her devotion to rescue work. Ann Cook's Weimaraner, the first to win an Obedience Test, was also a Grinshill, being Grinshill Rana Vanessa. This bitch, who also gained CDEx, WDEx, TDEx, was out of Shalina Dancing Diamond by Ch. Monroes Ambition of Westglade CDEx UDEx WDEx. She was bred by Mike and Vicky Bambridge. The Bambridges have also bred other dogs which have won working trial qualifications – Johnson's Beckstone Ambassador CDEx UDEx and Bellmont's Beckstone Hildas Megan UDEx. Their stock has also won well in the show ring and forms the foundation for other lines.

Jackie Atkinson also bred Suzanne Walkden's first Weimaraner, Sh. Ch. Grinshill Sweet Solario. Whelped in 1977, Sweet Solario not only gained her title in the ring but also Suzanne trained her to win CDEx UDEx and WDEx. The Walkdens bought their next puppy, from the Absaloms – Varstock Vermillionairess at Jazetas, who gained two Challenge Certificates before her untimely death. Fortunately Suzanne has a daughter of Vermillionairess, carrying the Plusila affix, by Tim Smith and Yvette Sinclair's Ch. Varstock Voyager of Roxberg.

The Smith-Sinclair partnership's first Weimaraner was Kisdon's Fiction of Roxberg who was the dam of Sh. Ch. Roxberg's Kamira. Owned by sisters Jackie Tranter and Sue Dennis, this bitch became a big winner handled by Nev Newton, who handled her when she won Reserve Gundog Group at Crufts in 1991 and he also steered her to win a Group at Championship level. Dianna Hill and her son Chris, Scalene, bred and owned Sh. Ch. Scalene Sportsman in 1981 and continue to breed and show. Beate von Dwingels-Lutten campaigned Sh. Ch. Wilhelm Maximillian to his title. He was by Hurstlem Hazard, a dog owned by Pamela LeMon, who was for many years Hon. Secretary of The Weimaraner Club of Great Britain. A lady who has campaigned Weimaraners over a number of years is Avril Aiken. She won two Challenge Certificates with her first homebred bitch, Savril Adeliq, and has since won a Challenge Certificate with Rhannigal Quota Queen of Savril. Her home-bred Savril Lucky The Reverant is the sire of McAngus's Sh. Ch. Tasairgid Ultra Easy of Greyfurs. Christine Simpson bred Quota Queen and has had Weimaraners for many years. Edward and Liz Hardman bred the Fairlies' first Champion in Sh. Ch. Bredebeck Ilka and continue to concentrate on field trialling.

Mike and Jane Thomas made their first Weimaraner into Sh. Ch. Deeta Jason and followed this with his daughter, Sh. Ch. Shermac Sandeeta. Before emigrating to Australia, Pam Lyons had an impressive record with her three bitches, Sh. Ch. Dach of Adel at Adlwood, Sh. Ch. Tynllwyn Belle Dee and homebred Sh. Ch. Adlwood Gingko Gem. Jo How's Pipwell affix has been connected with both Weimaraners and Viszlas. The Weimaraner Sh. Ch. Hansom Model Bee of

The first Weimaraner Association Championship Show – Joan Matuszewska's last judging appointment. (Back row left to right): Anne Harris (show secretary), Nev Newton (referee judge), Joan Matuszewska (bitch judge), Gillian Burgoin (president), John Taylor (dog judge) Gerald Harris (show manager). (Front row left to right): Stephen Hollings with Sh. Ch. Gunalt Obsession BIS, Pauline Brooks with Sh. Ch. Amtrak Ameros at Ormerod RBIS and Patsy Hollings with Gunalt Rover BPIS.

Pipwell was whelped in 1981 but Jo had her first Weimaraner from Jane Wright, Hofsetter, in 1977. Sandra Marshall's affix, Lowerden, is multi-breed connected. Her first Weimaraner was a dog who needed 'rescuing' at 12 months old. Off she went to meet his breeder, Di Arrowsmith, Fleetapple, and together they picked up Wilmar, alias Sam, who was whelped in 1974. Sandra campaigned Sam and he became Sh. Ch. Fleetapple Wilmar.

IRISH STOCK
A kennel founded on Strawbridge stock was Mrs Davis, Deerswood. Her Strawbridge Elfrida had five litters by Strawbridge Fury. Contemporary breeders in Ireland include Jim and Karen Gibson whose first male Weimaraner became the first Ch. and Ir. Ch. Gunalt Samco of Zilverein. Samco gained his Irish title in 1991 and English Championship in 1993. Tony and Madeline Rainey steered Kingsbeam Murphy Himself at Trilite to his English and Irish title. They bred Sh. Ch. Trilite Tegins Girl who was sold to Mr White and campaigned by Gerry Olsen.

THE WEIMARANER IN NORWAY
The Norwegian Weimaraner Club (Norsk Weimaraner Klubb) was founded in 1981 and presently has 65 members. The first dogs imported into Norway were from England and Denmark in 1964 and the first Norwegian puppies were whelped in 1968. Today the country has in the region of 100 to 150 Weimaraners. Norway follows the German thinking on the breed: no animal can be bred from unless X-rayed and free from HD, and working your dog is given priority.

Norway has imported dogs from Germany to help with the Klubb's breeding programmes. A male, Blitz von der Steinhorst, bred by Kal Heinz Frese, was imported in 1984 and was the male Nordic Winner in 1987. Blitz sired litters in Norway and one in Finland. He is owned by Eva Pedersen. Along with him came a bitch, Dana von der Wapelburg, owned by Lene Borud, who

Int N S UCH
Nordic Winner
1994
Faltherrens
Venus.

was the only breeder for many years. Two offspring from the pairing of these were NV-89 Felix and his sister NV-92 Ferra Die Grave. This kennel also used Ines Dawes' Euro. Lux. & German The Swagman of Equila.

Both have several CCs and CACIBs, Felix was BOB at the Klubb's first show in 1992 under British Judge, Marnie Marr. They also have awards in Field and Obedience competitions. Ferra gaining a first prize in blood tracking in Sweden, the first to achieve this. Ferra is owned by Eva and Kent Pederson, affix Hella. This kennel also owns Norwegian and Swedish Ch. Faltherrens Venus, bred in Sweden by Agneta and Lars Kilborn. This bitch is the first in Norway to get her title because she gained the necessary first in a field trial. She also won a CC under respected German breed Master Dr Werner Petri. She was mated to Aust. Sh. Ch. Bromhund American Express and offspring from this mating are winning well. This pair also produced two Longhaired Weimaraners, Hella's Fanny, owned by Solveig Overoie, and Hella's Fantasy, retained at Hella. Both have CCs and awards for hunting and retrieving. They have opened up an interest in the Longhaired Weimaraner in this country. Roald Lende imported Gunalt Cachet in 1987 from us. Sister to Gunalt Joy, the top brood retained at Gunalt, she is the breed's most successful show Weimaraner, with 70 CCs, CACIBs, BOBs and Best in Group awards.

THE LONGHAIRED WEIMARANER

The origin of the Weimaraner is hazy and the history of the Longhaired variant is even more so. First mention of the Longhair being shown was when Longhaired Weimaraners were exhibited at the Hanover Show in 1879. The first Longhaired puppy to be recognised was in a litter whelped February 7th 1933. Bred in Austria by Josef Schaffer, the puppy was bought as a Short by a Mr Pattay, who enquired as to why the coat appeared 'fluffy'. He was told the long hair would shed out in a short time. However, this was not the case and when Mr Pattay exhibited his dog Tell v.

Asta Von
Gut
Blaustauden

Aruni
Dinwiddi
From Seicer.

Stranzendorf in Vienna in 1934 much interest was shown. Major Herber researched the pedigree of this dog and after consultation with the German Club's meeting in 1935 it was decided to recognise the Longhaired Weimaraner as a variant of the Weimaraner. Initially the Longhaired was to be docked at the fourth vertebrae but it was later ruled that the dog should retain a full tail. However, docking was called for, to be at the second or third vertebrae, when the Standard was revised in 1952. Interestingly, this Standard states that the tail should be docked at 14 days of age. Today, any docking of Longhaireds or shorthaired Weimaraners is generally carried out before five days of age and usually at two days.

In 1965 Ken and Joan Fussell, Greyfilk, visited the World Show in Czechoslovakia and saw the Longhaired Weimaraner. On their return to the UK they brought photographs with them and wrote a report on Longhaireds for the Club magazine. It was Ann Janson who became interested in the Longhaireds and eventually imported Asta Von Gut Blaustauden from breeder Rev. Foster Rudolf Trost in 1973. I never saw Asta, but in her photograph she looks to me a lovely type, with a good body and balance all through.

This was not the first Longhaired in Britain. In Scotland on January 8th 1973, Mr Seymour bred a litter by Ortega Opal Mint out of Grey Moonshadow of Duenna who, in turn, was out of an American imported bitch. The resulting litter contained a Longhaired dog. It is thought another of the litter, who died, could also have been a Longhaired. This puppy was acquired by Joan

*Sh. Ch. Pondridge
Practical Joker:
The UK's only
longhaired
Champion, owned
and campaigned
by Shirley
Anderton, bred by
Gill Smith.*

*Photo: John
Hartley.*

Matuszewska and called Mafia Man on Monroes. Both his parents were shorts and, in fact, Commander Val Hawes traced back into the sire's pedigree and concluded that it was necessary to go six generations back before locating any Longhaireds. I find it amazing that no Longhaireds appeared in this country until Mafia Man, the same year the first Longhaired was imported into Britain. Ann Jansen then imported a Longhaired dog in 1974, again from Austria. He was Dino Von Der Hagardburg. Dino and Asta were mated to produce Aruni Dinwiddi from Seicer in 1975. This dog I did see and I must say, although my preference is for the shorts, I really liked him and felt it disappointing that he only won two Challenge Certificates – he deserved to be a Champion. However, he did make breed history. He was the first Weimaraner to win a Challenge Certificate in Britain. In 1970 Gill and Les Smith had their first Weimaraner, a short. It was in 1975 that Ann Jansen gave to the Smiths Dinwiddi's sister, Aruni Danya from Seicer. She was shown, and was the first Longhaired to win Best Bitch at The Weimaraner Club of Great Britain Open Show, in 1984. Along with her famous brother she qualified and was shown at Crufts. She also won a Certificate of Merit at a novice field trial. In 1979 the Smiths imported a dog from Herr Seidl of Austria, named Hasso Von Der Hagardburg. When he was mated to Danya, this produced the first puppies named with the Smiths' affix, Pondridge. It is Gill Smith who has produced the first Show Champion Longhaired from a mating of Hasso and Danya in 1981. Shirley Anderton owned Pondridge Practical Joker and campaigned him for 10 years, winning consistently and, despite Joker breaking a leg in 1989, Shirley produced him looking fit and in full coat in 1991 at South Wales Kennel Association to win his third and qualifying Challenge Certificate under breed specialist Stephen Hollings to great applause. Along the way this dog also won 7 Reserve Challenge Certificates, including a Reserve Challenge Certificate at Crufts 1988.

A top breeder of the short variety is Denise Mosey, Denmo. In 1991 Denise bought the dog Pondridge Pioneer of Denmo from Jill Smith and has campaigned him since. Always looking superb and in immaculate full coat, he has been consistently in top places alike under judges who favour the Longhaireds and under judges who generally only care for the shorts. To date, Pioneer has one CC and two RCCs. We obtained our first 'long' in 1993, a Pioneer daughter. It is through living at first hand with both that I have come to believe that somewhere in the distant past, Setter was introduced into the Weimaraner, giving coat and a very different personality. But this is a personal theory and has no proven backing.

Chapter Two

BUYING A PUPPY

Buying a puppy should be regarded as taking on a new member of the family – it is nothing like setting out to buy a new car! The Weimaraner is a beautiful dog, with a quite unique colour, and appears easy to look after. The dog has class, is aristocratic in looks and gives the impression that the owner of such a breed is high on the social scale. An excellent reason to buy a car! Not a good reason to buy a dog. The sticker in the back of the car stating 'A dog is not just for Christmas' is relevant all year round and a responsible person will realise that the commitment of a dog is with you for twelve or more years. Your dog will be what you make of him or her, providing you have a well-bred dog of the breed to suit you. I would sum up the Weimaraner with the phrase 'The Weimaraner does not suffer fools gladly.' This is an intelligent dog, questioning, courageous, powerful, extremely stubborn, sensitive, protective and biddable. You do not get 'owt for nowt' in this world. In fact the best and most fulfilling achievements are worked hard for, be they a good secure family or a well-reared secure pet. Therefore the ground work is essential. One will easily find a Weimaraner puppy for sale advertised in your local paper, but act in haste and repent at leisure. The size, protective instinct and light eye suggest to some misguided folk that the Weimaraner would make a guard dog. This is not the case. The Weimaraner is a dog who likes to be with people, not left to prowl a compound. I am not sure dogs of any breed should be exploited in this way, feeding someone's macho image.

CHOOSING A BREEDER

We have often invited people interested in the breed to visit our kennels, have a coffee, watch the dogs, ask questions and find out about the breed. Folk often take us up on that offer from all over the country. They go home, think about what they have seen and heard in the cold light of day, only then making their decision as to whether this is the breed for them. Once that decision is made, those people make fine owners. It is the people who find a half-hour journey too far, unless you have puppies available, who worry me. Are they working on impulse?

Research is invaluable. Ring the national club that governs the breed, or the governing body of your country, and ask for the name of a responsible breeder; buy the weekly or monthly dog publications applicable to pedigree dogs and check out advertisements. Read these publications as they also have results from shows – which will give a clue as to which breeder's stock is winning. Ring breeders and arrange to visit. Reputable ones who care strongly about their breed will be happy for you to come. It is these breeders who will be there for you, with support, help and advice, throughout your Weimaraner's life, rather like a doctor would be from the birth of your baby onwards. Talking to breeders gives an insight into their priorities.

A breeder will invariably have an affix. This is rather like a trade name and all dogs bred by that kennel bear their affix. For instance ours is Gunalt. The point of an affix is that different breeders can identify certain dogs by this affix, and looking into a pedigree shows various 'lines' to an experienced breeder. From the buyer's point of view you can easily research affixes in the dog press, as the names of winning dogs often appear there. Likewise you can look into the breeder's background, through other Weimaraner owners.

WEIMARANERS AND CHILDREN

Weimaraners are gundogs. Why gundogs make ideal family pets is because they are soft-mouthed. This means that, if the adrenaline is flowing due to playing hard with you or the children, and the dog resorts to instinct, the gundog's instinct is to carry, gently, the dead game, so that when returned to you, the game is still intact, not chewed and therefore still fit to eat. This of course means the gundog is less likely to snap or even bite. If one thinks of a terrier, for example, the instinct there is to kill vermin such as a rat by biting it at the back of the neck, killing the rat instantly. If the dog did not do this, the rat would soon bite its predator. Consequently, a terrier who is playing hard or is over-excited nips at ankles etc. Likewise Border Collies make headline news should they bite a child, but this is a herding breed and if provoked by

Weimaraner puppies are hard to resist, but you must weigh up the pros and cons before taking on a strong, sporting breed.

human or cow will resort to instinct. Having said all this, the Weimaraner is the strongest, both physically and in character, of the gundog group, and should be respected as such. If a father were asleep in a chair and a young child pounced on the father, the dog's 'instinct' would be to jump up and throw the child to the floor, alarming everyone. So always be aware that a dog may react on instinct if hurt or alarmed. A Weimaraner has a questioning intelligence and needs mental stimulation and therefore can find children boring. A child plays simple games over and over again. We are also owners of English Setters, and I remember my children, when small, played happily, leading a Setter around the garden, chatting for hours. The Weimaraner would only tolerate this for a short period of time and would possibly leave the child in the lurch very quickly. Obviously one does not buy a dog solely for a child, but a Weimaraner, while making a wonderful family pet, is too headstrong and powerful to be left in the sole control of a child. The Weimaraner is very protective and will often be found near a playing child, minding its own business, almost like a nanny, which can be very reassuring.

It must be stressed that while they are excellent for each other, children and dogs should be supervised at all times. Dogs can be taught black and white rules, a child is a free-thinking human who can only be guided, and may forget that puppies or even adult dogs need respect, and a child may pull at the legs of dogs, hurting them – or even worse. The animal's heart is suspended in the chest, therefore the front legs of a dog or a puppy should never be pulled apart, which appears to be a natural thing for a child to want to do – look at a child pulling a teddy's legs!

WILL A WEIMARANER FIT INTO YOUR LIFESTYLE?

If all occupants of the home work a nine-to-five day with the children out at school, you must weigh up whether your want of a dog will give that dog a good quality of life, or if you would be better suited to the more independent lifestyle of a cat. No dog, least of all a Weimaraner, can cope with a quick walk to the park five nights a week and then a hike over the mountains on Saturday and Sunday. Neither is this a dog who will sit happily hour after hour, chewing a bone while you are at work. The Weimaraner never does anything absentmindedly but will work out why and if, first. Consequently the dog who decides to chew can easily go through a door or take the plaster off a wall, and it certainly is not unheard of for a Weimaraner totally to destroy a settee. On the other hand if stimulated and occupied the dog may never chew.

Before embarking on a dog it is worth doing a little forethought into the future. Where will you be in five years' time? If one partner is at home, perhaps looking after small children now, they may wish to return to work at a later day. Your responsibility to your dog is virtually as great as that to your children. If this future could become a possibility, prepare when you acquire your puppy. It is neither fair nor easy suddenly to expect a dog that has had your nearly undivided attention, to be left for two or three hours on a regular basis. The rules you begin with are what your Weimaraner will expect to occur in future. So perhaps an outside kennel or run might be a good idea from the start, just for a couple of hours a day.

COST

Buying a Weimaraner is only the start of the costs. Like starting a family, unforeseen costs are always arising. The smart coupé may be great for the family but an expensive estate car is more practical, following the addition of a large Weimaraner. Once the estate car is obtained, one needs a dog guard. The clever Weimaraner soon fathoms how to knock the cheap guards down or squeeze through them – not only annoying but dangerous, as this trick is usually performed while the driver is the only occupant and should be

Ch. Monroes Ambition of Westglade: Weimaraners love to be involved with everything that is going on.

concentrating on the driving. Consequently a hidden extra is an expensive dog guard.

Veterinary costs, of course, can be great. Although the Weimaraner is generally a healthy breed, initially costs include vaccinations and worming. You can insure your puppy against veterinary fees and death but obviously insurance in expensive. An 'indoor kennel' or even dog basket and Vetbed also is costly. Feeding costs can make a big hole in the budget and of course one must also make allowances for kennelling fees, which can add up. It is not always fair to expect a friend or family member to take on the responsibility of looking after a big, active breed such as your Weimaraner, while you are away.

YOUR AGE

This consideration may seem a strange one – yet think about it. One soon forgets the bad things. The first couple of years of owning a puppy can have traumatic times, but these are quickly forgotten as your dog reaches maturity and settles into a routine with you. If you are considering buying your first puppy, that is one matter. But if you already have a dog, or have had one, that is different. In all probability you will not consider having a new puppy until your dog is eight or so. Forgetting the first difficult years, you are left remembering six wonderful years. *But* you are eight years older, your circumstances have no doubt changed – in fact it is going to be a whole different ball-game. So make sure you are honest with yourselves. On the other hand, you may find you have more patience, more free time and motivation, all of which will be ideal for a Weimaraner.

CHOOSING YOUR PUPPY

When you have decided on the Weimaraner and the 'line', be prepared to wait for what you want. If you want a nice, sound puppy as a pet you may not have to wait as long as if your desire is to show or work your Weimaraner. It will not cost you any more for a well-bred, typical puppy than for a badly-bred, unsound or untypical specimen, so be patient. Most folk find it fun and rather fulfilling to visit the puppy of the litter you have waited for numerous times during those first weeks of life, often recording the puppy's beginnings on photograph or video. We are happy for future owners to visit the litter and dam. It is good socialization for puppies. It shows the sound temperament of the dam. It helps owners form a bond. It also shows that puppies cannot be chosen at a very young age.

A puppy should go to the home where the characters of both the puppy and the owners gel. The puppy should show potential of personality to fulfil the owner's needs. This character is not sufficiently developed until at least seven weeks of age. For instance if Mr Brown wants to shoot over his puppy, it is no good him choosing the chap who is out for creature comforts and a quiet life. As the weeks progress the breeder, particularly, will be able to tell each puppy's character and if the breeder suggests to Mr Brown that X puppy is the inquisitive one, always going that bit further and carrying the brush or a leaf, then remember, the breeder wants the best for each puppy and is giving you good advice, matching like needs.

The prospective owner who has confidence in the breeder will realise that a good, caring breeder will not try to 'palm off' a puppy with a serious fault. So, listen to the breeder and go with their recommendation, as their aim will be to make sure owner and dog are suited, thereby giving a better chance of the relationship being built on sound foundations and an ultimate happy life for everyone for years to come. Because of this, breeders advise new owners to visit the veterinary surgeon soon after taking their puppy home. This gives the vet the opportunity to check the puppy over and gives the new owner a chance to check out the vet and make sure you have confidence in them. It is no good having to call a vet in an emergency and finding you are not happy with the treatment or the advice. If a puppy has a fault or problem, the good breeder will point these out to any prospective owner so that when that puppy goes to the new home everyone is happy, most of all the puppy.

ASSESSING A PUPPY
No breeder with any experience, or worth their salt, will claim to sell 'a definite show puppy'. I often remark "I do not have a crystal ball." Foreseeing the future is for people with greater powers than I. So much can happen and change, and to a great extent that is what is so fascinating about showing and, indeed, breeding dogs. The only sure way of getting 'a show puppy' is to go to someone having their first litter, or lacking real experience! The novice breeder, so full of enthusiasm, will see only good things about their precious charges and the faults will dull into obscurity. Only by seeing puppies of your line develop time after time will you gain an insight into what might happen. Therefore a breeder will suggest that this carefully reared, well-bred puppy shows more potential for the ring than the litter mate because of various points and will then point out the reasons for you to cogitate. When looking for a potential show puppy, a breeder will look for certain points. One puppy will often keep coming to the fore. This puppy will possess quality, something one can see but not often put one's finger on. As breeders, we never 'look' at a puppy's show potential until at least seven weeks of age and later if possible. Puppies change such a lot in those first weeks. We would then stand the puppy to survey construction and balance.

Balance is very important. At the head one is looking for good length of foreface, not narrow at muzzle, a sound, steady expression, no weepy eyes or eyes that are too round or bulbous. The ears should be of good length. The puppy should have well-constructed shoulders, with good layback of shoulder blade and length of upper arm and width between the front legs. We look for a good length of back – this is not a short-backed breed. We want a good bend of stifle with no sign of the puppy being cow-hocked. Watching the puppy trot up and down, we look for an alert, confident disposition, front legs turning neither in nor out on the move, hind legs moving fairly wide, almost

LEFT: Assessing puppies for show potential is never easy at this young age.

RIGHT: A show puppy must look balanced and in proportion. There should be a good length of foreface, and a sound, steady expression.

A 12-week-old puppy stacked in show pose to display her attributes. She has the correct length of neck with a distinct arch. The shoulder is well-laid with the correct length of upper arm. She has a good length of back and a strong topline. She has good angulation of hindquarters.

Photos: Keith Allison.

A 12-week-old puppy stacked in show pose showing his lack of show potential. The neck is shorter and weaker. The upright shoulder placement will lead to stilted movement. The ribcage is short and the loin is long. The stifle is straight (which often goes hand in hand with bad shoulder placement) which makes the puppy high at the rear-end.

bowlegged in appearance. Topline would be carried level on the move. One should check that the puppy has a scissor bite – that the top teeth slightly overlap the lower teeth. This may go wrong during growth but usually comes back in the end. A point often forgotten is that the puppy, if male, should have two testicles. The testicles can drop later but I usually find that if they are not in the scrotum by twelve weeks, the chances of them dropping later is much reduced. However, if the testicles are there at 8 to 12 weeks and then go back up, I have found they always come back down. The colour of Weimaraner puppies is usually lighter than adults, yet different shades are noticeable within the litter. Everyone has their own favourite point – personally, construction and soundness in body and mind and type come before shade of coat. In twenty years, I do not think I have seen more than one Weimaraner who did not comply to the standard on colour. In fact if you put the darkest coloured Weimaraner on a grouse moor, with solid liver GSPs and russet gold Hungarian Vizslas, you would still easily distinguish between the breeds on colour alone.

One colour which is totally unacceptable is 'mis-marking'. Some lines occasionally throw Weimaraners who, while primarily grey, have the markings likened to say, a Dobermann, in ginger – that is, ginger on the eyebrow, around the muzzle, under the tail root and on all four legs and feet below the knee. This is a serious fault and a Weimaraner having these markings should not be bred from, although it will make no difference to the dog physically, who can still enjoy a full life as a pet. Another colour fault is white markings on toes, and a full white chest. White spurs on the heels of the front feet are a fault but one not penalised too severely if all else is good, likewise white on the sheath of a male. White on the chest in the form of a stripe or small spot is perfectly acceptable.

DOG OR BITCH?

What are the differences between the dog and bitch? One hears that bitches are more loving, yet others state that dogs are more loyal. Both sexes are loving and loyal and it really is down to personal preference. The main differences are rather like the differences between male and female humans – while never humanising dogs! The bitch tends, rather like a woman, to be manipulative – what is she going to get out of the command, sit? Very sweet when it suits her, rather aloof when

Gil Averis's Sh. Ch. Benpark Strange Magic of Sireva: The female Weimaraner is loyal and loving, although she can be manipulative at times.

Sh. Ch. Monroes Nexus, owned and bred by Joan Mat. The male is a powerful animal, and if not checked, he can become bossy with other dogs.

it doesn't. The bitch usually comes into heat or season every six months and is in season for three weeks, so this can be tiring. The bitch may suffer a false pregnancy in varying degrees, from just getting quiet and broody, to making beds, digging up the garden and confiscating children's toys, becoming maternal and producing milk, even going off her food. We find that some of our bitches may become quick-tempered with their peers a week or two before their season. However, generally, bitches are gentle, loving and pleasant to live with.

Dogs on the whole tend to be more even in temperament than bitches; yes, very loyal, but only if they respect their owner. I often find a male more patient with children in the same way a father can be. The male, however, is often up to two inches bigger than the female and this does not just mean taller. To be balanced, the male is overall bigger and more powerful. He can, in adolescence, become rather like an eighteen-year-old youth, which means he could become physical, as impetuous youths do. Because of his strength and power, this can unnerve an owner not familiar with the breed, yet with support from the breeder, one can gain reassurance. Weimaraners on the whole are a protective breed, and as a pack animal, the male can see himself as pack leader, needing to look after 'his family'. While this is reassuring to the owner of the dog, if not controlled the Weimaraner can take this job too far, especially the male. As a male he can also become dominant if not checked, and bossy with others, particularly with other males.

SHORTHAIRED OR LONGHAIRED?

Is there a difference between the Longhaired and the Shorthaired Weimaraner, we are sometimes asked. The main difference is obviously the coat. To be honest, the sleek outline with obvious muscle delineation of the Shorthaired variety, is one thing that really appeals to me. More grooming is necessary with the long coat, plus a little trimming under the ears to prevent knots forming. The hair around the feet can also knot and, of course, collects mud, which causes more cleaning problems. The activity of the Weimaraner, and the way they wag their tails, must also be taken into consideration, as the long tail of the Longhaired variety can damage precious ornaments

The longhaired Weimaraner.

and can, itself, be damaged. Personally, I find a slight difference in temperament between the two varieties. The short is more clinging, while the long is often faster and more willing to range – and is also, in my opinion, more vocal.

TWO PUPPIES TOGETHER?

Many people feel that two dogs look good, are company for each other and ease the guilt feelings of the owner for taking one puppy away from the pack. Two dogs do look good together, but should definitely be of *different* ages. As the owner of many Weimaraners, I can honestly say two of the same age are not a good idea. The initial training of an intelligent breed such as this needs great effort, and the rewards are substantial. Training requires repetitive action and concentrated time on a one-to-one basis to achieve the best results. It is virtually impossible to expend this amount of effort on two puppies at the same time. For example, if one wets on the carpet, which do you reprimand? If one chews at the cushion, the other thinks, great game, and the house is covered in feathers!

Because Weimaraners are headstrong, one must put in a lot of work when lead training. Talking to the puppy, and repetitively making the baby pup walk to heel, using gentle restraint, stops your Weimaraner pulling when older. This is impossible to do with two puppies. Again, leaving one alone, while training the other, if they are an inseparable duo, causes traumas to both puppies and to neighbours having to listen to the screams of the remaining puppy. Not only this, but it is important for a puppy to have individual attention. A Weimaraner is very much a people dog, who loves being with humans even if it is only riding around in the car with you.

Adolescence, when your juvenile turns into a delinquent, can be hard with one dog. With two it is often a nightmare. Not only will the youngsters question your leadership but one may also want to establish leadership over the other, causing many problems and jealousy. Then there is the problem of both dogs reaching old age together, or even developing the same illness. If one died, the remaining one would be devastated, having never been alone. Much wiser to have a first

Taking on two puppies may seem like a good idea, but when they reach the adolescent stage, you could well have problems with two powerful dogs both testing your superiority.

Photo: Keith Allison.

Weimaraner who grows into a well-trained, well-adjusted adult and have the advantage of having that dog helping train a youngster.

GENERAL FEEDING

While cats are true carnivores, dogs are omnivorous, which means they can feed on vegetable material as well as meat. Feeding dogs in this day and age is so much easier than in our fathers' day, when one fed meat and crude biscuit or flaked maize. Often 'dog people' today swear by tripe or paunch – many Hunt kennels and big working gundog kennels feed raw uncleaned tripe. While this may be acceptable for kennel dogs, the smell of the food and the smell emitted from the dog after feeding can be unacceptable in a dog living in the home as part of the family. Also the 'old dog man' works on instinct in feeding, knowing just the right combination of meat and biscuit by looking at his charge and knowing the exercise regime to keep the animal in tip-top form. There is also the worry these days of uncooked meant containing various growth additives, which are added to farm animals and/or their feeds to fatten the animal quickly for the table. Likewise chickens can carry viruses, so it is perhaps wise to cook fresh meat. Today the big dog food companies make our job of feeding our animals foolproof.

Basically dogs need: protein for growth, energy and maintenance of body tissue; fat/oil for energy and to help the absorption of Vitamins A, D, E and K; carbohydrate as a filler and fibre, vitamins and minerals. One needs to get the correct balance of all these nutrients and this is where the big well-known dog food companies benefit us. Thousands of pounds are invested into research by these companies and the resulting product is balanced to fit the dogs' needs at each stage of development. As a general rule a Puppy and Junior requires between 25-35 per cent protein for growth and development. As maintenance for the average family pet 18-20 per cent is adequate. People often fall into a trap of giving their pet too high a protein food which results in the dog becoming hyperactive, loose in motions or indeed possibly aggressive. If one were to equate the Weimaraner with a horse, this is the thoroughbred of the canine world and if you want a

LEFT: The Weimaraner must be fed a balanced diet at all times of its life, but this is particularly important when it is growing.

BELOW: Offspring of Sh. Ch. Flimmoric Fanclub pictured (left to right) at one month, three months, six months and a mature six-year-old. Notice the rapid growth rate to six months, illustrating the need for good feeding and early training.

racehorse to win the Grand National you feed a high protein diet. So to do the same with your Weimaraner is winding the dog up, which can lead you into the trap of over-exercising to reduce this over-activity, forming a vicious circle – the more the dog gets, the more the dog needs. For a working dog or a pregnant bitch the protein and fat levels should be higher, in the region of 28- 35 per cent. In an older dog the levels change again. As activity decreases, the energy required from food decreases. Ideally a veteran dog requires a lower protein level than a normal diet and slightly reduced fat level with a higher fibre content.

Feeding a complete food is far easier than a tinned feed and biscuit. With the tinned meat and biscuit you need to feed the right balance of both to fulfil the correct requirement. Weimaraners are very cute and can pick out the meaty bits, leaving the biscuit. Therefore it is less of a headache feeding a complete food where every nutrient is formed into a dry, hard nut or shape. Putting a bowl of this down, not only fulfils all your dog's needs, but is crunchy, which helps keep teeth clean and strong, there is no smell, nor does the food go off or sour, therefore there is no waste. Obviously fresh clean water must be readily available for the dog at all times and especially when feeding a dry complete food. The only problem with this form of feeding is – it is too easy. We want to give our much-loved pet recognition that we care, and putting a bowl of dry food down is not conducive to this end. Another way of feeding a complete diet is with a flaked complete food. This usually takes the form of coloured biscuits, flakes and dried meat and looks rather like a muesli. It can be fed dry but usually is mixed with warm water which makes a gravy and a pleasing aroma for the dog. Because it is impossible to separate out the meaty bits from a complete food the dog can become picky. This leads to the owner worrying that the dog is not eating enough and therefore adding a tasty supplement to make the dog eat. The Weimaraner, being very astute, realises that by leaving the meal something more appetising will be added. We then hear the cry 'My Weimaraner won't eat unless I add chicken etc.' My husband summed up the scenario with the phrase 'My children would eat only chocolate if I let them'. It is exactly the same principle.

No dog will starve itself to death. However, a Weimaraner is extremely stubborn and can hold off eating for a long time if sure that you will give in first. This leads to much tension within the household, particularly when this dog is a much-loved and wanted member of your family. The tension goes through to the dog, who then worries, which, in turn, removes the desire to eat. If you worry at meal times, so will your dog. We never have bad eaters, because there is always some other dog here who will eat, if one wants to be picky, so all our dogs retain the eat-or-die instinct they are born with. Learn something from this or you will make a rod for your own back. Weimaraners go through various stages of eating but usually end up devouring anything and everything.

In an adult dog, we would always feed a Weimaraner twice a day even if the dog were overweight, due to the worry of gastric torsion. For this reason one should be careful about exercising before or after meals. We tend to avoid taking the dogs for walks or runs an hour before or after a meal, and after having exercise we refrain from allowing our dogs excess water to drink. If the dog is carrying too much weight, feed two smaller meals; and a useful thought, if your dog always seems hungry, is to add raw carrot or cabbage, as these contain nothing a dog needs but add bulk and provide something to chew, thus alleviating hunger pangs. It is rare for a Weimaraner to be overweight but this must be avoided. One hears tales of the dog hardly having anything to eat yet remaining fat. This is rather like a greatly overweight human, over-eating causes over-weight!

STORAGE, BOWLS AND BONES

It is obviously cheaper, when feeding a large breed such as a Weimaraner, to buy feed in bulk. Storage must be thought of and a plastic dustbin can be a good idea. This will keep vermin out and keep the food dry. Do not leave it in a place accessible to your Weimaraners as they are extremely clever at getting in feed containers or, indeed, fridges and most Weimaraner owners will be able to tell you where to buy a fridge lock!

Because Weimaraners are determined creatures I feel it best to invest in stainless steel feed bowls from the start. I have heard of Weimaraners trying to chew aluminium bowls, resulting in the dogs having to have chewed aluminium removed, by anaesthetic, from their teeth. Plastic dishes are often chewed and eaten. Again these can cause problems to the digestive system. Ceramic dishes are carried about by Weimaraners, usually as a party trick or when the dog, deciding it is teatime, drops it at your feet, smashing the dish.

I am always wary of giving bones to the greedy Weimaraner. They can get bored and then swallow large chunks causing blockages and other problems. So, if in doubt, do not, is a good rule. We only give the white sterilised bones, obtainable from pet suppliers, which are good for keeping your dog occupied and stimulating the jaw and gastric juices. Knuckle bones can be OK but if too rich can upset the dog's tummy. Hide chews are fine but we avoid the cow hooves, as again these can be swallowed, causing problems.

Chapter Three

CARING FOR YOUR WEIMARANER

There is a saying that 'all puppies are the same'. Not only is this thinking wrong but it can lead to real problems when bringing up a Weimaraner. The beauty of pedigree dogs is that you can research the breeds which appeal in looks and end up with a breed which appeals in character with a good degree of certainty.

UNDERSTANDING YOUR WEIMARANER

The idea of giving a puppy a toy to play with for the first six months and then start the training will suit some breeds but not a Weimaraner. The rules laid down initially are the rules the dog believes should apply for life. The Weimaraner is extremely intelligent, but not in the way that what you say goes, as with some breeds. The dog who is good at pure obedience, repeating commands machine-like until each step is perfectly rehearsed without question, is lovely to look at and great to live with – but is not the Weimaraner. The Weimaraner always says Why? Believe me, when you have lived with a Weimaraner for a year you will know exactly what I mean. As I have said, the Weimaraner does not suffer fools gladly. This does not mean that if you have a silly

Sh. Ch. Kisdons Derring Do: The Weimaraner is always asking the question, why?

Weimaraner you are a fool. It means that the Weimaraner does not respect you and therefore treats you with contempt. Some breeds of dogs, particularly gundogs, being soft-mouthed, are very easy-going. Often these will not mentally push you or decide to try for a higher position in the pack – but the Weimaraner will.

The Weimaraner being a hunt, point, retrieve (HPR) breed is rather a jack-of-all-trades, so has many facets. Originally bred to hunt in the thick forests of Weimar game such as wild boar, wild cat or deer, the Weimaraner is, and has to be, courageous and, because that game is extremely dangerous, very protective as well. As I have explained previously, being a gundog, the Weimaraner is soft-mouthed, yet has this protective streak, usually lacking in the more popular gundog breeds. Because the Weimaraner has the gundog temperament, coupled with courage and an acute protective instinct, the dog can be a great asset to the owner who understands this character properly.

CONTROLLING A PACK ANIMAL
We, as humans, think in an entirely different way to the way a dog thinks. I know from experience that a three-year-old little girl can point-blank refuse to put her good clothes on when going to visit a dear elderly aunt. Even at this tender age individual views are formed, in the free-thinking individual human being. To put that same child into an environment where she must be totally obedient, subservient to her genera, would stifle her mental development, possibly leading to psychological problems later.

A dog, on the other hand, is an animal, and also a pack-oriented animal. To live in a pack successfully, one must have some form of pecking order, so each member knows what is expected and where everyone fits in. Humans have domesticated dogs to fit into our lifestyles. Having an affinity with humans, dogs fit into this environment beautifully. Nevertheless, we cannot and should not try to change their natural way of thinking to fulfil our needs, but respect them as dogs, thus giving them mental stability. Therefore we give them rules and conditions to live by which give them confidence.

We have a responsibility to dogs to understand them. Treating them as a child, peer or surrogate comforter is putting pressure on them mentally which will disorientate them and could lead to instability in temperament. For example, there is the blue-rinsed lady with the toy poodle on whose chair no-one is allowed to sit or the poodle snaps. This is not because poodles are snappy dogs, but because they are intelligent and cannot cope mentally with being indulged in this way and not knowing where in the pack they fit in. The dog snaps out of insecurity through being treated as a human by the indulgent 'blue rinse', who requires a child substitute.

Consistency is needed with dogs. A puppy should never be teased by an adult or a child, for example by having a toy or chew taken away and then being repeatedly tempted with it. Likewise, a dog should never be allowed to assume ownership of a toy or chew, if a higher member of the pack – *you* – demands the toy. If you watch, as I do regularly, how members of a pack deal with this situation, you will see how the dog higher in the pecking order will approach, and then stand over, a subordinate. As the underdog submits, the higher pack dog takes the bone. This is done usually at a time when the underdog is in a vulnerable position, so avoiding a confrontation and probable fight.

If we work in this way we can also avoid confrontation most of the time. Always make actions clear and concise, leaving the dog in no doubt. So, to prove your higher placing in the pack by taking the toy or chew away, gently talk to the puppy, who can then tell that you are in a calm, not cross or threatening mood. Then approach the puppy and firmly take the toy or chew. Stroke and restrain the puppy, who will realise that grabbing the chew back is not allowed. Once you have the

This situation could be chaotic, but early training means that all the dogs know who is pack-leader.   *Photo: Keith Allison.*

chew, praise the puppy, who will then respect your prerogative to take what is yours, as pack leader. The puppy can then be given the chew back and praised for having good manners.

In your role as pack leader, you can gain respect from a youngster fairly easily. The tone of your voice, the inner confidence of what you are asking, play a great part in achieving this respect. A dam with puppies teaches manners and respect for elders in much the same way we do with our young. If the youngster goes too far in a game, instead of saying 'it will end in tears' as we would, the dam will give a disapproving look. If youngster pushes the situation further, the dam administers a 'short sharp shock' in the form of a snap and sharp growl. Puppy will often scream in response, but comply to the request immediately, watching and listening more intently to the signs next time. I have seen this action many times over the years and never seen a mark or wound on a puppy following such actions. The parallel action, administered by the human pack leader is a sharp smack on the bottom, stinging not damaging, simultaneously with a firm command of *No*. The Weimaraner puppy, next time, responds to the No and the sound of a clap of hands. The Weimaraner never forgets if taught something clearly.

Obviously youngsters accept rules (once learned) without question, but as with adolescent teenagers, adolescent Weimaraners think they know everything. Again I do not invent rules, I watch nature and deal with pretensions in the same way. Despite so-called equality in humans, dogs still respect the difference between male and female. Female adolescent canines try it on, but when told off verbally, usually act silly and avoid any real confrontation. The male can react more physically. We have a number of males in our pack, all differing in age by at least a year and consequently well aware of the pecking order. To reiterate, if possible try to avoid a confrontation, using mental strength to make your point.

With a number of dogs, if one or two are taken from the pack to a show, field trial or just for a walk, be alert when reintroducing them into the pack. It is wise to let them meet in the garden, so when greetings take place, precious possessions are not knocked over. Do not start petting any of the dogs, just talk calmly, settling the possible excitable situations. When all have greeted and sniffed each other, the pack will settle into normality.

INDOOR KENNELS

We have established that a Weimaraner is intelligent, and rules for life must be laid down from the beginning. The use of an indoor kennel is often your greatest asset. It is brilliant for stress relief for both owner and dog. For the owner it relieves the worry of getting up one morning to find a 'pile' in the middle of the lounge carpet, or a kitchen soaked in puddles. If the dog is left for a couple of hours during the day in an indoor kennel, the owner does not come back to find the chair chewed or the lino pulled up. This gives the owner mental control. By shutting the puppy in the kennel you are saying "If I have to go out, I will go when I want and walk you at my convenience," thus establishing the pecking order. The dog who has grown up knowing this cannot, even in adolescence, retaliate at being left by chewing something to defy you. From the dog's point of view the indoor kennel provides somewhere that is private – it will become the dog's sanctuary. We all know the feeling of security gained when we are in our 'own' chair or using our 'own' cup. The indoor kennel is the same for dogs. It is their 'own' place, a bolt hole to escape to from, for example, marauding children, a place in which they are never told off. Initially

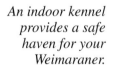

An indoor kennel provides a safe haven for your Weimaraner.

the dog may not appreciate these facts, in much the same way as we do not always appreciate what, in the long run, will benefit us. The first few nights of putting a new puppy to bed in an indoor kennel may cause sleeplessness for all. Remember the Weimaraner is very stubborn – this fact is often learned first-hand at this time. Do not give in: you are now setting a pattern for the future. Something which may help puppy become less hostile initially to the indoor kennel is to put it at the side of your bed. Each time puppy cries out, you can put your hand on the kennel telling puppy you are near and giving reassurance of your presence. After a few nights the kennel can be moved out of the bedroom and, eventually, placed in the room of your choice.

Apprehension is often the reaction I get when first mentioning the virtues of an indoor kennel. When thinking of acquiring any puppy, the last thing on one's mind is putting this 'precious being' in a cage. However, by the same token, when one has a baby no-one envisages putting that child behind bars, yet without exception we do indeed put a baby in a cot. These wooden bars give the child security but, as anyone putting a toddler into a normal bed for the first time will know, much reassurance is needed before the child adapts – exactly the same scenario as with a puppy and an indoor kennel. Another benefit of an indoor kennel is that, when going away in a caravan, the dog is safe in that kennel, in the awning, with no danger of escaping to go wandering. When taking a dog to a hotel, the advantage of an indoor kennel is that the dog is secure, in a familiar environment, and therefore will not bark or chew at the stress of being left. The one thing you cannot do is put an eight-month juvenile delinquent into the indoor kennel for the first time. The decision must be made initially. If an indoor kennel does not fit into your lifestyle, fine, but never think of the kennel as cruel.

OUTSIDE KENNELS

Many people who work part-time or alternate shifts successfully have dogs. Dogs who have plenty of quality time with their owners will not suffer at all. In fact, the person who works from home or has a small family to care for, may spend many hours with the dog, yet actually give that dog no individual time and little training because they are so busy with work/children etc. A Weimaraner is very much a people dog who will gladly go wherever you go, usually happy to sit in the car, just to be with you. In life we all have to do things we do not want to, be it work, or school, or being parted from loved ones. It is no different for your Weimaraner. In fact time spent apart can be good for all, allowing batteries to be recharged.

To leave a Weimaraner with the run of the home on a regular basis for three or four hours a day is courting trouble. That active mind will need stimulus, so rearranging the home or garden may be on the agenda. An outside kennel with run allows the dog freedom of choice to go inside or out, while keeping control of the canine imagination. It must always be remembered that a Weimaraner will explore all avenues before complying with your wishes. With this in mind the kennel run should be high enough so that the dog cannot jump or climb out. Six foot is not an inviting height to jump, so it is an ideal height for the run. It must be unchewable, so a good quality weldmesh will prove cheap in the long run. The run will also need paving or concreting. This allows cleaning to be more efficient and the dog will not be able to dig a way out. Pre-built kennels and runs can be purchased; otherwise partitioning the end of a garage may be a possibility, incorporating a bob hole to allow your Weimaraner into a run. A bob hole is useful because it reduces the chance of cold or draught infiltrating the rest area. If a type of garden shed is to be used as a kennel it is also a good idea to have a bob hole into the run for this reason, plus the door allowing easy access for you into the kennel to place bedding, cleaning it etc. Housing arrangements need some thought before taking puppy home. You will have trouble putting an older dog into a kennel, whether inside or out, while a puppy who is used to it initially will settle happily and grow up with it.

TRAVEL

As a breed Weimaraners love being with humans and usually will happily go with you in the car. Again, good habits need teaching young. The initial trip home is rather special. Everyone is excited and there is an element of stress involved for the new puppy, so being cuddled on your knee, with towels and a supply of kitchen paper handy, is acceptable for this first journey. Always have two people for this journey – one to drive and the other to care for the puppy.

One is advised not to take a puppy out until all inoculations are complete. This is OK in theory but in practice it means puppy goes home, and then to the vet for an inoculation, which is enough to make any dog wary of cars. I think commonsense can prevail. Obviously taking puppy on to pavements, into parks and the like can leave an uninoculated puppy vulnerable to diseases deposited by strays, or irresponsibly owned dogs, who are carriers of disease. I recommend taking puppy to friends or relatives who do not have dogs, or who have dogs which are vaccinated. After all, puppy comes from an environment of being in contact with other canines, even if it is only mother. I would advise carrying the puppy from the car to the garden of your destination, thus taking sensible precautions. Puppy can then become socialised at an early impressionable age when learning is very important.

Decide where puppy is to be in the car while travelling. Obviously a good place is in the back of a station wagon or hatchback. On initial journeys take a companion with you who can sit in the back seat and exercise restraint should the puppy try to climb over the seat. Do not make a fuss or puppy will be encouraged to want to climb over. Your puppy, if worried, should be talked to quietly, thus discouraging any upset. A concentrated effort for a few journeys will lead to a contented traveller in the future. If your dog suffers travel sickness, the best remedy I have found is to give travel sickness pills one would buy for humans. Your vet can only supply a sedative which does not really help, especially if you are intending taking puppy for a walk or to a show, as your puppy will be drowsy. On every journey give the puppy a tablet a couple of hours previously and, usually, within two or three months, puppy will have grown out of being sick.

HOUSE TRAINING

Think for your dog. Puppies should be popped outside after every awakening. Stand silently watching them. When finally they perform, which can take ages, quietly praise them. Other signs that they may need to go out are when they stop playing and start sniffing around – they can start to go round and round in circles in preparation for performing. Was it a long time since they went out? They may even go to the door asking to go out – Weimaraners learn very quickly. After a meal is another sure time. If you dog has an accident in the house, try to look on it as *your* fault for not being vigilant enough. Show disapproval by a stern *No*, take the pup out and wait. Read *War and Peace* if necessary! Again, make a positive show of approval when finally the puppy performs. This will establish the message very quickly that you are pleased when duty is done outside – not inside. If you get excited, get angry and make a fuss when your puppy has an accident inside, this can build up an association in the puppy's mind between the evacuation of bowels and bladder and your displeasure. This leads to the puppy doing these natural functions out of your sight, and refraining from 'going' when out for a walk or when you are about. In extreme cases this can lead to a puppy depositing a pile on the lounge carpet when your back is turned because, although the puppy does not really want to feel your wrath, yet even this is better than being ignored, which usually happens if the pup is put outside to perform when you are angry. The indoor kennel can be invaluable as an aid to night-time house-training, as the puppy can only go in the enclosed space and so will grow out of needing relief at night more quickly. Restricting late night feeding and water can also help.

TEACHING GOOD MANNERS

As with children, a well-mannered dog is an asset to you and an achievement you can be proud of. We have 20 Weimaraners, and folk old and young can walk among them without being 'mugged' or jumped all over. This is never achieved by cruelty but by starting as you mean to go on. Instead of greeting puppies by calling to them with arms outstretched, always go down to their level and if they try to jump on you with excitement, hold them down, while praising them and giving them the attention they require. This way no puppy will ever need to jump up and therefore it will never enter their head to try. When friends come round, instead of letting them fawn all over the puppy before they have even moved from the doorway, discourage any familiarity until they are well installed in the house and all have settled. Your puppy will not then get into the habit of throwing itself at the door every time someone arrives. This behaviour may be acceptable in a puppy but not in an eighty-pound adult. Always apply rules for your youngster that you want to be adhered to when your dog is an adult.

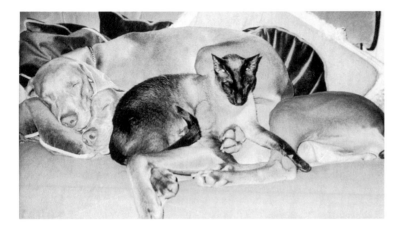

If Weimaraners are brought up with other animals they will live together in perfect harmony.

If introduced at an early age, Weimaraners will tolerate most pets.

TOYS

The point to remember when giving toys is that puppies must always be of the opinion that they are your toys which they are being allowed to play with. Take toys away from a puppy from an early age. Never tease, but only return the toy when your Weimaraner is respectful, not when trying to snatch the toy back. If by some chance at a future time a child, for instance, inadvertently goes to take something from the dog, the dog will then allow this to happen without snapping.

It is useful to have certain toys, bones, etc. for the dog to play with. Our Weimaraners love carrying and must be taught what is allowed to be carried. In fact we have a worn-out old slipper and the dogs will root this particular slipper out of a pile of slippers very successfully. 'Nylabones' made for dogs can give hours of enjoyment with no worry or harm, as can sterilised bones, obtained from your pet retailer, or a large marrow bone from the butchers. All these have the added advantage of keeping teeth and gums healthy and stimulating gastric juices. Because Weimaraners are such a determined breed, cow heels and smaller hide chews are best avoided. A Weimaraner who gets fed up chewing may swallow such chews whole, causing blockages and worse. Also avoid small bones of any description and if in doubt, best omit. A point worth mentioning when playing with Weimaraners with a toy – do not play tug of war games. This has the effect of encouraging them to bite harder to hang on to the prize, which can make them 'hard mouthed' – and in the future, if asked to retrieve something gently, the dog may bite harder to avoid losing the retrieve.

PLAYING GAMES
Any 'rough housing', or playing hard with your Weimaraner, should be done on a controlled basis, with you making sure the excitement does not get too far. A youngster who has been allowed to grab your arm, or old clothes, will think this is acceptable behaviour when adult. Many times I am told that Weimaraners are a highly strung and boisterous breed. I certainly do not find that. What Weimaraners definitely are is sensitive and very aware of your moods and therefore they can be easily 'wound up'. Because they put their heart and soul into whatever they do, this can lead to over-zealous behaviour or, with a young adolescent male, possible sexual excitement. We have never had a young dog 'riding a leg' but if over-excitement is developing, we quickly change the subject to relax the situation.

GETTING ON WITH OTHER DOGS
Many showgoers of other breeds are of the opinion that Weimaraners, particularly males, are aggressive with other dogs. Indeed many pet owners extol the virtues of their wonderful Weimaraners but add that they are unreliable with other dogs. This starts in puppyhood and can be avoided with all but very badly-bred dogs. Generally, bad temperament is really bad temper! When puppies go for a walk they, being naive, trustingly approach all dogs, wanting to play. Not all dogs are friendly. A puppy who rushes up to such a dog can be bitten. If that puppy is a Weimaraner, this experience will be remembered. Next time that Weimaraner puppy will be more wary and on guard. This can then lead to that puppy becoming too defensive and, ultimately, aggressive. As humans we do not approach strangers by throwing our arms around them – we are more polite, approaching with a smile and general greeting. Apply these rules to your Weimaraner. When you see another dog, put your puppy back on to the lead. You now have the choice of whether or not to let your dog play with the other, after conversing with the owner as to whether the oncomer is friendly. Always apply these rules. Then your dog will grow up not expecting to be bitten and will have confidence in you when you allow play, knowing then that there is no need to be on the defensive.

ADOLESCENCE
As a youngster your dog looks on you as the one who must be obeyed and, if you keep this attention, will generally respond well. However, as I have said, adolescent Weimaraners, rather

like human teenagers, think they know best. Haven't you noticed that, at seventeen, parents know very little, yet by the time you reach twenty they have learned an enormous amount in those three short years!

If a youngster starts to defy you at this stage, go back to basics. For instance, if your dog while on a walk starts to go further when called back, do not release the lead. Instead put on a flexi-lead and then, when the dog does not respond to your command, you have the power to dictate, thus reminding your dog of your higher standing in the pack. Once you have retracted the lead and your dog is with you, that is the time to praise and perhaps give a treat. Even though your dog did not instantly respond and had to be drawn in on the lead, your command has actually been complied with and therefore deserves praise. Alternatively, walk in an unfamiliar place which will make your dog feel vulnerable and more ready to return to you when called. Don't form a habit of sticking to the same pattern and, for example, always putting the lead back on at 'the third tree'. Change the routine, call your dog and give a tidbit, without putting the lead back on every time.

CHILDREN

If you teach your Weimaraners with love that they are dogs, they will have no hang-ups with children. It is unwise, indeed cruel, to indulge dogs as if they were human and then, when a baby comes along, suddenly change the rules. Children and dogs give so much to each other. Dogs teach children vital lessons, showing respect for other beings, loyalty and friendship. Weimaraners will protect all family members and, as I have said, are often found watching over a young child at play, without participating. Weimaraners can play hard, so games need overseeing. It is unwise to allow a young child, under mid-teens to take a Weimaraner for a walk unsupervised. If the Weimaraner reacted to a situation, a youngster may not have either the strength of character or physical strength to control a potentially sticky situation, with the headstrong Weimaraner taking charge. Much as you love your dog, respect the fact that this is a dog. I feel young children and dogs should never be left together unattended. A child may poke something into the dog's ear, purely out of curiosity. How else does the dog react to stopping such pain, but by the only defence available – biting? A child could jump onto a sleeping dog, innocently; again the dog's instinct will say 'predator', and cause a bad reaction. Don't rely on "my dog will never bite". Never say never, and foresee all eventualities – your whole family will ultimately benefit.

LIVESTOCK

We regularly walk up to twenty Weimaraners through fields of sheep. Many folk take Weimaraners shooting and the dog is asked to hunt through land with sheep and cattle. If trained, the Weimaraners will react as if the livestock were invisible, yet if they are bored, or left to their own devices, the Weimaraner is very capable of bringing down sheep, even worrying them. Quite often, the worst sheep-worrying breed is the Border Collie or Working Sheepdog. This is because they will work sheep. However, if underestimated, and once the adrenaline flows, one thing can lead to another and they can become a sheep worrier. Because of the nature of their inherent instincts, Weimaraners were asked to face and bring down wild boar or deer and therefore, once their adrenaline is aroused and if free from supervision, they could do the same with sheep. No responsible owner allows his dog to wander freely. It is your job to supply the stimulation for your dog. If you cannot do this, do not get a Weimaraner.

Many Weimaraners will exercise happily with horses. If properly taught to respect the heavy-footed creature they should come to no harm. Likewise with cats. If your Weimaraner is brought into an environment where cats are present you should have no problem. The dog will grow up being taught respect by the cat. Initially, however, watch carefully. An inquisitive Weimaraner getting too close to the cat may come away with clawed eyes! It is considerably harder to introduce a cat into the home of a grown Weimaraner and vigilance must prevail, otherwise one snap could fatally damage the cat.

BOARDING

As the owner of boarding kennels I dread boarding Weimaraners. This breed is so people-oriented and such a loyal companion they can suffer stress at being left, resulting in the fit dog you kennelled becoming a grey-covered skeleton on your return. I find it rare to find a Weimaraner sitting in a corner shivering, not wanting to eat. Indeed they enter into the spirit of the occasion well. But it is the inner stress and fretting which burns off the calories. In boarding kennels, we would feed a Weimaraner three times a day. The Weimaraners who settle best, in a boarding environment, are the ones who come at least once a year, possibly for the first time before

Dick Finch out hunting with his dogs. Many Weimaraners will exercise happily with horses.

they are one year old. They accept that you go, but do come back. Length of time actually in a boarding kennel matters little. Dogs are not conscious of time, be it one week or one month. It is when the dog is fully mature and left for the first time for over a fortnight, that you will find the most deterioration, so if your dog is older and has never been left before, make a point of leaving your Weimaraner in the kennels of your choice, for a couple of days, once or twice before you go on the World tour.

RESCUE

There is a saying 'There are no bad dogs, only bad owners'. While I do not wholeheartedly agree with this statement, it is fact that the majority of Weimaraners needing to be rehomed have problems caused by bad upbringing. When someone brings a 'rescue' Weimaraner here for us to rehome, we are always assured that the dog has no problems, is good in every way and it is a change in home circumstances, or the like, which has necessitated the parting. In my experience over the years only three male Weimaraners came as rescues on correct and honest terms. The other 'perfect' Weimaraners were described as such to alleviate the guilt felt by the parting owners. No-one enjoys being wrong.

The reason I stress this is because many people decide upon an 'older' dog, rather than a puppy, thinking they are missing a hard stage of dog-owning. Generally, with an older dog you may be swapping one set of problems for another. The older the dog the more set the dog's way. For instance, chewing in a puppy is one thing; severe destruction can occur when that dog is older. Defiance in a puppy can be easily rectified; in a two-year-old it can be very unnerving. If you want to give a caring, loving home to an older dog in need, think very carefully, making sure you have removed the 'rose-coloured glasses'.

Chapter Four

BREED STANDARDS

A pedigree dog scores over a mongrel because, with the former, you know your puppy's ancestry, what the full-grown dog will look like and what to expect about the temperament and characteristics of your chosen breed. Before breeding or judging you must understand the basic construction of dogs and have a thorough knowledge of the pertinent Breed Standard. It is essential that the Standard is interpreted properly. For example, all too often I read in so-called judges' critiques the words 'pale colour' relating to the Weimaraner's coat colour, yet in no Weimaraner standard I have read is the word 'pale' used.

We must adhere to the Standard of the breed as closely as possible. The Standard was laid down in this precise way because a dog of this construction, size, shape, colour and temperament would fulfil the needs of the fancier. The Weimaraner has indeed done this for centuries, before being recognised officially as a breed in 1896. We, the breed's present-day custodians, owe it to our Weimaraners not to change them just to follow the fashion of the day. All too often this has happened with other breeds in the past, frequently with devastating results and consequent breathing, hereditary and whelping problems. We can learn from this and keep our breed sound.

Everyone interprets the Standard slightly differently because of personal preferences. This is good, because these preferences usually balance out and the end result is that breeders are aware of the different aspects of the Standard. In fact this has happened with breeders of the Weimaraner in the UK, who have bred with their eyes open. This has resulted in the Weimaraner being, at present, one of the soundest breeds in construction in the gundog group.

Contributing to this in no small way has been the importation of dogs from the USA, particularly Jane George's Ch. Kamsou Moonraker von Bismark in the mid-seventies and Carolyn Alston's British-bred, of American-bred stock, Sh. Ch. Flimmoric Fanclub (mainly Nani's breeding) in the mid-eighties.

Reproduced are the British, American and German Breed Standards. The British Standard is the Kennel Club Revised Standard of 1987. The American Standard is dated 1972 and the German Standard 1990.

UK STANDARD

GENERAL APPEARANCE Medium sized, grey with light eyes. Presents a picture of power, stamina and balance.
CHARACTERISTICS Hunting ability of paramount concern.
TEMPERAMENT Fearless, friendly, protective, obedient and alert.
HEAD AND SKULL Moderately long, aristocratic; moderate stop, slight median line

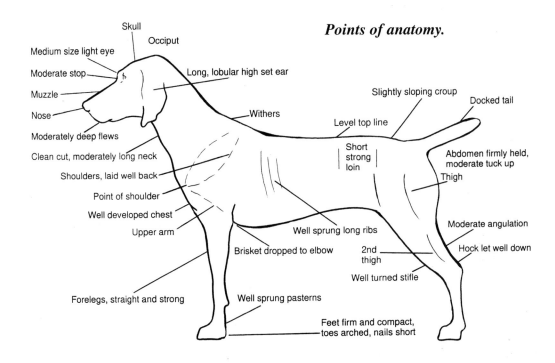

Points of anatomy.

extending back over forehead. Rather prominent occipital bone. Measurement from top of nose to stop equal to measurement from stop to occipital prominence. Flews moderately deep, enclosing powerful jaw. Foreface straight, delicate nostrils. Skin tightly drawn. Nose grey.

EYES Medium sized. Shades of amber or blue-grey. Placed far enough apart to indicate good disposition, not too protruding or deeply set. Expression keen, kind and intelligent.

EARS Long, lobular, slightly folded, set high. When drawn alongside jaw, should end approximately 1 inch from point of nose.

MOUTH Jaws strong with a perfect, regular and complete scissor bite, i.e. upper teeth closely overlapping lower teeth and set square to the jaws. Lips and gums of pinkish, flesh colour. Complete dentition highly desirable.

NECK Clean cut and moderately long.

FOREQUARTERS Forelegs straight and strong. Measurement from elbow to ground equal to distance from elbow to top of withers.

BODY Length of body measured from highest point of withers to ground. Topline level, with slightly sloping croup. Chest well developed, deep. Shoulders well laid. Ribs well sprung, ribcage extending well back. Abdomen firmly held, moderately tucked up flank. Brisket should drop to elbow.

HINDQUARTERS Moderately angulated, with well turned stifle. Hocks well let down, turned neither in nor out. Musculation well developed.

FEET Firm, compact. Toes well arched, pads close, thick. Nails short, grey or amber in colour. Dewclaws customarily removed.

TAIL Customarily docked at a point so that remaining tail covers scrotum in dogs and vulva in bitches. Thickness of tail in proportion to body, and should be carried in a manner expressing confidence and sound temperament. In long-haireds the tip of the tail should be removed.

GAIT/MOVEMENT Effortless ground covering, indicating smooth co-ordination. Seen from rear, hind feet parallel to front feet. Seen from side, topline remains strong and level

COAT Short, smooth and sleek. In longhaired variety, coat from 1-2 inches long on body, somewhat longer on neck, chest and belly. Tail and back of limbs, feathered.

COLOUR Preferably silver grey, shades of mouse or roe grey permissible; blending to lighter shade on head and ears. Dark eel stripe frequently occurs along back. Whole coat gives an appearance of metallic sheen. Small white mark permissible on chest. White spots resulting from injuries not penalised.

SIZE Height at withers: Dogs 61-69 cms (24-27 inches); Bitches 56-64 cms (22-25 inches).

FAULTS Any departure from the foregoing points should be considered a fault and the seriousness with which the fault should be regarded should be in exact proportion to its degree.

NOTE Male animals should have two apparently normal testicles fully descended into the scrotum.

Application has been made to the Kennel Club for the following amendments, some of which had been deleted from the previous standard.

HEAD AND SKULL Delicate at nostrils.

EARS To include the words 'set well back'

TAIL In longhaireds the tip of the tail may be removed.

COLOUR 'Usually' to be added to blending to lighter shade on head and ears.

Reproduced by kind permission of the Kennel Club.

AMERICAN STANDARD

GENERAL APPEARANCE A medium sized gray dog, with fine aristocratic features. He should present a picture of grace, speed, stamina, alertness and balance. Above all, the dog's conformation must indicate the ability to work with great speed and endurance in the field.

HEIGHT Height at the withers: Dogs 25" to 27"; Bitches 23" to 25". One inch over or under the specified height of each sex is allowable but should be penalized. Dogs measuring less than 24" or more than 28" and bitches measuring less than 22" or more than 26" shall be disqualified.

HEAD Moderately long and aristocratic, with moderate stop and slight median line extending back over the forehead. Rather prominent occipital bone and trumpets well set back, beginning at the back of the eye-sockets. Measurement from tip of nose to stop equal to that from stop to occipital bone. The flews should be straight, delicate at the nostrils. Skin drawn tightly. Neck clean-cut and moderately long. Expression kind, keen and intelligent.

EARS Long and lobular, slightly folded and set high. The ear when drawn snugly alongside the jaw should end approximately two inches from the point of the nose.

EYES In shades of light amber, gray or blue-gray, set well enough apart to indicate good disposition and intelligence. When dilated under excitement the eyes may appear almost black.

TEETH Well set, strong and even, well-developed and proportionate to jaw with correct scissors bite, the upper teeth protruding slightly over the lower teeth but not more than 1/16th of an inch. Complete dentition is greatly to be desired.

NOSE Gray.

LIPS AND GUMS Pinkish flesh shades.

BODY The back should be moderate in length, set in a straight line, strong and should slope slightly from the withers. The chest should be well developed and deep with shoulders well laid back. Ribs well sprung and long. Abdomen firmly held; moderately tucked up flank. The brisket should extend to the elbow.

COAT AND COLOR Short, smooth and sleek, solid color, in shades of mouse-gray to silver-gray, usually blending to lighter shades on the head and ears. A small white marking on the chest is permitted, but should be penalized on any other portion of the body. White spots resulting from injury should not be penalized. A distinctly long coat is a disqualification. A distinctly blue or black coat is a disqualification.

FORELEGS Straight and strong, with the measurement from the elbow to the ground approximately equalling the distance from the elbow to the top of the withers.

HINDQUARTERS Well angulated stifles and straight hocks. Musculation well developed.

FEET Firm and compact, webbed, toes well-arched, pads closed and thick, nails short and gray or amber in color. Dewclaws should be removed.

TAIL Docked. At maturity it should measure approximately six inches with a tendency to be light rather than heavy and should be carried in a manner expressing confidence and sound temperament. A non-docked tail should be penalized.

GAIT The gait should be effortless and should indicate smooth co-ordination. When seen from the rear, the hind feet should be parallel with the front feet. When viewed from the side, the top line should remain strong and level.

TEMPERAMENT The temperament should be friendly, fearless, alert and obedient.

MINOR FAULTS Tail too short or too long. Pink nose.

MAJOR FAULTS Doggy bitches. Bitchy dogs. Improper muscular condition. Badly affected teeth. More than four teeth missing. Back too long or too short. Faulty coat. Neck too short, thick or throaty. Low set tail. Elbows in or out. Feet east or west. Poor gait. Poor feet. Cow hocks. Faulty backs either roached or sway. Badly overshot, or undershot bite. Snipey muzzle. Short ears.

VERY SERIOUS FAULTS White, other than a spot on the chest. Eyes, other than gray, blue-gray or light amber. Black mottled mouth. Non-docked tail. Dogs exhibiting strong fear, shyness and extreme nervousness.

DISQUALIFICATION Deviation in height of more than one inch from standard either way. A distinctly long coat. A distinctly blue or black coat is a disqualification.

Standard as adopted 1971. Effective December 31st, 1972.
Reproduced by kind permission of the American Kennel Club.

GERMAN STANDARD

GENERAL APPEARANCE A medium large to large gundog. Effectively a working type, elegant, sinewy, with a powerful muscular system. The male and female sex must be clearly defined.

IMPORTANT MEASUREMENT PROPORTIONS Body length to wither height about 12 : 11. Length proportions of the head, from the tip of the nose to the start of the forehead slightly longer than from there to the occipital bone. Front legs, length from elbows to the middle of front middle foot knuckles, and length from elbows to withers, about the same.

BEHAVIOUR AND CHARACTER A versatile, easy-going, fearless and enthusiastic gundog with a systematic and persevering search, yet not excessively fast. A remarkably good nose. Sharp on prey and game. Also man-sharp, yet not aggressive. Reliable in pointing and waterwork. Remarkable inclination to work after the shot.

HEAD In proportion to the body size and with the facial structure in the dog broader than with the bitch, yet with both in good proportion in relation to the width of the top of the head and the total length of the head. On the centre of the forehead a groove. Occiput lightly to moderately protruding. Behind the eyes clearly visible cheek bone. Forehead area (Stop) extremely small.

FACIAL STRUCTURE Nose: Nose sponge large, pointing over the lower jaw, dark flesh coloured, receding gradually changing to grey.

Muzzle: Long and especially with the dog, strong in profile working almost to a right angle. Nose ridge straight, frequently a little raised, never dished.

Lips: Moderately overhanging, flesh coloured with small fold at the corner of the mouth.

Jaw: Powerful.

Cheeks: Muscular and clearly formed. 'Dry Head'. Set of Teeth: Complete, regular and strong. Cutting teeth moving in a grating fashion (scissor bite). Eyes: Amber coloured, dark to light with an intelligent expression. In puppy stage sky blue. Round, hardly slanted. Eyelids flat (well-fitting showing no haw.)

Ears: Broad and fairly long, reaching to about the corner of the mouth. High and narrow at the inset, rounded off into a point at the bottom. When alert, turned slightly forwards, folds.

NECK Of noble appearance and stately. Upper profile curved, muscular, nearly round, with a good reach and dry. Getting stronger towards the shoulder and harmoniously merging into the back line and chest.

BODY Topline: From the curved neck line over the well-formed wither harmoniously merging into the relatively long, strong back.

Wither: Clearly defined.

Back: Strong and muscular, without hollow. At the back not over built. (High behind.) A slightly longer back, as it is characteristic to the breed, is not faulty.

Croup: Pelvis long and with a moderate slope.

Chest: Powerful, but not too wide, with enough depth, nearly reaching the elbows and sufficiently long. Good curve, without being barrel shaped, with long ribs, front of chest well shaped. (Fore Chest.)

Belly-line: Slightly increasing, however belly not showing. Clearly defined flank. (Area below loin).

Tail: Set of tail slightly deeper under the back line than with other comparable breeds. Tail strong and well-covered with hair. In rest position hanging, when alert and in work, horizontal or also carried higher.

Sex Organs: Dogs must show two obviously normally developed testicles, which are completely in the scrotum.

LIMBS Forelegs: Generally legs 'high', sinewy, straight and parallel, but not broad standing. (Too wide)

Shoulders: Long and sloping, well (close) fitting, strongly muscular. Good angulation of the shoulder blade over arm 'hinge' (where shoulder joins to the withers).

Upper Arm: Set at a slant, long enough and strong (from point) of shoulder to elbows.

Elbows: Free and straight set. Neither turned inwardly nor outwardly.

Under Arm: Long, positioned straight.

Pastern Joint: Powerful, tight.

Pastern: Sinewy, slightly slanting.

Front Feet: Closed and powerful. Standing straight to body centre. Toes arched. Longer middle toes are characteristic to the breed so consequently not faulty. Claws light to dark grey. Pads well-pigmented, coarse.

Hindlegs: Generally legs 'high', sinewy, muscular, parallel in placing, not turned outwardly nor inwardly.

Upper thigh: Of sufficient length, strong and muscular.

Stifle joint: Powerful and tight.

'Under leg' (from stifle joint to hock joint): long tendons clearly protruding.

Hock Joint: Powerful and tight.

Hind Middle Foot: (Hock joint to pad.) Sinewy, nearly vertically placed.

Hind Feet: Closed and powerful, without dewclaws, otherwise like front feet.

MOVEMENT Movement sequence in all ways of walking free and flowing. Hind and front legs placed in a parallel fashion. Gallop long and front. In trot the back stays level. Pacing is undesirable.

SKIN Strong, good, but not too tightly fitting.

COAT Constitution: (a) Shorthaired: short, but longer and denser as with most comparable breeds. Strong, very thick, smooth flat top coat, with or without a small amount of undercoat. (b) Longhaired: Soft long topcoat with or without undercoat. Flat or a little wavy. Hair at the ear set long and overhanging. At the ear points shorter and velvety. With or without fringing. Hair length on the sides 3-5 cm, under neck, chest and belly usually a little longer. Good feathers and trousers, although at the bottom less long. Tail with good flag. Space between toes hairy. Head hair covering less long. A Sockhaarig (Wirecoat) with medium/long, dense and good-fitting topcoat, thick undercoat and moderately shaped feather and trousers appears occasionally with dogs of mixed breed (undesirable).

COLOUR Silver, roe or mouse grey as well as 'mergers' between these colour tones. Head and ears usually lighter. White markings are only permissible to a small extent on the chest and on the toes. Occasionally over the middle of the back a more or less obvious darker eel stripe. Dogs with clear red-yellow tint can at the most only obtain the score 'good'. Brown tint is a bad fault.

SIZE AND WEIGHT Wither height: Dogs 59-70 cm (23.25-27.5") (Ideal height 61-67 cm, 24-27"). Bitches 57-65 cm (22.5-25.5") (Ideal height 59-63 cm, 23.25-23.75"). Weight: Dogs: 30-40 kg (66-88 lbs). Bitches 25-35 kg (55-77 lbs).

FAULTS All deviations from the above mentioned points can be seen as a fault. The judgement of them is in exact relation to the extent of the deviation.

1. Distinct deviation in type. Sex uncharacteristic.

2. Large deviations in the proportions.

3. Slight character flaws.

4.1. Large deviations in size and proportions.

4.2. Facial structure. Large deviations e.g. lips too thick, shorter or snipey muzzle.

4.3. Jaw and teeth missing more than 2 P1 or M3.

4.4. Eyes.

4.5. Ears. Really short or long, not folded.

5. Throat. Large deviations in shape and muscle.

6. Back. Sway or roach backed, overbuilt.

6.1. Chest and Belly. Barrel-shaped ribs, insufficient chest depth or length, pulled up belly, too much tuck.

6.2. Sex Organs. Clear deviations in the shape, size or consistency of testicles.

7.1. Limbs. Large positional anomalies e.g. poor angles, outwardly turned elbows.

7.2. Hind Limbs. Marked 0-shaped legs or cow hocks.

8. Poor movement in individual ways of walking. Also faulty "forestep" or "forehove" – "stepwalk" (pacing).

9. Coat. Big inadequacies e.g. coat very fine or very coarse.

DISQUALIFYING FAULTS

Totally untypical, above all clumsy or weak.

Totally unproportioned.

Character flaws e.g. timid or frightened.

Totally untypical e.g. Bulldog-like top of head.

Absolutely untypical e.g. dished face

Overshot, undershot, further teeth missing.

Entropion and ectropion.

Ears absolutely untypical e.g. sticking out.

Exceptionally throaty.

Exceptionally sway or roached backed or overbuilt.

Ribs extremely barrel shaped or deformed

Monorchid or cryptorchid in dogs.

Legs rickety or deformed.

Hip Dysplasia.

Totally obstructed/restricted in movement.

Coat malformation and defects

FCI 1990 Weimaraner Standard

ANALYSIS

Basically all three standards are very similar. The British is more easily open to wrong interpretation by being less specific. The German Standard has the greatest differences from the British and American Standards.

GENERAL APPEARANCE AND TEMPERAMENT

All three Standards stress that a Weimaraner should have working ability. In an ideal world all Weimaraners would be shot over in one capacity or another – but then, in an ideal world I would not have to work! Whether you want a Weimaraner to work or not, that instinct is still and should still be there. It is wonderful to watch. This instinct takes over when out walking your Weimaraner, who will quarter, even in the park, and many Weimaraners will go rigid on point, even on an old discarded tennis ball, lost in undergrowth. I have proudly been presented with a slimy decaying skeleton of a bird, for which I have been truly grateful, on more than one occasion.

However, the Weimaraner makes a wonderful pet/companion, and an enjoyable dog should you want to compete in Working Trials and Agility. And many people show their Weimaraners with

**Sh. Ch. Gunalt Anais Anais pictured at three
different ages. Her basic outline is apparent
from puppyhood through to her veteran years
showing her true quality.**

*Seven months old: At this stage
she looked round and soft
– a typical puppy.*

*Three years old: In her prime,
showing excellent muscle definition.*

*Fourteen years old: Thickening
around the tummy and lacking
in muscle quality.*

great success. So this versatile breed lends itself to many facets. A priority when owning a Weimaraner is to provide stimulation. When reproducing the Weimaraner, in our endeavour to preserve the breed's characteristics, we should certainly only breed from dogs with an instinct to work, and make sure that the puppies are placed into homes which will utilise their inquisitive minds. We are not breeding a lap dog intent on lying in front of the fire all day. I would liken a Weimaraner puppy to a child of higher-than-average intelligence who, if placed in a class of average children would, because of under-stimulation, become bored and probably disruptive, even destructive.

The standard calls for a friendly, fearless, protective alert temperament. Bred originally to hunt game such as wild boar, wild cat, etc., the dog needed to be courageous and protective in case such dangerous game turned on its master. Working in thick forests in Weimar, the Weimaraner needed agility and alertness. To have such traits means the dog is brave and quick-thinking, and therefore needs a sound temperament.

This sound temperament should be to the fore in any breeding programme. While the German Standard calls for 'sharp on prey and game', both the American and UK Standards have no mention of such. We require any gundog to be soft-mouthed, able to retrieve game gently so that the master can eat that game. Here in the UK we never want a gundog 'sharp'. It is often thought that temperament cannot be properly assessed when judging. Gazing into the eye of a horse portrays the soul. So it is with the dog. So much can be read from the expression. The Weimaraner should have a steady gaze, looking back at you honestly, not flighty or nervous, nor with the pupil dilated except in excitement or work. Likewise the tail carriage sends signals which can be read. A tail clamped down suggests nervousness. Insecurity of temperament in this way is totally unacceptable and leads to biting out of fear. A tail carried high over the back can be a sign of aggression. – watch a terrier on the scent of a rat. The ideal position of the tail should be slightly higher than the level of the back, displaying a confident air. A youngster sometimes carries a high tail when at that stage of being full of self-importance – a stage which the dog generally grows out of.

Medium is a word covering the Weimaraner. The dog should be balanced throughout, each part fitting in harmony with the next, presenting a total animal which can work all day, hunting, galloping, jumping and carrying heavy birds or game. If, for instance, the forequarters are overdone, pressure on bones, muscles and vital organs results, shortening the efficiency of the animal and ultimately the dog's life. In the shooting field can often be viewed the most unsound, unbalanced specimens of certain breeds of gundogs, yet work they do – and extremely well. However, the thing keeping such an animal going more than anything is desire, instinct, 'a big heart'. When breeding we should do the best for our chosen breed and try to breed a dog who can live a long, pain-free life to the full. If I were to equate a dog to a horse, the Weimaraner is the canine equivalent of the thoroughbred. Athletic, powerful, muscular, a breath-taking sight when galloping.

HEAD AND SKULL
Although the head in a male is altogether bigger than in a bitch, neither of them should be coarse. There should be width of skull to allow for brain room (but the skull should not be domed), with the median line across the skull from ear to ear being slightly lighter in colour on the head. The length from occiput to stop, and stop to nose, is equal. This, coupled with the fact that the nose to stop should not be dished, and may even be very slightly raised, contributes to the snooty, aristocratic expression. The cheeks should be clean, not too wide or fleshy. The flews or top lip should cover a powerful jaw, without being pendulous or deep; nor should they be snipey or go to

a point drawing tight over the jaw.

Scent is taken by the nostril and therefore the nose should be large with open nostrils, yet not bulbous. The nose is grey not black as in many breeds. Heads develop at different times during maturity and can often appear unbalanced. A snipey head rarely develops into anything different. A broad, coarse head will rarely change either, yet a doggy head on a bitch, and a bitch head on a dog, will generally even out beautifully in a mature animal. Likewise a bitch with a plain head will often mature and develop following a season, as will the bitch generally.

EYES

The colour is quite unique, being a piercing blue in a youngster under about 18 months, turning to amber with maturity. The eyes should be round, well-set, not too deep giving a piggy appearance, nor bulbous, which could cause health problems. The skin around the eye should be close-fitting, showing no red, loose, haw. Otherwise, again this could be problematic. The eyes should be set not too close together, nor too wide but looking forward with that characteristic, aristocratic look.

EARS

The ears are set on high which goes with the broad flat skull. The domed skull tends to go with the low-set ear, as in Setters. The ear leather is fine. I tend to notice that any dog with a thick leather may be inclined to be coarse. The fine, long ear (finishing to within an inch of the nose, when held down towards the jaw) has a distinctive fold. In a young puppy the ear appears particularly long – imagination suggests that your puppy, at about 18 weeks of age, is about to take off and fly when running towards you with flapping ears. While Weimaraners do not often suffer from ear problems, they do often catch their ears, which then bleed profusely and end up with scars and bits missing.

MOUTH

The Weimaraner, being a retrieving breed, needs a strong jaw and complete dentition with a scissor bite. This means that the front teeth close with the top teeth slightly over the bottom teeth. If the gap is too great this is overshot and, in a youngster, I prefer to see a slightly overshot mouth,

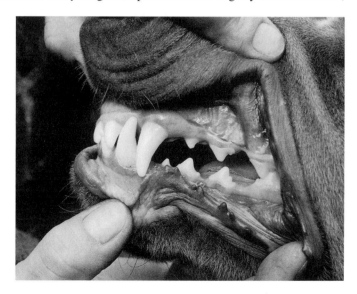

A good mouth: The top front teeth slightly overlap the bottom teeth, showing a correct scissor bite. The teeth are clean, and the gums are in good condition.

Photo: Keith Allison.

as the bottom jaw grows at a different rate, thus catching up and producing the correct mouth in an adult. An undershot jaw is when the bottom teeth protrude in front of the top. A wry mouth is when the jaw is slightly twisted. When breeding, mouths should always be considered. If a dog with a bad mouth is bred from, the problem is difficult to breed out and we must remember that the mouth is important to a dog whose job includes retrieving.

NECK
The neck supports the dog when carrying heavy game, often over obstacles and uneven terrain, so it must be muscular and strong. Too long and the neck loses strength, too short and the neck is cloddy, making picking game and scenting much harder work. The neck needs to be 'dry' or 'clean', without dewlap or loose hanging skin, except in a youngster, who often appears to be wearing an older dog's skin by mistake. The neck should fit neatly into the shoulders; this will be the case if the shoulders are correctly angulated.

FOREQUARTERS
The forelegs should be straight when viewed from the front, not bowed. The bone must be strong, not fine and weak, nor coarse, making the dog cloddy and clumsy. Neither should the feet turn inwards, which is a sign of bad shoulder placement or over-knuckling when the pastern is too straight. Nor should the feet turn out, east and west, which is a sign of weak pasterns. The movement accompanying this is that the dog throws out, and flaps, the front feet when moving. Sometimes an unbalanced youngster stands east and west, but this rights itself as the dog grows and strengthens. If an older dog stands east-west this shows a lack of exercise, or a construction

Hands positioned to show the length and lay of the shoulder blade.

Hands positioned to show length and angle of upper arm.

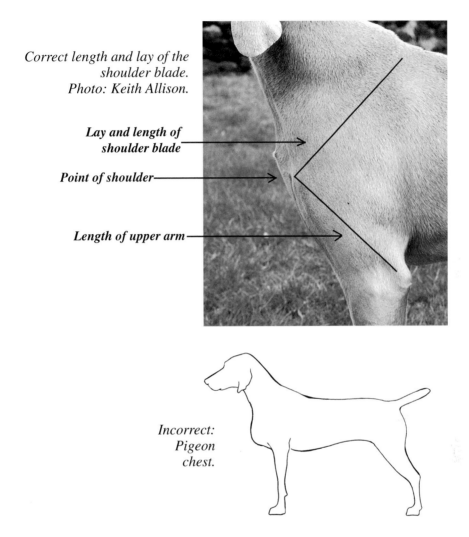

Correct length and lay of the shoulder blade. Photo: Keith Allison.

Lay and length of shoulder blade

Point of shoulder

Length of upper arm

Incorrect: Pigeon chest.

fault, and would be penalised. The pasterns, while not being weak, should have 'give' in them. If you think of the pastern as the shock-absorber, then if it is too straight, jarring will occur when the dog is moving and jumping. If weak, the pasterns will possibly let the dog down, especially with age. If front legs appear to be close together, the dog lacks forechest, which a Weimaraner needs, coupled with spring of rib and length of rib cage. In this area is contained the engine of this galloping breed and room is required so the lungs can function properly and there is heart room.

The greatest weight is carried by the forequarters so shoulders should be properly constructed. We require well-laid shoulder blades, coupled with good length of upper arm. Although an exact angle is not defined, it is generally accepted that an angle of 90 degrees is correct. This gives enough leverage of foreleg, which means the dog has good front extension when moving. If the shoulder blade is not laid correctly, the upper arm is short and the dog can only move forward by the legs being lifted in a hackney action, putting more wear on the dog's front assembly and using more energy. The shoulder blade will be wide at the withers. This can also have the effect of making the dog wide at the elbow, again obstructing free movement. When standing naturally, or 'stacked' for the show ring, the side view of the front assembly shows the shoulder placement and good front if the dog's elbow is in a straight line up to the withers.

BODY
The length of body of the Weimaraner is long in comparison to many breeds. Before judges understood the breed properly, many Weimaraners were penalised for being too long. All dogs have thirteen pairs of ribs. In a shorter-backed dog the ribs do not extend as far back as in a long-backed dog. Either way, no dog requires a long loin. The loin should be well muscled, giving support to the vertebrae, as this is 'the weak link' in the spine. Because there is no support over the loin other than muscle, the loin should be approximately the length of a hand span, so retaining strength. The ribs support the vertebrae. Ribs should be well-sprung, rounded and deep, not too

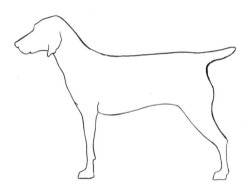

Incorrect: High behind, over-built.

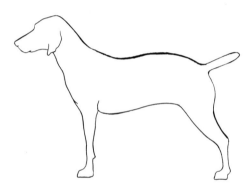

Incorrect: Roached back.

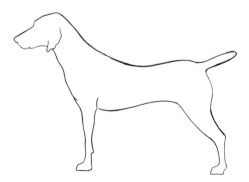

Incorrect: sway back.

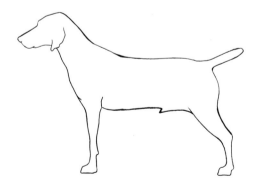

Incorrect: No tuck.

round or barrel-ribbed, which often goes hand in hand with a shallow body – the ribs not reaching the elbow – as this will not give room for the lungs and heart which, as previously stated, is needed in this galloping breed. Weimaraners need this fore chest and a hand-width between the front legs – again to allow for heart and lung room.

A moderate tuck-up means that the abdomen is firmly held but not pulled up, as with a Greyhound or Whippet. Not enough tuck-up can also appear when the animal is dipped in the topline. The topline will be level to the croup which is slightly sloping, giving a slightly lower tail-set than many breeds. When judging a Weimaraner the construction can generally be seen. The reason hands are laid over the ribs, loin and hindquarters, is to feel the quality of muscle or, indeed, fat. A Weimaraner should have hard muscle, not fat.

HINDQUARTERS
'Moderately angulated' is required in the UK Standard. The USA Standard calls for 'well angulated' stifles. This could lead to different interpretation of the original meaning and, when shown, there is a very different way of stacking the Weimaraner in each country. In the UK we stack the Weimaraner with a level topline and therefore moderately angulated hindquarters. In the USA the hindquarters are stood further back from the body giving a sloping topline and a much more angulated appearance to the quarters. If stood naturally the animal will not stand as angulated and the actual type of Weimaraner does not differ as much as one would assume when looking at photographs. Over-angulation can lead to the animal being cow-hocked. The thing we do strive for is balance. Exaggeration leads to weakness and strain on other parts which have to compensate for the weakness.

The angle of the bend of stifle is in sympathy with the shoulder angulation, thus producing correct movement where hind legs follow in the path of the front legs. If there is over-angulation in the hindlegs, the dog, when moving, can only 'crab' – that is moving with the hindlegs going to the side – because they go faster than the front legs or 'run up behind', which forces the topline to be higher than the rear. Any movement other than the desired leads to an imbalance, putting pressure on certain parts. The tibia should be of good length to allow the hock to be 'well let

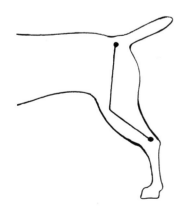

Correct angulation of hindquarters.

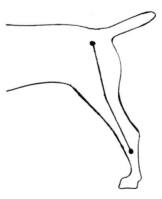

Incorrect: Angulation is too straight.

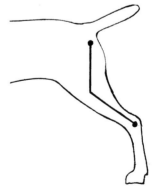

Incorrect: Over-angulated hindquarters.

down' or lower to the ground. This gives moving power, which produces better drive.

Just as the forequarters need to be soundly constructed because they carry the greatest weight of the dog, so the hindquarters need to be correct because they produce drive and lift, giving this hunting, retrieving breed the power to do its job. It is therefore very necessary for the dog to have good width and quantity of muscle. When viewed from the side, the width of second thigh shows between the hock and stifle joint. This should be full and wide. Above this the thigh muscle should also be full, with good density of muscle, not soft and spongy. Poor-quality muscle is due to lack of exercise which is abhorrent in an active gundog such as the Weimaraner.

When viewed from behind, the dog should have wide full buttocks, and the hocks should be parallel to the floor (not cow-hocked) or bowing, again a weakness. If the hip bones are narrow and muscle poor, often the dog moves close behind. I have also noticed that a young puppy can have super quarters, yet with over-exercise in a growing youngster (under one year old), this can lead to weakness and narrow quarters in an adult. We would not allow a 12 year old human to run in a marathon – neither should we walk a young dog's legs off. The Weimaraner has a big heart coupled with the desire to go, and will run as long as you allow, without appearing tired. So be patient – refrain from over-exercise until you have an adult.

FEET

While a Weimaraner requires tight arched feet, we do not want a round, cat-like foot associated with breeds such as the Golden Retriever. According to the German Standard longer middle toes are characteristic and could help to give the dog grip. The pads of the foot need to be thick and evenly padded. They cushion the foot and, if correctly proportioned, protect it from thorns and stones. It is essential that nails are kept short, otherwise the foot cannot function correctly. The dewclaws are removed within the first three days of life and can save much pain and distress later, should they be caught in thick undergrowth. The nature of the Weimaraner is brave – and perhaps even a little foolhardy – therefore the chance of the dog damaging an unremoved dewclaw outweighs the minor painless operation of its early excision. Presumably it is for this reason that the English and USA standards state that the dewclaws are removed.

TAIL

Much controversy reigns over the length of the tail – should it be docked or not? The Weimaraner has no undercoat, the undocked tail is unnaturally long and the tail is used in conjunction with working. In thick undergrowth it can be, and frequently is, damaged. Customarily docked (to cover the vulva in

A well-set tail showing slightly sloping croup, leading to well-muscled hindquarters. The second thigh has good width, the hocks are low, giving good drive and the toes are tight and arched. Photo: Keith Allison.

bitches), the tail is used to denote temperament, by how it is carried, and where scent is, when working. A sound, well-adjusted Weimaraner's tail will be carried at an angle above the body-line, denoting confidence. When out, either enjoying a walk or working, you will find the Weimaraner, when taking scent, will wag that tail incessantly. Whatever your reason for owning this wonderful breed, this instinct is the same and it is fascinating to watch, if only out of curiosity.

GAIT

The whole construction of these dogs allows them to fulfil their work as early as possible without stress. Therefore if they are made right, they will move right. There is no finer sight than watching these graceful, almost aerodynamically constructed dogs gallop over a grouse moor or move in unison with their handlers in a show ring, muscles rippling as the light catches, very like a thoroughbred horse performing. We must remember that the whole picture is taken into consideration when assessing a Weimaraner. As the owner of boarding kennels I see many 'good movers' in the form of mongrels, yet they have no type. Having said that, it is important for a gundog to move with drive from the hindquarters, that the front and hind are parallel (not crabbing or moving close behind or crossing in front). To assess movement at its best, good training is essential. If a dog trots along nose to the floor or jumps at the handler, nothing can be viewed except a disrespectful Weimaraner.

COAT

This is explained fully in the Standards. Suffice it to say that an animal in peak condition, mentally and physically, usually has a real bloom to the coat. Of course this will not be the case when the animal is moulting. I notice that Weimaraners who live out moult more frequently than those 'in house' and weather patterns dictate the moult to a large degree. Because Weimaraners have no undercoat, and therefore no added protection against thorns etc., their coats should be dense to give this protection to the skin. Nevertheless no judge worth their salt would penalise scars, from tears etc. In fact I know of a bitch who dived into water to make a retrieve, only to catch herself on an old, discarded wing of a car, ripping her chest and side open. This left a considerable scar, even though she was beautifully stitched by a vet who knew she was shown. She rewarded the vet by gaining her show title!

COLOUR

We must all strive to preserve the beautiful unique colour of this breed. The coat colour can be varying shades of the basic colour, as the standard states. We have 20 or so Weimaraners here and they nearly cover the whole range within the Standard. I have noticed not only genetics, but time of year, feeding and housing can lead to different shades of coat colour. However, coat colour can lead to dissension within fanciers of the breed. Some novice enthusiasts will be found to use 'pale' in conjunction with the colour; in fact 'pale' is defined in the dictionary as 'lacking colour'. What is meant by the inexperienced by the use of this word is that they prefer silver grey – as indeed many enthusiasts do. Funnily enough only the UK standard states 'preferred silver grey'. It must be remembered that each point of the Weimaraner is taken in context. A Weimaraner, even if very dark or muddy coloured and not ideal in colour, when put on a grouse moor with GSPs and Vizslas, for instance, will still be identifiable by colour against the other breeds. When the Weimaraner was nicknamed 'The Grey Ghost' it was with good reason. To watch this dog emerge from a mist, makes one gasp momentarily at the apparition. When moulting the coat can appear to have dark 'rain drops' all over the back as the woolly old coat comes out and the new coat takes on a darker shade, which lightens up when the dog has finished moulting. Feeding a small amount of cooking oil and, indeed, massaging the same into a moulting coat, can speed up the moult, leaving a lovely, shiny, new coat.

The only white allowed on a Weimaraner is a small amount on the chest. Sometimes a Weimaraner may have white 'spurs' (a spot of white behind the pastern) and while it is officially wrong, if the animal is of excellent merit, you will find this usually will not be penalised in the UK. However in Britain white toes will disqualify dogs from the winning line-up under the majority of judges, as would too much white anywhere else. One point to mention while on the subject of white, is that all puppies will at some stage, between three months and a year of age, develop white hair on the tail. Many breeders receive calls from alarmed would-be show owners that the beautiful puppy they own has white and cannot therefore be shown. Why the white develops on the tail is a mystery to me. I did think at one time it was a reaction to docking but I have since noted undocked and longhaired Weimaraners also have the white hair, just in the same place, showing, therefore, that docking is not the cause. The hair will eventually come out, leaving the original grey tail. No judge would penalise this.

MISMARKED

An absolute disqualification regarding colour would be if the animal were mismarked – although there is no disqualification as such in the UK Standard. The Weimaraner who is mismarked displays ginger markings on the legs up to the knee and hock, and would also have distinctive ginger on the muzzle, chin and eyebrows. Under the tail would also be ginger. In fact the dog looks rather like a washed-out Dobermann. These markings are evident from birth, they will never fade; in fact they become more prominent. They will not affect the animal's health, who can be a super pet, but should not be bred from, as the markings are genetic in origin. The dog's registration will usually be endorsed by the breeder to prevent breeding with the dog, who should never win in a show ring. These markings are thrown up occasionally, although not too often, as responsible breeders avoid doubling up on lines which are known to produce it. It must be remembered that during a moult or change of coat a Weimaraner may appear to have ginger bits. These are quite normal and will disappear as the coat is discarded.

SIZE

It is important that we strive to keep the size of the Weimaraner within the Standard. We all have the capability to produce a puppy on the periphery of the Standard but we must be careful when breeding. If we breed from such stock we will increase the chance of the resulting puppies being outside the Standard. Again, the key word is balance. A Weimaraner who is too big will not be able to fulfil any working potential because of undue pressure on bones and organs. Likewise, if too small, the animal would not have the stamina. When breeding from a Weimaraner who is outside, or on the periphery, of the Standard one should not necessarily use a dog of opposite proportions but look to the pedigree and, if possible, use the knowledge of a more experienced breeder – or do not breed.

One should try to retain all characteristics of the Weimaraner and objectively interpret the Standard, for the good of the Weimaraner. No dog is perfect, but the great dogs adhere to the Standard of the breed, yet possess an indefinable *quality*, which will set them apart from the rest.

Chapter Five

SHOWING YOUR WEIMARANER

Most folk initially get into showing by accident. If they have researched the breed, gone to the right breeders, accepted good advice and taken home a puppy which is their pride and joy, the next step on the ladder of enthusiasm is to pop along to a local show to see the Weimaraners being exhibited. Once there, with like-minded people, one gets caught up in the excitement of it all and goes home with dreams of one day winning Crufts.

FIRST STEP ON THE LADDER
Show training classes, or matches which are held in some countries, are the best place to start. Puppies learn invaluable lessons, whether or not they are ultimately shown. They have to behave and sit next to other puppies of different breeds while the show training is in progress. They learn that barking at other dogs is unacceptable, as is jumping on other puppies, dogs or humans. There is a time and place in which to act silly and play, and the match meeting or the training class is neither, thus teaching the puppies good manners. A puppy has to trot up and down the 'ring', which is usually the middle area of the hall, while all other dogs and handlers sit around it, which gives good ring training and also good lead training due to the repetitive action of going regularly. Also, at these gatherings, one gets the opportunity to find out when shows are going to be held, and often schedules for forthcoming shows are available. One can discuss which classes to enter with more experienced showgoers and even go along to shows with such folk, who will help you. The dog also learns about being handled by strangers – and potential judges often hone their skills at these meetings.

PRESENTATION
Despite all the work and enthusiasm of the first-time show-goer the major placings and awards, particularly at Championship shows, often go to 'big names' or experienced breeders and handlers. This is not because judges are influenced by previous wins by the dogs, the handlers or the breeders but because, generally, the more successful the breeder, the greater the likelihood of that breeder only showing very good-quality exhibits in tip-top condition. Successful breeders have the ability to see faults in their dogs and therefore can take precautions to try to eradicate these faults through careful breeding programmes, thus producing, more consistently, top-quality stock.

Because dog showing is, on the surface, a beauty show, presentation is very important. At Championship shows these days we expect to see in the region of 150 Weimaraners entered in about 12 classes; this averages about 12 dogs per class. Of these there will probably be six very sound, typy exhibits in each class. Therefore a judge will have to resort to considering the condition of the animals, and how well they are presented, to assessing their movement, and to personal preference for a particular point, to distinguish between the placings. As a judge I am offended to judge a dog which is in poor condition, or soft in muscle tone, or who has splayed feet, or is not going at one with the handler. So if you do not want to work, but just want the glory, dog showing is not for you.

If dog showing is for you, great enjoyment can be gained, friends will be made countrywide, you find boredom is a word never on your lips, you rarely have a chance to fall out with your spouse – unless only one of you is involved, in which case time away from home and money spent are the main bones of contention!

SELECTING A SHOW DOG

When one has been 'bitten by the showing bug' the next step is to acquire another Weimaraner specifically to show. Do not rush off to the sweetest person on the dog-showing circuit or the breeder having their first litter of which 'all will be Champions'. Instead, look at dogs that you admire and check in the catalogue how that animal is bred. You will find a pattern develops and find you like dogs going back to the same line. Approach breeders, talk to them about what you like. Take time to see where you want to go with your future in dogs. Remember a puppy once purchased is going to be with you 12 to 13 years. You will only show the dog for six or seven of those years and rushing into buying and breeding will find you 'dogged up' very quickly. For instance you start with one pet, then when that one is two years old you acquire another. Within another two years you progress to breeding and keep a least one puppy. This is a conservative estimate of the development of dog-showing in a lot of instances. When the youngest of these animals is five and coming to the end of a showing career, the oldest is only eight. Not many folk have the facilities to keep any more dogs.

Someone I really admire showed a mediocre dog, regularly winning only minor placings. He approached us and enquired when we would have a dog puppy available of a breeding he liked. It was over a year later that he took his 'promising' puppy home. He reared the puppy and won nicely with him. At two-and-a-half the dog started to fulfil his early promise and by three-and-a-half the dog became a show Champion, winning prestigious awards at major shows. The man had been patient and the sensible approach paid off.

DEVELOPING THE PUPPY FOR THE SHOW RING

So you have taken the promising puppy home, having been shown the puppy's good points by the breeder who has stood the puppy for you. Weimaraners are generally presented 'stacked'. This means holding the head and tail with the legs in the best position to show to advantage the animal's conformation. Training the puppy to stand is useful as a general discipline, conditioning the pup to thinking of you as one who must be obeyed as pack leader. Any training must be administered kindly, with the handler being in the correct frame of mind. It is no earthly good deciding to stand a puppy when you are stressed or in a hurry to do something else, as a puppy can instantly feel the kind of mood you are in. So, when all is calm and you have loads of time, take the telephone off the hook and proceed by holding the puppy by the skin under the chin, with a gentle but firm hand. With your other hand, lift the puppy between the back legs and 'drop' the puppy to stand squarely. Still with your hand between the hind legs, talk gently and keep stroking with your fingers to give reassurance, and keep your puppy standing, even if a tantrum is brewing. Only when it is understood that you will not let go until the puppy is still and obedient can you then calmly release the pup with a small pat and a gentle kind word. Change the word of praise each time otherwise the puppy will associate, for instance, 'good boy' with being released and subsequently, if the words are uttered in the ring, will feel enough has been done and it is time to

Hold the head and lift with the other hand to drop the front into the correct position.

The legs should be under the body in a comfortable position, showing correct shoulder placement.

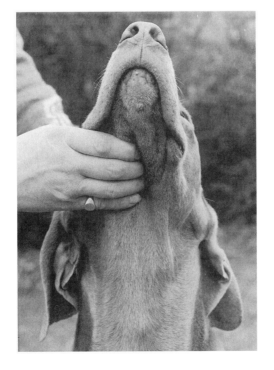

Photos: Keith Allison.

Correct position of the hand when holding the head in showing position.

The position of the hand, viewed from the off-side. The fingers are underneath the jaw and the thumb is held against the cheek, giving leverage to move the head.

Photos: Keith Allison.

This is the picture you are presenting to the judge, with your hand obscured so that it does not spoil the outline of the head.

Sh. Ch. Hansom Portman of Gunalt in correct show pose. The handler's hand is holding the head at the right level without being visible and spoiling the outline. The front legs and hind legs are not over-stretched and so the dog is able to show off his correct construction.
Photo: M. Trafford.

This dog has good hindquarters, but bad handling can give an awkward and unnatural appearance.

Incorrect: The hindlegs are too close together.

Incorrect: The hindlegs are overstretched giving an unnatural stance.

Correct: The dog is now handled to show the correct width of hindquarters, with excellent muscle, and it is also possible to see the neck, which is of good length, flowing into the body.

Photos: Keith Allison.

jump about. This procedure needs doing fairly often to start with, perhaps three times a week, in different places, with different distractions, so puppy will obey on command. Many distractions occur at dog shows. Keep lessons short and sweet – showing is a hobby which both of you need to enjoy to get optimum results.

MOVEMENT

Lead training having been completed, puppy needs to be trained to trot at your side, head up. This can be achieved when out for a walk to give different environments and distractions to puppy. It is worth remembering that your stride will reflect the puppy's stride or vice versa. I often watch a handler tiptoeing down the ring with short stilted strides and the exhibit will also move in this manner. Long free strides from the handler will show a dog's free driving movement off much

Correct: The front legs are moving in a straight line showing the correct construction of the dog. The forequarters are not too wide, which would put the elbows out. The feet are turning neither in nor out. The hindlegs are moving parallel with good width. The hocks are not pointing in (cow hocks) nor out.

Photo: Keith Allison.

The dog's body is moving in a straight line with hindlegs following front legs. If the hindlegs crab to the side it would suggest unbalanced construction with over-angulated hindquarters moving faster than the forequarters.

Photo: Keith Allison.

The handler is moving with long strides, which enables the Weimaraner to move freely, retaining the correct topline.

When the handler moves with short strides, the dog bunches and the movement alters.

better. Many experienced handlers even race round the ring in the misinformed belief that the faster you go the better. This is not the case; one should work with one's charge to exploit the dog's virtues. Learn to move in a triangle. Many judges (ring size and shape permitting) require the dog to be moved in a triangle. This is so that hind movement can be judged as the dog goes away, side movement as the dog goes along the top of the ring, and front movement assessed coming back to the judge. Many 'triangles' take the form of a circle and nothing can be assessed from this as the dog is always on the turn and therefore the legs are not moving at the correct angle. A judge, when asking for a circle, will stand in the middle to watch the dog's topline and extension of movement, and may also ask for a circle at the start of the class to help settle the dogs to the job in hand.

During the summer months shows are held outside on grass and various smells prevail. Indeed at a Championship show, held over three or four days, a dog in a previous class could have been in the ring with in-season bitches. This can cause problems for you in keeping your charge's head up so movement is not impaired. During training, keep the lead right under the chin, so your dog cannot even think about putting that nose down. Encourage your dog to think right by having a tasty morsel in your other hand to keep interest alive. These habits need to be instilled from the beginning and then your dog will be easier to handle. Once you have that attention, do not trot along waving the tidbit in front of your dog, who will then be encouraged to jump at it and will not concentrate. The tidbit is only to get initial attention.

WHICH SHOWS TO START WITH

We pay an awful lot of money to show dogs, into the tens of pounds per entry at Championship shows. Petrol, time – all come into consideration. All these points are to be considered when starting out. Should you start out at open shows or go for the Championship shows? To build up your experience it is, therefore, in the UK, probably wise to commence with the open shows, staying with the shows easily located around you. This not only is economic sense but also gives you an insight into the shows without getting too bored. If you enter Championship shows you are obliged to stay all day. In most cases, it is against the rules to leave before a set time, and to a novice, who is concentrating on one breed with not many friends in dogs to start with, this can be rather tedious.

ACHIEVING CHAMPIONSHIP STATUS

Achieving Championship status in the US is entirely different to the process of gaining three CCs in the UK. In the US points are won at the shows, and the number of points depends on the number of dogs competing. So that dogs do not become 'cheap Champions' by rushing around winning one point in poor entries, at least two 'Majors', which are three to five point wins, must be won under different judges. This is rather like the system for becoming an Irish Show Champion, but in Southern Ireland green stars are awarded instead of points. To become a Show Champion in the UK, a dog or bitch needs to win the CC at three shows under three different judges. At least one of these wins must be after the dog is over a year old. This sounds relatively simple, but in the UK one competes for the CC against *all* unbeaten dogs and bitches, so one is up

Showing in the USA: Joan Valdez with Ch. Valmar's Yours Truly.

against top winners and multi-CC winning animals. In the USA, and many other countries, once an animal is a Champion, that dog does not compete for points, but enters in a Specials class. Therefore many more new dogs become Champions than in the UK.

Most breeds of dogs gain the title Champion (Ch). In the Gundog Group in the UK, the dog must be called a Show Champion (Sh. Ch.). The way a gundog becomes a Champion is by qualifying in the field – the job for which the dog was bred originally. You can enter your dog at a Field Trial for a show working certificate, which is relatively easy. The judge has to see that the Weimaraner is capable at hunting, pointing and retrieving. One can enter the Field Trial, in which case the dog has to work in a more efficient and professional way and win an award, at least to a Certificate of Merit, against other dogs entered, which, of course, is altogether more difficult.

In Europe, the governing body, the FCI, offers a two-tier system of Champion, which is the National Certificate, CAC, and the International Champion, CACIB, the international certificate. This is because of freedom of movement between the countries in Europe. Each dog is graded by the judge and an individual critique is written by the judge, which is then given to the exhibitor on completion of the competition. Only dogs who have been awarded an Excellent grade are eligible for the CAB or CACIB.

In Australia Challenges are awarded. Due to the vastness of that country, most people exhibiting will attend possibly two shows in the same area over a weekend period, and will barbecque and have a get-together, making for a slightly more relaxed atmosphere. While the US presents a very professional image to dog showing, with immaculately presented handlers and almost exaggerated exhibits, competition in the UK is fierce, yet handlers are more casual, with dogs in a more natural pose. However the often shorts-clad Australasian exhibitors present their charges in a more American stance, an acknowledgement of the large number of imported American stock. However, whatever the style of presentation, the overall impression is of like-minded people from a myriad of countries, each of whom thinks they have the best Weimaraner in the world!

SHOWS IN GERMANY
The German Kennel Club is called VDH and the main headquarters are in Dortmund. Dog showing in Europe involves much travelling, as it is possible to show your dog in many different countries. Probably for this reason each dog entered has to have an up-to-date inoculation certificate and without it no dog is admitted, no matter who that dog is. As dogs enter the show, each one is thoroughly checked by a vet or vets. This involves examining eyes, ears, rectum etc. and making sure each animal is healthy.

Shows are generally held in big halls, with a full range of facilities such as restaurants and banks – even standpipes near each breed's area, so water is easily accessible. The rings are spacious and usually carpeted. Dogs are not benched as we know it in England, but cages are provided of different sizes, even 'family'-sized cages can be made available. Sophisticated the shows may be, but also expensive; entries are about £30 per dog. There is usually a facility for late entries, closing only 10 days before the show, which can prove very useful, but for this privilege you would pay in the region of £45.

Numbers are small in comparison with the UK. In fact no country has generally the numbers that the UK does, but Britain, being a small island, provides greater ease of travel, and most exhibitors can feasibly attend all the Championship shows without too much trouble. For comparison the Championship shows in the UK will generate an average of fourteen thousand dogs, and over twenty thousand at shows such as Crufts, whereas in Germany the attendance of dogs will be in the region of three-and-a-half to seven-and-a-half thousand.

The big shows are held in many of the major towns such as Berlin, Munich and Dusseldorf, with the big all-winners show being held in Dortmund in the autumn. There is also a Special held in Spring, the Eurochampionship Show. These shows attract entries from all over Europe. In these shows every dog has a written critique which the judge dictates to a typist who is there all through judging for just this purpose. Obviously, this is brilliant for exhibitors, who can read these critiques, and it means the judge must have adequate knowledge of the breed being judged, because the critique must be detailed. While this is a good idea for shows in Germany and Europe, it would be impossible to implement given the numbers of dogs in the classes in the UK. In a German dog show all the dogs are graded. The grades are: V1 – Excellent; SG – Very Good; G – Good; and Genugend – Sufficient. If this is the only mark gained, it really means your dog is not good enough. To be considered for the CACIB you must be graded V1. In Germany a dog is required to win the equivalent of four Challenge Certificates, while three are needed in the UK. These are best of sex awards at Championship level and in all Europe these awards are known as CACIBs. Between the first CACIB and the qualifying fourth CACIB, one year and one day must have elapsed, so a dog cannot be 'made up' in three shows, as can occur in the UK. For an International Show Champion, again the four CACIBs are necessary but two must be gained in other countries and the judge must be from an international panel. Great kudos is bestowed on winning dogs – each Best of Sex wins a case of food. BOB usually receives a piece of engraved crystal. Winners are entertained in a lounge, the Best of Breed winner gets a champagne afternoon tea. Group winners receive even more prizes and all expenses for accommodation and meals are paid if Best in Show is on a following day. If a judge has bred or owned an exhibit, that judge is asked to leave the ring while an independent judge is brought in to assess that particular dog. This judge's marks are collated along with the appointed judge's marks of all other exhibits and dogs are placed accordingly.

Since the Berlin Wall came down and former East Germany became accessible, the town of Weimar, which is in Thuringia, has staged an annual Weimaraner Classification and Beauty Championship Show. The town promotes the show and donates big cash prizes for Best Dog and Best Bitch. It is hoped to hold this show every June and a great effort is made to encourage as many visitors as possible. Great store is put on winning Best in Show there and the 1995 winner was Bustian Von Zenthop who, along with BIS, was awarded V1, the top award possible. This V1 (Excellent) was the only one awarded this year – in fact in the last five years only six to eight V1s have been awarded. It is fitting and a rather poignant tribute that this dog was bred by the great Heinz Reuper who died in this year. Ines Dawes (affix Aquila) was a great help to me with information on the Weimaraner in Germany. Ines commutes between various countries but spent a considerable time in Germany with her Euro. Lux. & German Sh. Ch. The Swagman of Aquila. Known as Banjo, he started life in the UK. He is by Ines' import Sieger Sascha Vom Zehinthof at Aquila and won in puppy classes in the UK before leaving with his owner to be campaigned in Europe. He gained the BIS at The Weimaraner Klub (German) and was awarded V1/V1, of which Ines was justly very proud. Before returning to the UK he also won 7 CACIBs and four Gundog Groups. Ines also owns English Sh. Ch. Varstock Vicereine of Aquila and is now resident back in England where she hopes to settle to her breeding programme.

Another 'ex-patriot' to campaign a Weimaraner in Germany and Europe was Kevin Bingham with his wife Julie. Kevin, who is a Major in the Army, bought his dog in Ireland, while a serving officer there, from Jim and Karen Gibson. NL. Lux. D. (VDH) Euro. Ch. Zilverein Captain's Lad won very well in Europe when Kevin and family were serving in Germany. He gained 27 CACIBS, 300 CACs, 6 group wins and 2 Reserve Best in Shows at championship shows in Europe. He also took BIS at the Belgian Weimaraner Club in 1992, Best Dog in 1993, and Best Dog at the Dutch Weimaraner Club in 1994. The Binghams returned to England in 1994 bringing

Captain's Lad and the Hungarian Vizsla NL Lux. D. (VDH) Ch. Chilsham Special Envoy and have since imported a Wirehaired Hungarian Vizsla.

ENTERING THE SHOW

No matter what country you live in, the general format of dog showing remains the same. After looking in the dog papers at the list of forthcoming shows, you will have selected the ones you want and have sent in a SAE or rung the secretary for the schedule to be sent to you. It is wise just to enter your breed puppy or relevant age class to start with and possibly the Any Variety Puppy class under the Group judge at an open show. Entering too many classes will bore both of you. Although, at first glance, the schedule will look as if written in code, on further inspection you will realise J stands for Junior, PG for Post Graduate etc., and towards the back of the Schedule age or win classes are explained fully. It is worth marking your schedule with the classes entered, so you do not forget; and then file the schedule in a safe place, as it will also give times and place of venue.

PREPARING FOR THE RING

We do not always bath Weimaraners for a show as we would an English Setter. In fact too much bathing removes the natural oils from the coat, can give the dog a chill, and can also leave the coat with scurf. Because of this I would bath a Weimaraner, if necessary, two days prior to the show to allow the shine to return to the coat. When bathing use a propriety brand of dog shampoo. Avoid the eyes and ears and make sure all shampoo is rinsed out properly to avoid any reaction which could cause itching. Take care around the tail of your dog. For some unknown reason dogs can develop 'dead tail' the day after a bath. This means the tail when lifted sticks out about an inch and then drops as if broken. The dog has no control over the dead part of the tail, it simply hangs. It also appears to be painful if touched. It will return naturally to normal the next day and needs no veterinary treatment. A chamois leather is ideal for drying the coat and stimulating the circulation but do keep your dog away from draughts after the bath. Check your dog's teeth are clean and make sure nails are short, otherwise the feet will have the appearance of being splayed even if they are not. Pack your dog bag the day before – you may need to set off at the crack of dawn on the day of the show. You will require a show lead. We generally use a nylon lead with one ring, forming a slip lead. Heavy chain collars and leather leads get in the way and spoil the dog's outline, as do leather collars. Remember the schedule, so you know where you are going. A pen is useful so you can mark winners in the catalogue, which you can buy when you arrive, telling you the names of dogs in each class. You need a ring clip for your number, which needs displaying when you are in the ring so that the steward can mark you off as present and the judge can check against your name, after judging, when he writes his critique – if you are lucky enough to be among the winners. Then you need tidbits, a chamois leather, a rug for your dog to sit on, and a towel for drying your dog off if it is wet or after being soaked in cold water to cool off on a rare hot day. A poop scoop is very important, so that you leave no excrement at the venue or in the surrounding area. A water dish and bottle of water are essential in case your dog needs a drink. And don't forget your exhibitor's pass, which is very important because without it no dog is allowed in or out, so keep it safe. This is to safeguard against dogs being removed without the owner's permission.

BENCHING

If it is a benched show you need a benching collar and lead. Benches are a wooden platform with partitions to which your dog is fastened for the duration of the show. It allows your dog to be viewed by spectators and also the dog can rest without distraction. Weimaraners have a bad reputation for attacking other dogs which come too near their benches so it is worth doing some training in good manners on the bench. I often see folk trailing their dog around the show all day. This just serves to fray tempers, not only in the dog but also in the owner.

With youngsters, I will keep them with me initially, usually until they have been in their class. By then they are tiring. I will then fasten my young dog to the allocated bench and sit there to give reassurance. When my Weimaraner has settled and, perhaps, fallen asleep, I will move away – but the bench is always in my sight, although my dog cannot necessarily see me. I stay around and take the dog off the bench after an hour or so. This helps the dog get used to the bench without feeling deserted. At the next show leave the dog a little longer, until benching is happily accepted .

Always make sure your Weimaraner's lead is short enough so that your dog's nose can reach no further than the end of the bench. This way your dog cannot get into the habit of lunging at passing dogs. Should any nipping then ensue it will be the fault of the other dog, who must have put an inquisitive nose into your dog's bench, thus invading territory. Many breeds, particularly gundogs, do not have the protective instinct of the Weimaraner, which lulls many show-goers into a false sense of security, and they do not always watch their charges' manners when passing other benches. If your dog does bark or lunge at some passing dog, do not become aggressive to the alarmed owner. Apologise and keep the situation calm. This will not wind your dog up further, nor damage public relations between the Weimaraner and other breeds.

PROCEDURE AT THE SHOW

After settling your dog and making sure everything is OK, get your bearings. Find your ring, check times of judging, make sure you are ready. I always take a change of clothes from the usual jeans and sweater I travel in. I think it is only fair to your dog and, indeed, to the judge to look tidy. You do not need to go over the top. I remember once seeing a lady who, in her desire to win, put on a tight-fitting outfit with plunging neckline when she thought it would influence a male judge. She did not win, but it gave spectators a lot of amusement!

However, do think about clothes. Colour can be important. Weimaraners are not the most eye-catching of dogs, especially in the group ring, so wear a colour that complements the breed, yet is not too bright or gaudy. If the dog requires tidbits, you will need pockets to put them in. Keep shoes flat. I think it is positively dangerous for a lady to be around dogs in stiletto heels, apart from it being impractical. Keep cardigans and jackets fastened, otherwise they flap around when moving the dog. Leave whistles out, they are invaluable for training or at a field trial but do not impress judges who know their stuff. If it is wet, you will need a coat. However, I find it near impossible to exhibit and make the most of my charge, wearing a great wax coat or the like. I would rather get wet and do my job efficiently. Make sure you have your ring clip for your number. It is useful to watch the procedure for your particular judge so you have an idea what will be required when it is your turn.

Take your dog off the bench in plenty of time, so you can check your dog's mood and that there has been no stiffening up and consequent lameness. Go for a walk so your dog can loosen up and spend a penny; perhaps finding a quiet corner to stand and move your dog, who will then realise where you both are and what is expected. Check the ring and sort out where you want to be. If, for example, your charge is on the tall side you do not want to be stood where the ground rises, making the dog look bigger.

IN THE RING

Look in the catalogue to see your number. When you enter the ring, you can recite your number immediately to the steward and place yourself where you want to be with no bother. Make sure you have your charge stood, for when the judge surveys the ring of dogs, first impressions count. If the judge asks you to do something, even if he did not ask the others, you should obey. He may require you to move again or turn your dog the opposite way round. If you find it difficult to stand your dog the opposite way, you could try doing the placing with your back to the judge and when the dog is stood correctly, you simply swap sides so the judge has a clear view. It is not your place to question why the judge wants something. In fact it is against Kennel Club rules to have a conversation with the judge while in the ring. You should only answer any questions the judge might have; usually the judge will ask "How old?".

Do not complain. Remember it was your choice to enter under that judge, who may not be an ace handler but, on that day, is the judge and deserves your respect. In fact it is sensible to have a good attitude throughout showing and have good manners in the ring. Do not stand too close to another exhibitor, so as to let your dog sniff at another – for a start, the recipient may not be too friendly. Do not stand chattering. There is plenty of time for that outside the ring. Concentrate on your job and your dog. Read your dog who, if young may be nervous of the procedure – just like you – or maybe bored and start whining or pulling to leave the ring. Do not scold. Reassure, stroke and talk to your dog. Always address the judge and stewards as Sir or Madam and expect them to address you in a similar manner. Do not stand round the ring backbiting. We all see things differently and experience frustration and jealousies or we would not be human, but save them for the journey home. You cannot change any results, the judge's decision is final. Accept it, congratulate the winner and vow to do better next time, letting the winner have their glory.

When you win, remember your dog will 'read' your euphoria and possibly act excitedly, barking and jumping up and down. Remain in control. I have often noticed, particularly with inexperienced handlers – let this situation get out of control and the next thing a fight develops in the ring. Not good for you, the dogs or the breed. Remember you are an ambassador for this wonderful breed, and in the show ring for pleasure, so do not make life difficult for yourself.

JUDGING

The natural progression from showing is judging. Everyone seems to be in a hurry to judge, but unless you have been patient, watched, talked and learned, you will quickly realise that you are, and will be seen by others to be, short of knowledge. A very useful exercise for potential judges is to offer to steward at shows. This gives you a close-up view of dogs, how judges handle animals and ring procedure. Stewarding for other breeds is enormously useful; it gives you an eye for construction and movement, without knowing particular dogs or handlers and being swayed by their record.

When judging, the reason you go over a dog is to assess conformation, type, temperament and condition. When you hold a dog's head, looking at eye placement and expression will give an insight into temperament. Feeling the thickness of ear tells you a lot about the quality of the dog. If the leather (ear) is thick the dog may be cloddy, if fine and supple the dog is often in good condition and of nice quality. Open the dog's flews or lips to view dentition. Also one can check that the lip is not snipy. If the weather is hot and the dog is panting, one cannot see if the lip is drawn back to pant. Run your hand down the neck to feel strength. Put your hand behind the shoulder blade to see how it is laid. Gently grasp the front leg to feel bone. Pick up the foot and look at the padding of the foot, to see if the padding is good and not flat or unevenly worn, which could be through unsound construction and movement. Put hands either side of the ribs to check spring rather than fat. Check with outstretched palm for length of loin, from end of rib to pelvis. Feel hindquarters to test correct muscle tone and depth of second thigh, and check, in a male, to

Patsy Hollings officiating as judge, with Carolyn Alstosn and Sh. Ch. Flimmoric Fanclub (left), and Rachel Barney with Sh. Ch. Verrami Joint Effort.

see if he has two testicles. A very experienced judge may go over your dog virtually without touching the animal. That judge's eye, particularly on the short-coated Weimaraner, will tell him what he needs to know; so do not think he does not know his job. I feel that obviously going over the dog settles everyone to the task in hand. Also one is seen to be doing one's job and giving the exhibitor the feeling he has had his money's worth.

I always address exhibitors and stewards as Sir or Madam. This is good manners and also it looks bad to address an exhibitor you know well by their christian name. Knowing exhibitors is part of the game. A good judge will judge the dogs on the day, not on personality of owner, or reputation of handler, or indeed on what the animal will be. Today is all that matters. One cannot please everyone and if 'friends' fall out because of placings they are not worth having. Likewise a judge who is intimidated by exhibitors should not be judging. When judging, you are there to do your job. Relax, enjoy it and be aware that your decisions could influence the future of the breed. Winning dogs are bred from.

Organise your ring and get a pattern of your classes sorted in your head. I stand new dogs to my left, seen dogs (been in a previous class, and therefore do not need going over) to my right. If the ring is big enough, it settles all to send the exhibitors round the ring once in the younger classes. After going over the dog, I move each animal in a triangle, then up and down the ring for assessment. If the ring is very small, twice up and down will do as well, with the judge moving to watch side movement on the second run. Do not dither around; sort the dogs out in your head and place them. Changing places shows up a judge's lack of confidence in his decision. Do not play Lord for a day. The exhibitors have paid for your opinion as a judge not an entertainer.

It is a wise judge who puts a dog up on merit, not down on faults. All dogs have faults and fault-judging stops one judging the overall animal.

Chapter Six

THE WORKING WEIMARANER

The Weimaraner is one of seven breeds classified under the heading Hunt, Point, Retrieve, or HPR. The breeds within this group are Brittany Spaniel, German Shorthaired Pointer (GSP), German Wirehaired Pointer (GWP), Hungarian Vizsla, Italian Spinone, Large Munsterlander and Weimaraner. Because these are dogs who will lend themselves to different working facets, they are rather 'Jacks of all Trades' and consequently need an enquiring mind to cope with the different work requirements. This is exactly what Weimaraners have, which is why they would not make good couch potatoes. In all gundogs the original instinct can be noted at some time; even 'show types' display their inherent instinct to some degree. For example, the Golden Retriever always wants to carry something, the Irish Setter ranges the park at speed, the Cocker Spaniel merrily seeks in undergrowth – yet many gundog breeds, including the aforementioned, have split into two totally different types, either for working or for showing.

Three gundogs (left to right): the Hungarian Vizsla, the Weimaraner and the English Setter. All three are good specimens of their breed. Each one is completely different in shape and size. Note the Weimaraner is longer and more powerful than the others.

Photo: Keith Allison.

Pictured left to right: the longhaired Weimaraner, the shorthaired Weimaraner, the Hungarian Vizsla and the English Setter. The Weimaraners have the same expression and head-shape. The Vizsla's head is more gaunt and the Setter's is more rounded and moulded with a lower ear placement.

It is generally accepted that the HPR breeds that are shown are more likely to have retained working instinct, good conformation and temperament. The breeders of HPRs, and Weimaraners in particular should, and hopefully do, work to preserve them as one breed, learning from the mistakes of their predecessors with other gundog breeds. It is a wonderful sight and feeling to see your Weimaraners fulfil their inherent desires; yet not all owners wish to shoot over their Weimaraner. In my opinion, if your dog is stimulated and fulfilled, then so be it. After all, if we go back to our instinct, man would probably drag his 'woman' around by the hair, and rush about killing his 'meal' with his bare hands or primitive tool! You can, however, 'work' your Weimaraner without actually going out with a gun and shooting over the dog.

THE WORKING TEST

This is an ideal environment in which to stimulate your dog and have a great day out meeting new friends. In the UK these events are now licensed by The Kennel Club and are held on ground which is privately owned by someone interested in the sport, so good manners are essential for both owner and dog. Being a member of the breed clubs and/or gundog clubs in your area will give you information about when or where working tests are held. The beauty of these events is that they can take place all year round, so many field trial enthusiasts and shooting men also partake . Usually the working test comprises a Puppy Class (6-18 months), a Novice Class (open to all who have not won a novice, graduate or open test), and an Open Class (open to all regardless of wins). More often now a Graduate Class is included, as the jump from novice to open is great. The puppy test may have heel work, possibly winding through canes, a sit and stay with recall plus a seen retrieve, maybe even a shallow water retrieve.

Progressing through the classes the exercises set will be harder. The Open class could have hunting and pointing on caged game which is hidden under branches or grass, blind retrieving of game, possibly over water and retrieving with the distraction of a dummy launcher, or a fur-covered dummy attached to strong elastic and released across the path of the retrieving dog, who is expected to ignore it. Dogs under six months of age are not allowed to enter because it would be too much pressure on such a baby, but it is before this age that the basic training is given.

FIELD TRIALS

Again these are licensed by The Kennel Club, and are competitive events designed to assess the ability of the gundog. They are divided into four groups: Retriever and Irish Water Spaniels; Sporting Spaniels other than Irish Water Spaniels; Pointers and Setters; and breeds which Hunt, Point and Retrieve. A Field Trial is run on ground where live game can be hunted, shot and retrieved. While being an enjoyable event for all, dog and man, it is also a showcase which helps breeders assess which dogs have the correct ability and instinct, thereby enabling breeders to retain working ability, in much the same way as dog shows look at conformation and temperament.

Weimaraners are expected to work, as are the other HPRs, yet this breed thinks differently, so it can be difficult and frustrating for handlers hoping to win awards. There is only one Field Trial Champion Weimaraner in the UK. He is Di Arrowsmith's Wobrooke of Fleetapple, a real credit to dog and handler. Generally, serious Field Trial enthusiasts would probably stick to the GSP, an ideal dog for the job, who tends to be faster than a Weimaraner because of being a more natural air-scenting dog and thus able to cover ground more swiftly and efficiently. This leaves the

Ch. Wobrooke of Fleetapple completing a perfect retrieve to handler Di Arrowsmith. Note the 'grey ghost' appearance against the moorland.

The Weimaraner uses speed, agility, power – and a soft mouth – when retrieving game.

Weimaraner open to criticism by the judges who are more used to the thinking of the GSP. The ground scenting of the Weimaraners slows them, as they need to be more methodical in their hunting, but this, coupled with their stubborn 'I know best' attitude, make them a great asset to the rough shooter. The disadvantage with ground scenting is the risk of the dog alerting the bird by getting too close, rather than taking the scent from the air and going on point, allowing the gun to position himself, ready for the flushing of the game.

TRAINING

It is obviously important to train your dog from the beginning to get into good habits and channel all instincts in the right way, whether you intend to compete seriously either in field trials or working tests or just go rough shooting or, indeed, beating with your Weimaraners. Even if your Weimaraner is purely a pet, you both will benefit immensely from correct training from the word go. The training regime used is basically exploiting the dog's inherent instincts. The Weimaraner is intelligent and will remember all initial training, which can be taught using repetitive actions, keeping it short and sweet to avoid boredom. The dog's need is to please you. I stress again, do not attempt training unless you are in the correct frame of mind. If you are rushed, irritable or stressed, your dog will sense this, will gain no pleasure from training and will not give optimum co-operation.

The result of training should be a biddable companion who is capable of hunting and finding game, pointing the game for the gun, on command flushing that game, sitting to the shot and retrieving gently that game, back to the gun, on command. With patience, determination and the instinct to work you will have a dog who is welcomed on a shoot, a good ambassador for the breed and a credit to you, the owner. To reach this stage, go to classes offered by your breed clubs, listen and take advice from anyone and everyone more experienced, gleaning the relevant information applicable to you and your charge.

I have included basic fundamental training methods to start you off but one book which is easy to understand and a great help in training to gundog work is David Layton's *The GSP Today*. Although obviously written for GSP enthusiasts, David's training methods are intelligent, easily interpreted and equally applicable to the Weimaraner. It is important to start with correct training methods, otherwise you could find bad habits hard, if not impossible, to correct.

OBTAINING YOUR PUPPY

As stated earlier, the Weimaraner has remained undivided as a breed; however, as with showing, not every puppy will be best suited to every job. You should have confidence in the breeder of your puppy and be guided by what that breeder tells you about the litter and their characteristics. You should be taking note that the puppy who is alert, wants to be first out, is off 'hunting' and carrying leaves or twigs is the puppy who will be of interest to you. We often find that if a toy is thrown, even at seven to eight weeks of age, some puppies will happily retrieve for you. This is the puppy showing an aptitude to work. Avoid a shy or nervous puppy. Look at relations, dam or sire: do they have an aptitude to work? It will help.

STARTING TRAINING

Your puppy will have inherited instincts and your job is to bring those instincts out. A puppy has a short concentration span, rather like a child. So training is kept short, finishing while interest is still high, so boredom does not set in. Working together to build a good partnership is essential and takes time, but it will show even if you only work with your dog for an hour a week! There will be times when everything goes wrong. Recognise the signs that puppy is becoming distressed by your attitude, otherwise confidence in you will be lost. If you have a bad day, mentally close the book and do something else. Use the time before puppy can go out to start good habits through play. An old sock knotted makes a great first dummy. While watching TV throw the sock for puppy, using "On and fetch". When puppy is near the sock say "Hie Lost". The puppy, having picked up the retrieve, should be called back using the instruction "Fetch". The puppy will be proud of this prize

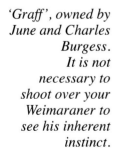

'Graff', owned by June and Charles Burgess. It is not necessary to shoot over your Weimaraner to see his inherent instinct.

so, as the puppy approaches you, do not grab at the sock. Instead, put the puppy gently into the sit, say "Sit" and open the puppy's mouth by putting a finger in the corner of it, then gently take the retrieve, saying "Dead". Only repeat this 'game' once or twice, so puppy does not become bored.

All these actions will 'condition' puppy into good habits. After all, we are all creatures of habit, animals more so than humans. For instance, I have never seen a cow with a watch, but you will always see cows standing waiting to be milked at the gate at 4 o'clock on a summer afternoon. So this conditioning is not cruel but leads puppy into a secure environment of knowing right from wrong. At feeding time use the whistle, even when puppies are in the nest. All useful conditioning!

LEAD TRAINING

Because the majority of handlers carry their gun in the right hand, it is easier for all to train the dog to walk on the left. The soft cotton-rope leads with one ring, forming a type of 'choker', are excellent for lead training and, indeed, any field work. They are light, do not burn the hand when wet, do not make any noise and are easily slipped into your pocket when not needed. They are also very gentle and kind on a puppy, and do not 'cut' the hair on the neck. A fundamental point to remember is to make sure you have the lead on the right way up so that, after it has been tightened, it will automatically release when slackened off again. The ring through which the lead passes is at the side of the handler; the lead passes through this, goes over the dog's neck then back through the ring. When lead-walking a puppy, or indeed any dog, that is exactly what we do. We lead. There is no sniffing the grass, or pulling allowed, from the beginning. The puppy is walked with head level to body. We talk reassuringly at *all* times on these first few walks. The effort will pay many dividends later when your Weimaraner weighs 70 or 80 lbs and walks sensibly, not dragging you along!

SIT

Even before all inoculations have been completed a puppy can be taught 'Sit'. Put your hand on the puppy's bottom, gently press down and say 'Sit'. Hold the puppy down, and calmly, so that the puppy does not get excited and want to jump up, tell the pup how clever this is. One can progress later with asking the puppy to sit in anticipation of receiving tea, by putting the left hand, palm forward, up and saying 'sit', at the same time stamping the ground with your left foot. In time the puppy will identify these actions with sitting. Once these actions are totally familiar, you can substitute the whistle for the voice, using a long single blow of the whistle. The reason hand, foot and whistle action are advantageous to a shooting dog is because wild life will not be disturbed by these sounds and actions, while a voice will alert game to impending danger. If, when your dog is close, you stamp your foot, the vibration of the action will tell your dog your requirements.

STAY

Your youngster, having complied with the command of 'sit', can then be taught to stay. Using feeding time can again prove very effective. Ask for 'sit' while holding the feed dish. Then step back one step and say 'stay'. Put the dish down, continue to say 'stay', holding the palm of the hand forward towards the puppy. Once this action is mastered, practise in the field or park but away from any distractions. Leave the lead around the puppy's neck, who will then have the feeling of being controlled. Keep lessons short and do not go too far. Just make sure that if you have started this training exercise it must be finished, to gain compliance of command. That way the puppy will develop the knowledge that, if you ask for something to be done, you must and will always be complied with. Weimaraners who think they can get away with something, most definitely will. They are always of the opinion that they know best.

RECALL

When teaching "Stay" always go back to your puppy, never let your puppy return to you unless you ask for this, and recall should not be attempted until you and your dog are in total agreement as to what "Sit" and "Stay" mean. Make sure, as with all training, that you have your dog's interest and attention. While your dog is at sit and staying, always face your dog with your arms open wide in a welcoming gesture. Then bend forward and call "Come". To keep the attention you can slap your hands to your thighs. Once you have your dog's understanding of "Come", you can then introduce the whistle. Sound two short blasts, accompanied by the action instead of the voice.

If a distraction occurs, another dog or even a rabbit, stop calling or, better still, do not start calling. An impetuous youngster will not wish to respond to you and could very easily get into bad habits. In fact if a youngster dashes off, the best course of action is to attract attention by voice, whistle or whatever means, then make haste in the opposite direction. This will have the effect of knocking your dog's confidence in the situation and will usually result in your dog following you. Running after your charge will usually result in the dog thinking it is a game and thus continuing to run away. On completion of a successful recall, occasionally reward with a tidbit, varying with praise or a pat. Do not let your dog become complacent; one who always expects a reward will get into the habit of dropping the retrieve in order to receive it.

HUNTING

Any dog working with a gun, in whichever sphere, needs to have a degree of steadiness and obedience. However, the dog must not be controlled to the point where there is no willingness to hunt on. This is a mistake I made with Portman: he is thorough, but keeps looking round to see where I am – lovely when rough shooting but frustrating when ground needs covering at speed. Ideally, find a quiet spot on open moorland, or ask a local farmer for a place where you can take your dog to run.

The owner of one of our offspring told us how his wonderful charge had been 'zigzagging' across the dales while on holiday. The young dog was, in fact, using his instinct and quartering the ground, taking the scent. As the chap said, a wonderful sight, even though the chap did not know why. It is no good having a brilliant retriever and pointing dog if he cannot find game for you. Both dog and handler need to understand how game think and which way the wind is blowing. Fundamental? Not always that easy in practice. Go to as many classes as you can, listen and learn, so you can be instrumental in guiding your dog properly.

In initial training, using a 'head' wind is the most easily understood. This is when the wind is coming straight at you, so that you can work your dog into the wind. Once you introduce your dog to game finding, you need to think where game will be. On a warm sunny day, the game can be in the open, basking in the warmth. On cold days, game is more likely to be taking cover in hedgerows and the like. While most Weimaraners have the instinct to hunt to some degree, you can help by working out the correct hunting pattern. Basically, when hunting and quartering, the dog is taking scent of the game from the wind. Simplistically the dog would hunt into the wind, moving across the beat (the area of ground to be hunted by the dog) between the guns without passing through the guns' line of fire.

Obviously the dog should not gallop off, otherwise this could put up game which is out of range. It is no use a dog disappearing and going on point if you have no idea where the dog is. To encourage a dog to quarter, choose ground to use as your 'beat'; this would normally be not more than about 20 yards each side of the handler. Start by sending the dog out to the left. Give a short pip on your whistle and a clear hand signal, lifting your left hand out, with palm clearly visible up and outwards. You go to the left, your dog will then go with you. As the dog goes, you turn and repeat in reverse. This will encourage the dog to move quickly across the beat, wasting no time. Be careful not to run in front of the dog or you will be in danger of disturbing any game. In the first stages of training it is wiser to use land clean of game as this removes any distraction and allows the dog to learn the job. Once game is located, the dog should point and never be allowed to flush game except on command.

POINTING

Again, pointing is down to instinct but that instinct can be exploited. Working tests on caged birds are helpful in encouraging it. You know where the game is, so can steady the dog onto the scent and then, by keeping quiet and calm, hold the dog onto the point with little physical contact. Once on point, whisper to the dog, whom you can lightly stroke from head to tail which will help to keep the dog steady and holding the point. To see a dog point is breathtaking. Man has knowledge to send rockets into space, make babies from eggs fertilised in test tubes, yet man can never emulate nature and can never reproduce the sight of a dog on point, quivering in anticipation, stonelike, following the thrill of the hunt and with the expectation of the retrieve. On no account allow a youngster or novice, in training, to go on and follow through the point with a retrieve. The dog must be old enough and mature in attitude before this can happen, otherwise it is possible to have the dog wanting to retrieve unasked and this will result in unsteadiness.

RETRIEVING

This is the exercise which is the ultimate for the dog. The work of hunting, quartering the ground, pointing and flushing the 'prize' all lead to the end result of retrieving. It is the exercise we use to finish a training spell because we have then ended on the high note of the day and it leaves the dog wanting more. From the first 'dummy' of the sock we move onto the canvas dummy, which is made specifically for the job, in weight, shape and fabric. We have established that your dog looks on you as pack leader. The dog must also be of the thinking that any retrieve, be it dummy or game, is yours and it is a privilege to return it to you. Do not give a dog a dummy to 'play' with. The dog must be respectful of your dummy or 'game' at all times. Again, make sure training sessions are kept short, in a place void of distractions.

Your dog should be taken to the training ground, then should then be seated at your side, initially on the lead, and shown the dummy, which is then thrown a short distance. Use On and Fetch while encouraging the dog forward. Once the dummy is retrieved, call the dog to you and take hold of the dog, with praise. *Never* grab the dummy. This will only serve to make the dog hang on to it tightly, which is the start of making the dog 'hard-mouthed', a great sin in a gundog, whose job is to bring your 'dinner' in good condition, so you can eat it. A hard-mouthed dog will, at best, have shattered the ribs, rendering the breast of the game inedible.

The dog should also be of the opinion that the retrieve is only allowed on your orders, so at odd times throw a dummy, leave the dog in the sit and retrieve the dummy yourself. Also as the training progresses, throw two dummies, ask your dog to retrieve only one, or one and then the second, never all at once. Once mastered, the unseen retrieve adds variety and more scope for your dog. Weimaraners love jumping, in my experience, and asking them to 'on and fetch' over a wall is something the Weimaraner will readily accept. Not only is this stretching them physically but it allows them to use their initiative, another thing the Weimaraner enjoys.

The training done in front of the TV using the 'Hie lost' – which means the dog is close to the retrieve – comes into its own in the blind retrieve. To start with, you should always know where the retrieve fell, so you can confidently encourage the dog on; this convinces the dog that you should be obeyed, that you always know best. Vary the dummy as time progresses by fastening

Teaching the retrieve

ABOVE: Command your dog to sit, and with your palm forward, show him the dummy.

LEFT: The dog is sent out to retrieve.

RIGHT: The dog picks up the dummy.

pheasant wings on, giving your dog the introduction to game. You can then go on to cold game. If you use pigeon, because they have many loose feathers, they can put a young dog off, as during the retrieve all the feathers end up in the dog's mouth; so secure the feathers to the body of the bird with elastic bands.

Another retrieve your dog will encounter is a water retrieve. The best way of giving a dog confidence to enter water is to follow you. Obviously this is much more pleasant in warm weather, so don the waders or swimming costume and make a pleasant game of going into water. Throwing dogs into water only serves to frighten young ones, and can put them off for life. Once they have confidence in water, a dummy of an old washing-up liquid bottle, sealed and covered in a sock so it can be easily gripped and will float, is the ideal first dummy to be used in water. Until the dog is mature and totally confident, avoid very cold and foul stagnant water; once put off it is very difficult to build the confidence of a young dog.

WHISTLES
The whistles used by the trainer of a gundog are a pea whistle and a panic whistle, rather like a referee's whistle used in football matches. Any gun shop or gundog class usually has whistles and dummies for sale. The pea whistle is used as described throughout the training. The panic whistle, being extremely shrill, is used only if a dog is doing something very wrong, e.g. running in, chasing sheep or disappearing into the wild blue yonder. The shock of the sound should have the effect of stopping a dog in its tracks, rather like the slap on the bottom in the short, sharp early discipline. It is essential that a Weimaraner is taught obedience with livestock, especially sheep, at a young age, and therefore grows up with no thought of chasing them. Failure in this renders your Weimaraner useless as a gundog. Finally, don't forget to find out the dates of the shooting seasons in your area.

WORKING TRIALS
Many people get mixed up with Working Tests and Working Trials. One does not instantly associate Working Trials with gundogs, as Working Trials lend themselves to the ability of the 'working breeds', e.g. German Shepherd Dog, Border Collie or Giant Schnauser. These breeds are often used by the police and the exercises are applicable to police work. In the US this discipline comes under the catgory of Obedience Trials, and the categories, in ascending level, cover similar ground. The titles to be gained are: CD Companion Dog, UD Utility Dog, WD Working Dog, TD Tracking Dog, PD Patrol Dog.

LEFT: Paul Dodd with Metpol Monroes Thor PDEx (left) and Metpol Monroe's Prangen CDEx, UDEx, WDEx.

ABOVE: Paul Dodd working with Thor – a dog needs total confidence in his handler to achieve such a feat.

ABOVE: Ch. Reeman Aruac CDEx, UDEx, WDEx, TDEx.

LEFT: Ch. Monroes Ambition of Westglade CDEx, UDEx, WDEx negotiating a 6ft scale.

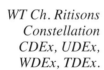

WT Ch. Ritisons Constellation CDEx, UDEx, WDEx, TDEx.

Barbara Rushbridge's great Ch. Amstud Steely Dan ADx, CDx, UDx, WDx. His sire is NZ Am. Ch. Nani's Totally Awesome (USA import) out of Aust. NZ Ch. Bromhund Aleeta. He is eight years old and Barbara is currently training him to TD level. He is a member of the canine Agility Display team where he jumps through fire hoops on a two-tiered dog walk which is over 30 m long and 2.5 m high. Barbara and Khan live in Christchurch, New Zealand.

The enquiring, determined mind of Weimaraners, coupled with their inherent protective instinct, lend them to being acceptable participants in this discipine. Many feel that, as gundogs, they should not be seen in the same light as 'guarding' breeds, and their trait of being 'soft-mouthed' should not be put in jeopardy by using them in this kind of work. As a gundog their initiative should be exploited only in gundog work. I have a leaning to agree with these thoughts – in an ideal world this would most probably occur. However, as thoughts and ideals change in this 'modern' world, we must congratulate anyone who is valuing and stimulating their dog, whichever breed is chosen.

Training needed is similar to that initially needed for Field Trial work, with the emphasis more on obedience, although 'control' is the word more commonly associated with Working Trials, because the dog needs to respond immediately to commands, yet have the ability to think independently. The beauty of Working Trials is that they are run in much less space than a Field Trial needs and without the use of game, so they are accessible to a greater number of participants. Your dog must be able to retrieve and must complete the 'send away', which is running in a straight line until told to stop by the handler. So instead of encouraging 'quartering', do the training alongside a wall or fence. Put a toy alongside the wall, both of you go back a few yards, then you ask the dog to 'get on'. You go with the dog, whom you tell to 'down' at the toy. Never allow a retrieve and never call the dog back. You go to the dog with praise. The dog must learn to 'stay'; this is initially a two-minute 'sit' with the handler out of sight in a CD stake, building to ten minutes in other stakes.

The dog is required to track, following a human scent for up to half a mile. Gwen Sowersby, who successfully runs classes for Weimaraners, advises scent training by trailing a piece of tripe along, then placing one of the dog's toys in the trail. Then release the dog who will then start to track. Agility is something Weimaraners enjoy, but the dog is required to clear a 3 ft jump and a 9 ft long jump and must also scale a 9 ft obstacle and return on command. So start small and build up.

Chapter Seven

BREEDING WEIMARANERS

Producing offspring from something you love dearly and admire for companionship, showmanship and working ability is a very natural desire. However, reproduction in dogs, as with humans, requires much thought and, indeed, dedication.

WHY BREED?
Letting your bitch have one litter 'because it is good for her', is a fallacy. What she has never had, it can be said, she will never miss. Or 'because she suffers false pregnancies'. In my experience if a bitch has false pregnancies prior to a litter, she most certainly will have one on subsequent seasons, usually made worse because she has whelped and produced milk. Nor is it a good enough reason to breed just because she has the best temperament and is lovely to look at. Pat yourself on the back – if she is well-behaved, you have reared her correctly. If her beauty and temperament are

Jane George with the American import Ch. Kamsou Moonraker Von Bismark – a top stud dog who did much for the British Weimaraner.

excellent, you obviously went to a good breeder. In which case your bitch very probably will produce good puppies, provided you have used the right 'stud dog' of comparable breeding, and not 'the dog down the road' because he has a cheap stud fee and is handy. To produce the one puppy you require, you will invariably produce seven or eight puppies.

It is a *not* a reason to breed because you wish to recoup the costs of buying your pedigree dog, or heaven forbid, that you need a new carpet or want a foreign holiday! When I have seen people breed 'for money' I tend to notice things can go wrong. They end up paying a stud fee and buying a whelping box, bedding, extra feed, only to find that their bitch 'misses' (does not produce a litter). These costs are not refundable. Or the bitch could need a caesarean section and even lose her puppies, incurring veterinary fees.

To produce and rear a litter properly is very expensive and time-consuming, and you definitely need the facilities for housing growing puppies. Puppies at three weeks of age, when mum is cleaning and feeding them, are very pleasurable. Puppies at eight weeks, needing feeding at least four times a day, cleaning out even more regularly and requiring the stimulation of human contact and play, are another matter. Weimaraners are the strongest of the gundog breeds. One should not buy a Weimaraner on a whim, neither should one breed on a whim.

I have often heard, in the media, that pedigree dogs are 'highly bred' and silly. This implies that pure, carefully line-bred dogs, produced by a breeder, are to be avoided in favour of a mongrel or of one of a 'homebred' litter produced in ignorance. The truth is the opposite: *indiscriminate* breeding produces the most problems. So before embarking on breeding from your Weimaraner, make sure you have researched all angles thoroughly.

BREEDING PRINCIPLES

At shows you will meet like-minded people, and can look at the stock exhibited. More importantly, you can assess the progeny of certain dogs and look at what is being produced by breeders. Is it sound, consistently good in temperament, of correct type? Showing may appear to be a 'beauty contest' but underneath the surface it gives breeders first-hand knowledge of what is being produced, which, in turn, gives breeders the ability to breed better dogs. Likewise field trials also tell you if the dogs produced are retaining the instinct for which they were originally developed: working – hunting, pointing and retrieving. These things are inherent and cannot be put there with training if natural ability has been lost through ignorant breeding.

In many gundog breeds – English Setters, Golden Retrievers and Cocker Spaniels to name but three – the ones kept as pets or shown, bear little resemblance to the 'working strains', indeed, they have little working instinct either. It is therefore essential to all who have the Weimaraners' welfare at heart to try, when breeding, to preserve the breed without losing its instincts or changing the standard of the breed.

So look at your bitch: is she good enough to breed from? A breeder once informed me that a particular bitch would be a good brood because she was big and could carry lots of pups. Size is not what constitutes a good brood. Her pedigree is obviously important. The bitch who produces sound healthy puppies and produces good quantity and quality of milk is necessary. Also she requires a sensible disposition. It is very tedious if you have a bitch who does not have the temperament to settle and look after her litter. The puppies not only suffer physically, unless you are very careful, but also mentally, without the stability of a quiet, caring dam. Make an appointment to go to more experienced breeders to ask their opinion of your bitch and pedigree, look at their stock, listen to what is important about the breed for them – is it comparable to your values?

In my experience from over twenty years of breeding dogs I find it hard enough breeding good dogs from good well-bred, sound dogs; it is damn near impossible to breed good dogs from bad ones! Everyone loves their dog the best, and rightly so. However, we should look objectively at her, when contemplating breeding. If you are kennel blind – meaning that you see no faults – how can you breed to correct faults? Likewise, if your bitch is too small, it is no good putting her to a big dog. You will not end up with medium-sized puppies, but with some too big and others too small.

When you have established that your bitch is of breed type and is sound, so therefore will have the potential to produce puppies of quality, you *must* also investigate whether your bitch carries any hereditary problems. Although HD is not solely hereditary, you should have your bitch X-rayed and scored under the KC scheme as explained in the chapter on health. Also check that entropion is not carried in either the bitch's line or the stud dog's pedigree. The pedigree of your bitch is also important. One can look at it and match it to a potential stud dog's pedigree to see how relations 'tie in' within the two pedigrees. This is line breeding. It must be remembered that ultimately you are mating animals and not paper pedigrees.

ACQUIRING AN AFFIX

As I said, when discussing choosing the breeder from whom you should buy your Weimaraner, an affix is a like a 'trade name', protected by your country's governing body, which can only be used by the holder. When we acquired our affix, we paid a fixed fee for life, to the Kennel Club. These days an annual fee is charged by the Kennel Club. Both ways the affix is yours and only dogs bred by you can bear your affix as a heading. The only alteration to this is if, for example, a Gunalt-bred bitch (our affix) who is owned by someone else is mated to a 'Gunalt' bred dog, we can head the resulting puppies 'Gunalt', simply because these puppies, although not bred by us, are all of our breeding. By the same example, if we bring a puppy into our kennel, not bred by us, or bearing our affix as a heading, we put Gunalt after the name – as in Sh. Ch. Hansom (the affix of Dick Finch) Portman of Gunalt. The usefulness of an affix is that you can look at a pedigree of a dog, and the names bearing affixes tell you who bred that dog or which 'lines' the dog goes back to.

FORMS OF BREEDING

Line breeding is the most used form of breeding to produce puppies with distinct similarities through the generations. It is generally the most successful. Line breeding, in simplistic terms, is a mating of grandfather to grand-daughter, uncle to niece, relatives once or twice removed within the pedigree. The point of doing such a mating (which appears to be very close to a person unfamiliar to dog breeding) is that you can, through generations of careful line breeding, see conformity of type of dogs produced. Knowing the lines of dogs bred gives a knowledgeable breeder the ability to double up on the good genes and dilute the bad genes, thereby producing better dogs, with better temperaments. Knowing lines and dogs within certain lines and pedigrees also helps breeders to avoid unwanted hereditary conditions.

Line breeding is only useful if you know the lines. An inexperienced potential breeder decided to use a certain stud dog on her bitch because the stud was the bitch's grandsire, with the phrase "This is a good mating." What this lady did not know was that the sire in question had an unstable temperament and produced puppies with an hereditary eye problem. Through lack of experience but loads of enthusiasm the lady would have produced a litter with definite problems, due to doubling up on such genes.

By outcrossing, which is mating far-removed relations or unrelated dogs, you can do just as much harm. You will in effect be throwing a dice and seeing how it falls. The more you outcross the more different genes are introduced into the pedigree, giving you less knowledge about which genes will feature in the resulting puppies, with therefore less control over how the puppies will grow up. Outcrossing is necessary to introduce other lines or 'fresh blood'. Too much line breeding reduces 'hybrid vigour', which is what produces a healthy constitution. I think this is nature's way of stopping too close breeding, too often, which could ultimately result in such a small gene pool leading to deformities. Out-crossing often gives increase in size of the gene pool. In humans, sisters and brothers can often look quite different. This is because humans tend not to marry relations and therefore they increase the gene pool. However, the natives of a particular area or country of origin can often share characteristics and this is not just the colour of skin. Take for instance the Irish. Irish folk I know seem to have a certain look and of course those 'Irish eyes' which do seem to be similar.

In-breeding should only be done with eyes wide open and only with extensive knowledge and experience. An inbred mating sometimes tried by breeders is brother/sister or parent/offspring. By doing such a mating you are simply doubling up on the genes, not introducing new ones, therefore you will have double good genes but also double bad ones. Knowing lines and how to go forward to produce good dogs of consistent type is, therefore, a daunting prospect, so use the experience of the long-standing winning breeders. Most breeders will be very happy to help the less experienced or genuinely interested folk starting out. Everyone has their own priorities in what they are wanting in a Weimaraner. An experienced breeder will help, without trying to influence the bitch's owner into using their stud. Just remember, avoid the instant experts! It is useful that breeders want different things. At some point when you need to 'go out' to a different line, your line can benefit from the new blood, using a dog with characteristics you are lacking.

THE BROOD BITCH

You have done your homework and heart-searching and want to proceed to breed your bitch. Any time after six months of age your bitch can have her first oestrus cycle – season or heat – but she should not be bred at this time. There is no particular pattern, although if her dam came into heat early and has regular seasons, the daughter can adhere to this. We find bitches who come into season early, before 12 months of age, usually come into season regularly every six months. We have one bitch who came into season at six-and-a-half months and she came back into season every four to five months, which was a bit of a nuisance. After three years of age this did regularise to five-and-a-half months between seasons, which was slightly better. We have found that a bitch not having her first season until nearly 18 months of age often results in that bitch only having a season once a year. The thing about Nature is that she is in control and we cannot say anything is normal – one must plan it by ear with each bitch. However, if a bitch has not had a season by the time she is 18 months, it is a good idea to have a word with your vet, who may suggest giving her a hormone injection to bring her into season. There is a slight possibility that the bitch could be barren, without ovaries or with malformation of the ovaries. If an injection is administered and proves effective, it is unwise to mate her on that season; wait until she has a normal one. If you have more than one bitch you will often find a 'maiden' bitch can be brought into season for the first time by her kennel mates. We find this happens quite often. We will end up with half our bitches in season together and the other half do the same. It is rare that one bitch is in season alone. Bitches can continue to have seasons well into old age. I know of a Labrador bitch having a puppy by accident at 12 years of age, fortunately with no ill effects, but this is not something to be recommended. The ideal time to breed a maiden bitch is between the ages of two and three years. The first season matures a bitch physically and I feel also helps in her mental development. It would therefore be totally wrong and unethical to expect a bitch to cope under the age of 18 months in either department – after all what is the rush?

SPAYING YOUR BITCH

Although most vets advise spaying of bitches before the first season – my theory on this is that it is easier across the board to eliminate the chances of unwanted puppies by getting bitches into the surgery early – I do feel the bitch should be allowed to develop properly with the help of that first season and then, if puppies are not wanted, in order to eliminate any uterine problem, or problems with unwanted stray males or mess in the home, have her spayed. One must weigh up both sides before contemplating spaying. There is a slight chance of problems and this is best discussed with your vet. Overall, if I did not want to breed I would not hesitate to have my bitch spayed. The old adage that as a result of being spayed she will get fat, holds no truth whatsoever. But having her spayed, then overfeeding and under-exercising her, well then yes, your bitch will put weight on. Spaying will not change her personality. It usually coincides with the bitch gaining maturity, which is why she can appear more sensible or quieter. It is worth noting that if you show your bitch and have her spayed you must inform the Kennel Club.

MONITORING THE BITCH'S SEASON

It is useful to watch your bitch closely during her first and second seasons if you wish to breed. Note the first day of colour, count days, monitor when she goes out of colour and when she is most receptive to a male. When a bitch ovulates she will sidle up to a male and flirt, she will stand arching her back, tail pushed round to the side of her, in anticipation of accepting a male. She will often back up to another dog, sometimes even a human if no dog is available, her instinct to reproduce taking over. It will be far easier from your point of view if you have a chart telling you on what day of the season this appears to happen, so when you want to mate her you have a good idea when you expect to take her to the stud.

On the first season the blood (colour) discharge often appears to be exceptionally heavy, more so than on subsequent seasons. This is accentuated by the fact that your bitch is unsure of what is going on and does not clean herself too well. On subsequent seasons, when she has the hang of things, she can be meticulously clean and if you are not careful you could miss day one. It is therefore a good idea to watch carefully for blood when you know the signs. Usually a fortnight or so before the bitch comes into season, neighbouring dogs are aware and start sniffing round. If you have dogs and bitches, you find your males follow a bitch who is about to come into season. They will lick at her vulva. The vulva starts to swell. We had a bitch who we always knew when she was due in season as she obviously got a form of PMT and would sit in the field looking sorry for herself. Her normally pleasant disposition would change and if any other of our canines went to pester her she would send them off with a stern word.

The start of the discharge can often be dark reddish brown but will quickly turn to clear fresh blood. Usually the discharge will change to a pinkish or clear colour around 10 to 11 days into the season. The bitch will throw her tail to one side at this time. We would mate the bitch about two days after this has occurred, not immediately. So, normally, you would mate your bitch on her twelfth or thirteenth day of season, although each bitch is unique. I know of one English Setter who ovulated on day one of her season and it was only after the bitch had a blood sample tested to see when she ovulated, having missed three times when mated, that it was found to be so. We have one bitch who always had puppies when mated on her ninth day in season; her daughter and grand-daughter followed suit.

If you are unsure when your bitch is ovulating and have a long way to go to the stud dog, it is a good idea to consult your vet and discuss the possibility of blood-testing her. The test needs doing every other day and gives you one of three results: (a) the bitch has ovulated; b) the bitch is not ovulating; (c) the bitch is coming to ovulation. So it is important to be ready to go when you receive the result. This is an expensive option but worth considering to ensure you have the right time. Although a bitch usually conceives if mated on the same day of the season as previous conception, this is not a hard and fast rule. Bitches do not necessarily ovulate on the same day of every season.

One mating is sufficient providing you have the correct time and a pre-potent sire. Some folk like two matings, which is a useful form of insurance. This would be done two days after the first mating thus giving you a greater chance of covering the ovulation time. It used to be thought sperm lived only a few days but now it is known to live eight to nine days. It is also only recently that I discovered that the bitch will usually whelp 63 days to the date she ovulated (which makes sense when you think about it) as opposed to previously thinking that she would whelp to the date of mating. Funny – knowing all this we would assume a bitch would never miss, yet they do, of course. Another case of nature informing us that she knows best!

The length of a season from first day of colour is three weeks – 21 days. The in-season bitch must be segregated from males for the whole of this time. However, I have known bitches to stand like the proverbial hussy after this time and be mated. I can recall one time a friend called, many years ago, with a bitch 25 days into her season. The bitch was let out into the field to play with her best friend, a male. As we chatted, I realised the male was paying particular interest to the rear of the bitch. We decided to intervene too late and we, vet and experienced breeder, with red faces had to stand seeing our charges tied for 20 long minutes! The bitch was injected to make sure she did not conceive, resulting in her having three further weeks of season. We had a bitch of our own who always conceived on her twelfth day of season and, when introduced back into the pack, was always mated, though by only one of the dogs, on her 28th day in season. We never had her injected – it would have been a mating we would have done anyway, but she never conceived when mismated in this way.

A point to remember is that when a bitch is ready for mating, she may decide to take matters into her own hands, act completely out of character and disappear looking for a mate – so keep a very close eye on your bitch at this time. When taking her out for a walk it is worth putting her in the car and perhaps going to a different, more isolated place so no trail to your door can be followed by astute males. Try to avoid going out at the most popular times; that way you are neither pestered nor cause trouble to dog-walkers with males. Even letting her out into the garden to relieve herself becomes a time-consuming exercise, no matter how well-fenced your garden is to keep her in. Rampaging males can scale anything in the quest for a mate.

The smallest Jack Russell can achieve his desire with a little help from an accommodating bitch in season. I once had a frantic telephone call from a breeder whose bitch had just produced 10 puppies to her own six-month male. She had seen them tied but never thought he would be fertile at such a young age. The moral is, always watch your bitch during a season and never let any male near her. As with humans it is sensible to have your bitch in tip-top condition. We usually give mineral tablets a month before the bitch is due in season to help give her an extra bloom.

ETIQUETTE OF MATING

To breed responsibly you should decide upon your potential stud in advance of your bitch's season, when the planned litter is to be tried for. So write, ring, or enquire at shows and Field Trials to the owners of stud dogs you are interested in. Stress that you are making an enquiry and not asking to use their dog. Nothing is more likely to put a stud dog owner's back up than being asked if you can use their dog only to find later you have changed your mind and gone off to another stud. No stud dog owner minds giving out copies of their dog's pedigree for appraisal. In fact most will be only too happy to help, if asked, as to whether a particular stud will gel with your bitch. Once the choice is made, book the dog in advance. If you leave this until your bitch is in season, you may find the stud's owner will not let you use their dog, or has a bitch booked for the same time. At this time, you can check that the stud is Kennel Club registered, an absolute must. Ask if he has been used before. You may not want to risk travelling a long distance with a maiden bitch to an inexperienced stud. A strange anomaly is that a bitch will stand for most mongrels and a young virgin mongrel stud can usually mate anything in season, but this is not always the case in an orchestrated mating. At this time enquire about stud fees. If you find the fee unacceptable, you can change your mind beforehand, not after the mating. A young dog, whose progeny cannot be assessed yet, or dog with a poor track record of producing quality puppies will have a cheaper stud fee. You should expect to pay more for a dog who is very well bred and capable of producing consistently good-quality stock.

Make sure the stud owner is happy with your method of paying and arrange whether you will be given a free return if your bitch does not produce. Would the stud owner take a puppy? If this is the case, you must discuss: Will this be first choice puppy? What if she only has one puppy, or only one of the sex both of you require? If all angles are discussed to satisfaction before the event, no one will fall out later. It is rare that a stud owner would consider returning a fee. It is generally thought among dog folk that you pay for the service of the dog, not for puppies. Mostly, you are given a free return, though it used to be that the first service of a maiden/virgin dog was free. However, with rising costs and puppy prices, it is generally thought unfair now. It is now more acceptable to decide on the price of the stud before the mating, to be paid on production of puppies for a first-time stud. If this is to be the arrangement, or a puppy is taken in lieu of a stud fee, the stud owner would reserve the right not to sign the Kennel Club registration form, needed to register the resulting puppies, before payment is made. Once all terms are agreed between both parties, no further contact is needed until the bitch commences her relevant season.

On commencement of this season, it is sensible and good manners to inform the stud owner. You can decide whether to have the bitch ovulation-tested or on what day approximately the mating should take place. You cannot be exact but a rough idea gives everyone time to sort out commitments and work round them. However, it is no earthly good deciding to go on her fourteenth day (let us say a Saturday) because its convenient, if the bitch is ovulating on her eleventh day. Rather forget the whole thing and mate the bitch when you can give commitment more fully. It is always expected that the bitch will go to the stud dog, unless extenuating circumstances prevail.

Chapter Eight

WHELPING AND REARING A LITTER

When your bitch has been mated, hopefully she will already be having a very good quality diet plus any supplement you wish to include. Do not 'kill her with kindness' by giving too rich a diet or too much supplement, as this can do more harm than good. By overdoing supplements puppies can have abnormal bone growth and even possible malformation of jaws. Read instructions very carefully. As with humans, no extra food is needed during the first weeks of pregnancy. We would give three smaller meals and introduce milk for a pregnant bitch during the last two or three weeks. Exercise can remain as normal, neither increasing nor decreasing until common sense will tell you when your bitch should slow down during the last two weeks or so. We tend to discourage any jumping of high obstacles and avoid letting a heavily pregnant bitch squeeze through small spaces. Generally, Weimaraners are very sensible and tend to behave in a manner befitting the condition.

SIGNS OF PREGNANCY
Often the owner is impatient to know if the bitch is in whelp. There are various signs which can help. Between three and four weeks the puppies can be felt, rather like golf balls. However, a vet or an experienced breeder should be the only ones to attempt this. It is not wise to poke about if you do not know what you are doing. No-one worth their salt will say definitely either way but an opinion can be offered. Some bitches can have sickness during the first week or two. Another sign is that your bitch may need to spend a penny more often at this time. Her behaviour can change from normal, for example at three weeks often going off her food, then by five to six weeks eating ravenously. Often a sign at about three weeks is that the teats start to become red and stand out, quite pronounced. At around five to six weeks a good sign of pregnancy is that the bitch is in fabulous condition, thickening in the flank (waist) and with the ribs springing more. A good sign at six to seven weeks is if the bitch tends to be plain over her back, the back bone becoming more prominent even when the bitch is obviously not thin. In a false pregnancy, a bitch can show many signs of being pregnant. Many people have been fooled, not just novices. However, I have yet to see a bitch displaying a false pregnancy who is very plain over her back.

A sure sign that your bitch is in whelp is if a vet categorically states she is not! No experienced vet will say 'definite' either way, unless the bitch has been ultrasonically scanned or X-rayed. Ultrasonic scanning machines are increasing in popularity and many vets have them, or can refer you to a practice that has. It is one sure way of knowing if your bitch is in whelp but, at the end of 63 days, you will know anyway! During the last week of pregnancy it should become evident. In fact generally you can see the puppies moving about inside the bitch when she is lying asleep, particularly in the shortcoated Weimaraner. It is a fascinating spectacle for me, even after all these

Gunalt Joy: A top brood bitch for the Gunalt kennel, 56 days in whelp. Owned and bred by Patsy and Stephen Hollings.

Photo; Keith Allison.

years. Pregnant bitches and puppies are real time-wasters it must be said. At this time we would bring the whelping box into the maternity unit and sleep the bitch in there. It is funny, but our bitches, although they have never lived alone, never cry for their peers at this time. They are happy and settled in the quiet whelping box alone. Maiden bitches can often whelp three days early, but we once had a bitch whelp seven days early, with no problems, so it is wise to prepare the whelping box early. As the birth becomes imminent, we would move the whelping box into the house. We feel it is easier to oversee the whelping from the comfort of the home with the use of a TV and video, rather than sitting in the stark surroundings of the maternity unit.

THE WHELPING BOX
Our whelping box is custom-made to specifications we find work ideally. Too big, and the bitch is constantly up gathering her brood to her; too small, and the chance of lying on the whelps is increased. The ideal measurements for our Weimaraners, whether the bitch is big or small, are: 43 ins (109 cm) x 30 ins (76 cm) with a 4 ins (10 cm) high side and a 4 ins (10 cm) turned-in lip,

which acts as a safety rail. If a whelp is asleep in a corner, or against the side, the bitch cannot inadvertently smother the puppy, because of the gap caused by this lip. Alternatively you can have high sides with the front hinged to drop down, allowing the bitch easy access, yet restraining the puppies within the box. If a high-sided box is preferred, a rail set into the box, at the dimension expressed for the turned lip, needs to be added as the safety barrier. This can easily be included using holes drilled into the sides of the box with broom handles slipped through. Cleaning the whelping box is imperative. After use, we wash it with a proprietary disinfectant and leave it outside for nature to do her work inflicting on it all weather conditions. A month before a litter is due the box is again disinfected and put inside to dry. The maternity kennel is treated in a similar manner.

As bedding for the whelping box we always use the synthetic, veterinary, sheepskin-type bedding, cut to size. We have at least two pieces which are alternated as necessary. This bedding is very hygienic: it can be washed in the washing machine, it reflects heat back to the puppies and it allows any liquid through, keeping the puppies warm and dry. It also lies flat, whereas normal blankets tend to gather up, so puppies could inadvertently be caught up in them and smothered or squashed. Furthermore, it gives a good grip for puppies to hang on to, giving them greater mobility at a younger age – an invaluable addition to the whelping box. We always put a layer of newspaper under the bedding, which soaks up any liquid and can be easily and frequently disposed of, alleviating the build-up of harmful germs.

HEATING

It is imperative that puppies are kept warm, particularly when new-born. A constant 24 degrees C (74 degrees F) is about the right temperature. We find the best way of heating the box is by a heat lamp. Farmers use these in farrowing units for baby pigs so, if you have difficulty obtaining a lamp and holder, go along to a farm-requisites dealer, who should be able to supply you. The lamp is hung from above, about 3 ft from the base of the whelping box or high enough so the bitch does not knock herself on it (the lamps are very hot to touch and in danger of exploding if touched). Not only does this provide heat, it also provides a focal point for the puppies to head towards, and light for you and the bitch to see what you are up to. If the box is too hot, puppies will head out under the rail and the lamp can be lifted; if too cold they will huddle on top of each other. We prefer a normal 'white' bulb. There is a thought that the red one promotes unnatural growth. They also give an unnatural light and puppies cannot be as easily scrutinised for potential problems. Always make sure draughts are avoided, as puppies can catch a chill. If a bitch whelps unexpectedly and is found with cold puppies, the best way of warming them is to fill a container with blood-heat water and submerge them up to their necks. As the puppies warm, they can then be towel-dried, thus stimulating circulation and keeping them warm until they are returned to the dam.

FADING PUPPY SYNDROME

Having experienced this condition many years ago I write this with trepidation. I would not wish fading puppies on my very worst enemy. I include this here because it is thought that cold could contribute to the occurence of this condition. There are other theories but none proven. In describing 'fading puppies' I would liken the syndrome, in a way, to cot death. It generally occurs in very young puppies who, although born healthy and apparently thriving, will start to go dark in colour and become lethargic, often squealing an unnatural noise. They die by simply fading away. As a farmer's daughter I have many times revived baby lambs and piglets, so to be helpless when faced with this fading puppy syndrome is devastating. Fortunately the condition is not common.

THE WHELPING

It is normal for a bitch to stop eating a day before she whelps. Yet most of our Weimaraners eat between whelps! Which just goes to prove, you can read the book, but you need common sense and a good back-up team! A day or two before parturition, your bitch could determinedly start 'looking' for a place to whelp. She may dig a hole in the bottom of the garden or disappear into your bedroom, scratching a bed for herself in the middle of your bedding. Her temperature will drop from the normal 38.5 C (101.5 F) to 37.5 C (98 F). She will look uncomfortable and probably want to go out and relieve herself an unnatural number of times.

As the birth becomes imminent, you will notice contractions of her abdomen, she will shiver and possibly the waters will break. This is normal. Once she starts bearing down – pushing – you need to monitor time. If this stage goes on for too long without anything happening, it could result in complications. If a birth has not occurred within a good half-an-hour, take her out and see if this will 'stir her up'. If this does not work, consult your vet immediately, who may suggest that you should take the bitch to the surgery. This is not because the vet is too lazy to come out but because the car journey often gets a bitch going. Many a puppy is born in the back of the car as you pull up in the vet's car park. If nothing has happened, once at the surgery your vet can see whether she needs an injection to help the procedure or if it is necessary to perform a Caesarean section – another good reason to be at the vet's surgery.

It is worth noting that most whelpings occur at night, so whenever you take the bitch out, either to get her going or to let her relieve herself, even if you are sure she has finished whelping, always take a good torch. It would be devastating to find a dead whelp next morning, when you thought she had just squatted to relieve herself. I know of bitches whelping eight puppies in a morning, yet we once had a bitch take a full 24 hours to produce four whelps with no ill effects, so there is no set pattern to follow.

If your bitch has gone more than three hours between whelps, it is worth having a word with your vet to explain what is going on. The vet can then make a judgement on when to intervene. Generally Weimaraners are very sensible. Once they get the hang of what is happening, just

A newborn litter on completion of parturition. Notice how striped Weimaraner puppies are.

Photo: Keith Allison.

Newborn puppies of the longhaired variety. These puppies do not have stripes and the coat has a woolly appearance.

overseeing the whelping is the order of the day, as opposed to having to gather scissors, towels etc. However, the first birth for a maiden bitch can shock her. If your bitch seems in pain or very distressed, watch carefully that she does not turn round and nip the puppy before she realises what is happening.

Puppies, as with most mammals, are usually born head and fore-legs first. However, it is not unusual for puppies to come back-legs and tail first. It can be a little more tricky if just the tail is present, as this leaves a large area of puppy to be delivered. If any puppy appears to be stuck, act calmly and gently without rushing. Hold the protruding part gently. With your other hand pre-soaped, run your finger around the vulva, and ease the puppy out in time with the contractions. If in any doubt at all, consult your vet.

Usually Weimaraners will instinctively cut the cord and lick the puppy to stimulate breathing and to get the circulation going, so do not always rush in. After all, it is her job and it helps with the bonding. The dam may appear to be extremely rough with the new whelp. This is natural. If, in rare cases, the dam does not cut the cord, I recommend severing it between thumbnail and finger, being particularly careful not to pull the cord from the body. The reason I would never cut the cord with scissors is because I am aware that a sharp open wound could lead to bacteria and infection being free to enter, causing many problems. The jagged graze of a thumb-nail seals the opening of the cord more successfully.

KNOWING WHEN TO INTERVENE

Each puppy has a sac and an afterbirth, or placenta. You may not notice this if the dam is fastidious at the birth. The bitch instinctively cleans up all afterbirth, a biological capability left over from the wild, when it was imperative to leave no trace, thereby reducing the chance of predators thinking they were in for an easy meal. Do not be alarmed if the discharge during birth is black or dark green as well as containing blood; this is normal. The first puppy can come in for much cleaning from mum, and I must say I am always happy when number two is born giving her something else to think of!

If the whelp is not cleaned by mum, or the sac broken, you should intervene. Break the sac, thus allowing the whelp to breath and rub the whelp gently but briskly. Put your finger in the pup's mouth to remove mucus. If a bitch has been whelping for a long time and is very tired she may suffer from uterine inertia. This is the inability to contract, which stops puppies being born. Your vet needs to be consulted, who can then give an injection to counteract this.

In the event of a Caesarean section having to be performed, you need to take precautions when taking the mother and offspring home. Due to the anaesthetic, the bitch will not react normally for a while. Stay with her, so she does not inadvertently lie on the pups. Watch very carefully that she does not try to pick up the pups, as she can bite hard without realising it and damage them. Or she may not be interested in her family initially. Do not worry; as she recovers, nature will take over and, as the puppies suck, she will come to.

POSSIBLE POST-WHELPING PROBLEMS

Once cleaned by their mother, Weimaraners display their determined temperament, even at this early stage, by fighting their way to the teat and sucking heartily. I have noticed English Setters do not have the same temperament and often lie squeaking until popped on a teat. I do like to make sure all puppies have sucked. The colostrum – the first milk produced – contains antibodies which line the whelps' stomachs, giving immunity to infections. The more the puppies suck, the more milk is produced. It is not necessary to have a great full udder for the bitch to feed her puppies heartily, but liquid creates milk, so do give the dam plenty to drink during lactation. Immediately after the birth of all puppies, we give the bitch a drink of milk with an egg and glucose. If you have trouble getting your bitch to accept liquid, we find it rare for one to refuse a drink of warm sweet tea – our bitches love it.

Once all is finished with the whelping it is wise quietly to check the puppies over. Fortunately we have never had a cleft palate in a Weimaraner, but I have seen it in other breeds. I find the condition most distressing, as the whelp appears perfect. On close inspection of the roof of the mouth a split can be visibly seen. The puppy will have to be put to sleep to save suffering, except in extremely mild cases. I feel there is an hereditary element involved when this occurs, therefore the dam should not be bred from again.

Often, a day or two after whelping, you may find your bitch becomes a little unsettled and starts scratching her bed up. This is usually caused by after pains. The normal dark discharge on completion of parturition will turn clear red and can quite normally persist for a week or so. Only if the discharge is very heavy or cloudy and smelling foul should you need to consult your vet. Do not waste any time if this is the case. You do not want a seriously ill dog when she has a young family to support.

Metritis (inflammation of the uterus) is a condition which should be watched for in the first days after whelping. The temperature of the bitch will rise, she will have an unnatural thirst and the discharge will be foul-smelling. This can be caused by a dead puppy or a retained afterbirth and can affect lactation. You should also be vigilant about watching the udder of a lactating bitch for signs of mastitis. This is where segments of the udder become hot, red and hard. Again consult your vet. If possible expel milk from this gland and bathe with a cold compress. Be careful, as the affected gland will be very painful.

Another complaint to watch for in a new mother is eclampsia or milk fever. This is caused by a sudden drop in calcium in the blood, often caused by the bitch producing a rush of milk. If she is in poor condition, this can also be a cause. The signs are restlessness – the bitch is unsettled and may collapse. An intravenous injection of calcium may be necessary, administered by the vet. You should watch for any recurrence throughout lactation.

HAND-REARING
Should a bitch became ill or die – which is highly unlikely, I might add – you must have some knowledge about hand-rearing puppies. While this is generally successful in these circumstances, we in 25 years, have never successfully supplemented a weak puppy in an otherwise healthy litter. I am a great believer in nature knowing best and have known bitches rear 14 puppies, no problem, yet another litter of four would be very uneven in growth rate. In the case of a big litter, we would pop the small one on a teat every time we passed. That puppy, if healthy, will thrive and be no different in growth at 12 months of age.

If hand-rearing is necessary, always use a bitch-substitute milk, not cow's milk as this has the incorrect nutrient for puppies. The puppies will need feeding every three hours and their genitals will need rubbing gently with damp cotton wool, far better than fingers which could introduce infection. The dam normally would lick the puppies to stimulate them to pass faeces and urine and it is essential that this is done.

DEWCLAWS AND DOCKING
Before five days of age Weimaraner puppies need their dewclaws removing, to save the pain and stress of tearing a dewclaw at a later date, and hopefully their tails docked. Docking of puppies' tails can only be carried out by a vet and many vets feel it unnecessary so will not perform the task. Breeders who love and know the breed well will move heaven and earth to find a competent vet willing to dock. This is not because Weimaraner breeders wish to have tails removed to make the dog look better but for the good of the dog. The removal of a tail or of dewclaws (if done properly) is not cruel. It causes no more pain – if as much – as tearing a nail too short in a human. Yet if blackthorn catches a tail, or the tail is bashed on furniture, or walls or barbed wire when out on a walk, a full anaesthetic is needed to amputate the grown dog's tail, followed by stitches which the dog may try to remove, as the healing of a tail wound in an older dog can be a long process, often resulting in gangrene. Once docked and with dewclaws removed, puppies sleep contentedly. From this time they seem to take off and grow at an alarming rate.

THE FIRST EIGHT WEEKS
Week 1: Puppies at this stage sleep and eat. Mum cleans up and, apart from being time-wasters, they need little from you. Weimaraner puppies are striped at birth. This usually lasts up to about three or four days. If puppies are to have white on their chest or indeed anywhere else, this will be evident from birth. Sometimes puppies are mismarked. This would not hamper the dog's life but would not be acceptable for showing or breeding. Mismarking can take the form of the puppy having white on the toes, or having ginger hair rather like Doberman points. Although not easily noticeable at birth, these offensive ginger markings will be evident from the beginning and will not fade.

The bitch needs a good-quality food at least twice a day. Initially she may need tempting to eat – she will have consumed so much afterbirth and be so tired, all she wants is liquid. We always give the bitch a drink of milk at bedtime. The milk we use is a powdered ewe-substitute powder mixed with warm water. Ewe milk is the nearest to bitch milk and we find it has reared many litters successfully for us when given to the dam and to weaning puppies.

Weeks 2 and 3: From ten days puppies start to open their eyes. Very occasionally you may have a

The puppies instinctively search for the teat. The first feed contains colostrum which has antibodies from the mother.

sticky eye in a pup, where it seems to have pus at the corner. Boil some water, dissolve salt into it and leave until just aired. This can be used to bathe a sticky eye. Always use clean cotton wool to avoid re-infection. We always cut puppies' toenails from this time, then weekly. If needed, at three weeks one can introduce a little food for puppies to try.

Week 4: Worm puppies and dam with a wormer your vet prescribes. Introduce food. In a shallow dish put warm, soaked puppy food or Weetabix. Take the puppies out of the whelping box into the kennel area and put around the dish. You could gently touch their noses into 'porridge-type' food, so they get the taste, but puppies usually dive in when they are ready. The first feeding is administered at a time when the dam has been out for an hour or more and the puppies are therefore hungry. After feeding, let mum in to clean up puppies and dish. By this time puppies will be strong on their feet and starting to play with each other. They will start to have a little bark – all fascinating stuff.

Week 5: Puppies will be fed three or four times a day at this time, jumping out of the box on hearing your voice or the food bin, one of the most important things to them. They will also play

Six-week-old puppies need the stimulus of toys, but they also need lots of rest in order to develop correctly.

At eight weeks old, the puppies are ready to leave home.

heartily but more with each other than with you. We would slightly reduce the bitch's food and liquid supply at this time in anticipation of full weaning.

Because the dam can stop cleaning up after puppies at about this stage, we put shredded paper, bought in plastic covered bales, in the sleeping quarters and wood chippings in the play area.

Week 6: Puppies are self-assured and should be eating heartily. The dam can be weaned at this time, but play it by ear – remember no hard and fast rules, we are dealing with life not machines. Cut the bitch's milk out, thus enabling her milk supply to diminish. Increase her exercise to get her back into condition. Worm both puppies and bitch. Do not forget the toenail cutting.

Week 7: Now puppies are getting more interested in you as a human rather than as a supplier of food. Human contact and play starts to dominate their thoughts as opposed to mum and food. We always say that puppies have to pass an examination in 'shoe-lace untying' and by this stage they are taking every opportunity to practise! They will enjoy stimulus from toys and chews at this time and the more you watch, the more you will notice how different they all are in personality and looks. We start to build a picture of which puppy will be right for which owner and their requirements.

The puppies will be totally weaned onto four feeds: Breakfast – Complete puppy food, soaked or crisp at this stage, followed by a drink of milk (ewe-substitute powder, diluted carefully into warm water); Lunch – repeat; Tea – repeat; Supper – Weetabix and milk or cereal or rice pudding.

Week 8: How can you part with them? Believe me the amount they eat, the amount they dispose of and the amount of noise – easily! Really though, at eight weeks a Weimaraner puppy is mentally ready to learn, and needs human company and stimulation. If you have eight eight-week-old puppies you cannot successfully give them what they need in mental terms. If they are going to a well-prepared, good home, as all of them should be, we are happy to see them go. Puppies are fed a diet as Week 7. Bitch and puppies are again wormed but toenails are not cut at this time.

Chapter Nine

DISEASES AND HEALTH CARE

My advice to new puppy owners is, as I have said, take the puppy along to your vet to be checked over. This also serves to introduce you to the vet and find out if you have confidence in the vet and the practice. One hears horrific tales about some doctors' receptionists and, likewise, if you find the receptionist at the veterinary surgery is unsympathetic, this will not instil confidence in you if you need a vet in an emergency. If you do not gel with the vet, this will leave you feeling vulnerable when you need reassurance most – when your Weimaraner is unwell or hurt. Generally vets are supportive, have the welfare of your pet at heart and are not out to make just a 'quick buck' out of you, but this first visit can give you that vital reassurance. Remember, if you are not happy it is your prerogative to go to any vet you like. "He who pays the piper, calls the tune." We do not register with a vet in just the same way we do, in the UK, with a doctor. Having said that, our vets are brilliant and I respect them totally; consequently, I receive excellent treatment and if my vet says "Come to the Surgery," I know that he will have a valid reason for saying that and it is not that he just cannot be bothered to come out.

THE FIRST AID KIT
Weimaraners are generally healthy as a breed but it is as wise to have a small first aid box for them as it is to have one for the human members of the family. It is best to include in this box the following:
Salt or TCP
Scissors
Cotton wool balls (Cotton)
Bandages
Liquid paraffin
Thermometer
Potassium Permanganate
Toothbrush
Syringe (Plastic)
Ear cleaner (obtained from vet)
Flea spray (obtained from vet)
Worming tablets (obtained from vet)
Nail clippers.

Although salt does not really need to be in the First Aid Kit, you can find it one of the most useful 'cure-all' remedies. Salt has great antiseptic capabilities, so boiled water with salt dissolved in it can be very useful for cuts, to stop infection and greatly aid healing. In fact, because

Weimaraners are so active, cuts can generally be the main problems for the breed.

On one occasion I had a two-year-old male who had barged through a small space, catching his side on some protruding metal, causing an inch-long slit on his ribs. Had it been any bigger he would have needed stitches – that would have entailed an anaesthetic, then ten days with a plastic bucket or Elizabethan collar strapped round his neck to stop him turning round to lick the cut, or even remove the stitches. Because the cut was not severe, I made up a saltwater solution and bathed the cut four times a day. The healing process was speeded up with the salt, no infection occurred and within five days the wound was virtually healed, saving the dog many traumas of head restraint and being isolated from the rest of the dogs. Obviously it must be stressed that if any doubt, the vet's advice must be sought.

Salt can also be useful, again diluted, if the dog needs to be made sick, following an inquisitive Weimaraner eating some poisonous substance or the like. The plastic syringe comes into its own here in administering the salt water down the dog's throat. Salt water is not the most pleasant substance to take! A strange anomaly: why does a Weimaraner so heartily consume slimy, rotten carcasses found when out on a walk, yet pick at the food at home? The syringe will also make the taking of liquid medicines a much easier alternative to trying to pour liquid down the throat with a measuring spoon.

Cotton wool balls, or just cotton as it is often called, are so useful for applying pressure to a cut to stem bleeding, for administering the salt solution, for cleaning out the ear etc. I must stress here that one should never poke about in a dog's ear with anything smaller than a cotton wool ball because one can so easily damage the fragile ear canal. If ear cleaner and cotton wool balls do not clean or relieve ear wax, it is best to get professional advice.

Potassium Permanganate is invaluable to stem bleeding. Weimaraners are notorious at catching ears on barbed wire or thorns, and once caught, the ear bleeds profusely, covering everything. A piece of damp cotton wool dipped in dry Potassium Permanganate crystals can instantly stop the bleeding. Likewise if one cuts the toenail too close to the quick, dry Potassium Permanganate can also be used as an antiseptic solution diluted in water. A word of warning, Potassium Permanganate stains, so be careful. It will eventually wash from fingers, but carpets and clothes do tend to remain stained. (My mother told me that during World War II Potassium Permanganate was diluted in a bath of water and then you sat in it, saving the need for stockings – very inventive!)

A thermometer is a useful addition to the First Aid box but do not be ruled by it. The normal temperature of an adult dog is 38.5 degrees Centigrade (101.5 degrees Fahrenheit). A youngster under six months may have a temperature of 39 degrees C (102.5 degrees F) without problem. If a dog is stressed, or hot or cold due to weather extremes, or if the dog has just participated in exercise, the temperature may be raised or lowered and yet the dog is not necessarily unwell. Only take the temperature if some other sign of illness is showing in the dog. The thermometer should be checked to ensure the mercury is down. Insert into the rectum of the dog for a minute and you will obtain a correct reading. If the temperature is not normal (being higher or lower), you must assume something is wrong and veterinary advice should be sought.

Liquid Paraffin is useful for dog or human. If a blockage is suspected, or constipation, a 15 ml dose of liquid paraffin with the syringe can save a trip to the vet. If this does not relieve symptoms, obviously something more serious could be amiss and the vet's advice should be sought.

Nail clippers are self-explanatory. Weimaraners hate having toenails clipped, yet look awful with great long talons distorting the toes. A vet will often offer the advice, at vaccination time, that your puppy will wear the nails down when walked on pavements or concrete. In my experience this is not necessarily so. All our Weimaraners live in the same environment, yet with some I never need to cut the nails, while others need nails cutting regularly. The best thing is to cut nails fortnightly in a young puppy to acclimatise the animal to the procedure, who is small enough at this stage to be restrained. This practice also teaches puppy that if you say it is nail-cutting time, this fact must be accepted. It also keeps nails really short, thereby reducing the risk of the nail bed becoming longer as puppy grows. If one meticulously performs this ritual, one finds that cutting of toenails is acceptable in an adult and the need to cut nails is reduced.

Flea spray is useful to have around. This really should be obtained from your vet and used with his advice, but as fleas are in the grass they are easily picked up. As with nits in children it does not mean you are uncaring or dirty if your dog picks up fleas. Because the Weimaraner has a short, fine coat, fleas can be easily spotted, the dark droppings of the flea are very easily noticed attached to the hair of the dog, usually around the ears, under 'arms' and along the back. Because the eggs are laid in the coat of the dog, a repeat treatment is recommended. It is useful to note that the bedding, carpets and chairs the dog uses should also be treated, as eggs can be laid there, also increasing re-infestation. Fleas are also an intermediate host for the tapeworm, so one should be vigilant in checking for fleas especially in warm and wet weather when they are at their most prevalent.

MITES AND TICKS

Late summer is usually the time when harvest mites occur most frequently. They tend to be present deep in the ear, virtually undetected by the eye. Affected dogs will scratch their ears and shake their heads causing irritation, an increase in wax and, in progressive cases, haemotoma of the ear where excessive shaking bursts a blood vessel, filling the ear. If left to its own devices, the blood will eventually dry away leaving the ear thick and shrivelled up. For this reason an operation is usually performed by the vet. Weimaraners can also receive a haemotoma following a knock, often on the occipital bone, but I have also seen them on the ribs. Then the haemotoma will form to protect the bruise or injury and, if left alone, will go, leaving no mark. However, if drained surgically, the haemotoma can reappear and accentuate the problem, plus, of course, leaving a scar; so leave well alone. The vet will prescribe drops or cream to kill the mites and the irritation.

Ticks are commonly known as sheep ticks and your dog can pick them up running over moors or through fields. I remember in my youth shearing a sheep for a farmer and it was covered in ticks – most unpleasant. Dipping sheep against various parasites has reduced the problem but I found a tick on a Collie only last summer. The tick shows itself fairly easily on the short smooth coat of the Weimaraner. They appear as a fat, light coloured growth, about the size of a baked bean. They are attached, in fact, by the head and because of this must be removed carefully. If pulled off, the head is invariably left on, causing infection. The vet can prescribe an effective remedy. I have heard of removing a tick by applying lighter-fuel to the body but be extremely careful or you may do more harm than good.

COMMON AILMENTS AND DISEASES

ANAL GLANDS These glands are located at twenty-past and twenty-to the hour, each side of the anus and are there to secrete lubrication fluid which helps dogs to pass their faeces more easily. However, these glands can become blocked and need emptying. A sign that the anal glands are blocked is often shown by dogs shuffling their bottom along the floor. Another sign could be the dogs biting at their rump and even hair falling out of the dog's back at the rump. Another sign of blocked anal glands shows itself in a general lack of condition which has no other obvious cause. To empty the anal glands, cover the anus with a big piece of cotton wool or kitchen paper and squeeze the glands with your thumbs, thus forcing the contents into the paper. The substance expelled is foul-smelling so be careful not to get it on your clothes. The contents of the anal gland can be released naturally by the dog if badly frightened.

ARTHRITIS This is not too common in Weimaraners – probably because this breed is sleek, not prone to being overweight and therefore retaining suppleness well into old age. However, if this condition does occur, drugs can be prescribed to relieve the pain, and oil of evening primrose or other herbal products are useful, as they are with humans.

BLOAT/GASTRIC TORSION This is the worst fear of the Weimaraner owner, and is one of the few true veterinary emergencies. It is one of the most common problems suffered by this breed. So what is gastric torsion – also known a bloat? It is where the stomach fills with gas and distends. The reason Weimaraners are prone to this condition is that they are long-bodied and deep-chested which allows this distended stomach to turn, rather like a balloon filled with water would, if each end were pulled. Once the stomach reaches this point and turns, nerve and blood supply is cut off, and the stomach swells dramatically, putting pressure on the adjoining organs, often rupturing the spleen. *Death will follow unless the vet operates immediately.* Even if the operation is successful, death can occur up to a week or so later because of shock or complications. Prevention is obviously the best course of action, and for this reason Weimaraner owners are advised to refrain from letting their dogs have exuberant exercise an hour before and after a meal. Because Weimaraners do everything to excess, given the chance, it is best to feed two meals rather than one big one, at which they will often gorge themselves, and if your Weimaraner is particularly greedy, a big stone, or the like, can be put in the dog's bowl. This makes the dog rummage for the food, which can help slow down the speed of eating.

No-one knows fully why gastric torsion occurs but there appears to be some similarity with colic, hence these preventative measures. It is also thought that white bread can help prevent gastric torsion, so a slice in the dog's meal may be an idea. One should also curb giving unlimited water to a very thirsty dog. Nevertheless, following all these guidelines, I have known a Weimaraner who had gastric torsion but when the vet opened the stomach, the only content, other than foam and gas, was one blade of grass. So one should not blame oneself – just be vigilant in recognising the symptoms. These include: restlessness, unnatural distension of the stomach, the dog trying to vomit to no avail, and general worry and obvious pain. If gastric torsion is suspected, ring your vet immediately to allow him to prepare for your arrival and get to the surgery quickly. If surgery is in progress, do not wait your turn, tell the receptionist it is very urgent. If it is the middle of the night, do not take no for an answer from your vet – it is better to end up embarrassed because you were wrong than end up with a dead dog.

BURNS Because the Weimaraner has a fine coat, if this is accidentally scalded or burnt the damage can be dramatic. Treat quickly with cold water and if it is severe, contact the vet immediately.

CONSTIPATION If your dog has bones to chew this can cause constipation – treat with liquid paraffin. Bran added to the diet can relieve constipation but if a problem persists, consult your vet because feed is so well-balanced these days that this should not be a real problem.

CRYPTORCHIDISM This is a heredity condition where the testicles are retained in the abdomen or inguinal canal (the passage by which the testicles travel to the scrotum). If both testicles are retained it usually means the dog is sterile (unable to sire puppies), but if one testicle is retained (known as monorchid), the dog is still able to reproduce and therefore should be castrated. Another reason to castrate is because the testicles retained in the body are in too warm an environment and can turn cancerous. An operation is usually suggested if one or both testicles have not dropped when the dog has reached 12 months of age, an operation which removes any fear of reproducing the problem or of future malignancy.

CYSTITIS This is as painful as with a human and shows itself in much the same way with loss of bladder control, traces of blood in the urine, etc. It is usually due to an infection and therefore the vet should be consulted.

DEPRAVED APPETITE This is the most anti-social behaviour of dogs eating their own or other dogs' excrement. It does tend to be habit-forming and once started can be hard to stop. Cleaning faeces up immediately will obviously prevent the dog from eating them but this is not always possible. It is often thought that a dog will start this habit through shortage of Vitamin B and the introduction of yeast tablets can help. I find bitches are more likely to eat faeces, due in part, I think, to the fact that a bitch will naturally clean up all that her puppies pass for the first four weeks of life. Bitches also tend to be more greedy than dogs.

DIARRHOEA Kaolin and morphine is invaluable in liquid or tablet form in the treatment of upset tummy problems. Weimaraners are sensitive to change, be it diet or your mood – either can upset their tummies. For this reason, do not dash off to the vet at the first sign of loose stools. Boiled rice and something light, such as fish or chicken, can alleviate this problem, but if it persists or you are worried, do see the vet. Because diarrhoea can cause dehydration, ensure the patient is encouraged to drink plenty, be it water, or tea which most Weimaraners take heartily. Too much milk can accentuate the problem.

ENTROPION This is a hereditary condition and very distressing to the recipient. The lid of the eye turns in, and as a result the lashes rub on the cornea. An operation to remove the offending layer of lashes can be performed, usually very successfully, so I am told. Of course, animals with this condition should never be bred from.

HEART PROBLEMS A dog who suffers a heart attack will suddenly collapse and may appear dead or with the eyes rotated upwards. There could be involuntarily emptying of the bladder and bowels. When the dog recovers sufficiently, do consult your vet. In an older dog heart trouble can be diagnosed by a cough which has no other obvious cause. Also heart problems can show up by an otherwise fit dog becoming short of breath in normal exercise. Always consult your vet.

HIP DYSPLASIA This condition is a malformation of the ball and socket which make up the hip. If the head of the femur, or socket, in which the hip joint fits, is deformed in any way then rubbing of the offending joints occurs, with bone on bone causing pain and discomfort. In severe cases surgery may be needed to give the animal a good quality of life but this is an extreme measure and every care should be taken to avoid the problem. Hip dysplasia can have both inherited and environmental causes. To be responsible, many breeders have breeding stock X-rayed, which in the UK can be done under a scheme run by The Kennel Club and British Veterinary Association, when the dog is over a year in age, usually under anaesthetic or heavy sedation. The dog is laid down with hind legs spread-eagled, the legs must be positioned correctly and the X-ray very clear to obtain the best picture of the hips. This X-ray is then sent before a panel of experts who evaluate it and grade each hip score. 0 - 0 means the dog has 'clear hips' or is clear of hip dysplasia. If for example a dog receives a score of 3 - 5 = Total 8, this means the dog has hip dysplasia. However, such a score would be considered low and the dog could still be bred from. I have noticed a Weimaraner with quite a high score, 46, showing no problems – in fact the animal in question is a true working dog. So reading scores must be done keeping everything in perspective. To avoid undue pressure on the growing dog and especially on bone and muscle development, it is wise to curb the desire to over-exercise a youngster under a year in age. Because the problem is only partly hereditary, it is difficult to eradicate. When breeding, so many things should be taken into consideration, e.g. soundness, temperament, type; one should not become blinkered by hip dysplasia when so many other factors are involved. In the United Kingdom we are fortunate that we are not dictated to by The Kennel Club, as happens in some countries. We can therefore let experienced breeders, with the welfare of the breed at heart, control, to a great extent, how to progress with breeding programmes taking everything in context, to produce an overall, sound, typy Weimaraner.

KENNEL COUGH Despite the name, kennel cough is not caught just because your dog has been in boarding kennels. It is a virus, and like a common cold in a human, its different strains make it difficult to vaccinate against, and dogs can still catch kennel cough despite vaccination. The vaccine is administered via nose drops straight into the nostrils of the dog, which is distressing to the animal, and often makes it difficult to administer, especially a repeat dose. As the vaccine only lasts up to six months, this can become a very tedious procedure. So go on your vet's advice as to when, or even if, to vaccinate against kennel cough. The symptoms are generally a rasping cough, usually after exercise or in the evening when the dog is in a warm, stuffy environment. Often the dog (rather like a child with a cold) seems fine playing out during the day, particularly when the weather is dry and crisp. If the animal appears to have a headache and sore throat, an Aspirin and Benylin can work wonders. The condition usually runs its course in a couple of weeks with no permanent problem. However, one should be vigilant, particularly in an older or younger dog, as if complications set in, this can lead to bronchitis or pneumonia. Therefore, if Kennel Cough does not start to clear up or if the symptoms get worse, then it is wise to go to the vet, who can prescribe antibiotics. Because kennel cough is an air-borne virus and is spread very easily, you should keep your dog away from others until the problem subsides. Nothing is more infuriating than to come home from a show and five days to a week later have all the dogs coughing. Naturally it can be worrying if one has a litter of puppies at home; the risk to them is great.

LUMPS When one thinks of lumps or growths, usually cancer springs to mind. While I think cancer appears to be on the increase, so cures seem to be more possible, much the same as in humans. Mammary tumours develop more often in older bitches but are easily spotted around the teats of the bitch. A good vet will advise whether to operate or not. We had a 10 year old bitch who had small, pealike growths in her teat. I mentioned this to the vet who decided it was best to monitor them but leave well alone. Fortunately they only grew very slowly and at 13 years still caused the bitch no problems. In a young dog detection of growths early can and does often result in complete recovery. Older dogs may develop a variety of lumps and bumps. If a malignant growth is found one must weigh up the pros and cons of surgery – remember it is about quality of life and if a painful operation would lengthen the dog's life by only a few months it may be kinder to let things alone until discomfort becomes too great and then have your dog put down.. Often Weimaraners can get sebaceous cysts, a marble-like growth under the skin which is not attached to muscle. These are obvious to the eye due to a short coat. They are best left alone, unless they grow, attach themselves to muscle or cause discomfort.

PYOMETRA This is an infection of the uterus. An open Pyometra shows itself by a discharge from the vulva, cloudy and pinkish brown in colour. This pus is recognisable because it is foul-smelling. The bitch will have a raised temperature and is usually drinking excessively and possibly vomiting. If it is caught in the early stages or in a mild form, antibiotics can remedy the condition. However this infection is potentially life-threatening and more often a hysterectomy is necessary. It was thought that maiden bitches, i.e. bitches never having had a litter, in middle age were most susceptible, but we have had bitches who have whelped and later developed pyometra, so the old adage 'a bitch should always have a litter for the good of her health' has no foundation here. A closed pyometra is obviously harder to detect and, because the pus is not being discharged, more dangerous. If in doubt, seek professional advice. It is also a useful thought to have your bitch spayed if you do not intend to breed or when she has had all the litters you require.

UMBILICAL HERNIA This is a non-heredity hernia often caused by an over-zealous bitch breaking the cord. In minor cases the small hole can be felt and fat just pops through, showing as a swelling at the navel. This hole often rectifies itself with time and very rarely would it cause the dog problems. Only if the hole is very big would a small operation to sew the hole be necessary. It is wise to leave well alone, certainly until the puppy is six months old, unless complications arise.

INGUINAL HERNIA These are hereditary and can be more of a problem. A soft, mobile lump in the groin can cause problems if it breaks through into the bladder or intestines. If this happens the bladder can become strangulated, thus cutting off blood supplies and causing serious problems if a corrective operation is not performed.

WORMS Roundworms are internal parasites. They only cause problems if one is casual about prevention and treatment. One hears so much from anti-dog people about humans, particularly children, picking up roundworm eggs (Toxocara canis) and becoming blind. If the dog is wormed regularly every six months, there should be no danger of this happening. By the same token, if dog owners are responsible and pick up any faeces deposited by their dog, this also reduces any chance of disease spreading. The Tapeworm is another worm which occurs in the UK. Fleas, lice and rodents are intermediate hosts, so cleanliness and vigilance of the dogs and their environment are of the utmost importance. Walking your Weimaraners through farmland, as I do, where sheep and rabbit droppings can be eaten, can also infect your dog. Tapeworms can be extremely long, but are made up of segments. The segments break off and are passed out in the dog's motions. They are rather like grains of white rice. Normal worming preparations are not sufficient against tapeworm but if suspected your vet can easily prescribe adequate medication. Do follow the instructions to the letter to be sure of eliminating all the worm.

Hook or whipworms are uncommon in the UK but endemic in other countries. They are not visible to the eye and a sample of the suspected faeces must be sent for testing. Loss of condition and general debility are the usual signs of hookworms. Heartworms are not a problem in the UK due to our climate not being warm enough, but are widespread in USA, Australia and New Zealand. Generally carried by the mosquito, they are passed to the dog when the animal is bitten by the mosquito. It is advisable to use prevention measures, as damage to major organs can occur before the worm is detected. Signs of heartworm include shortness of breath, coughing and tiredness.

WOUNDS As previously stated, minor cuts and tears can be treated with salt water. If the active, inquisitive Weimaraner is injured by a car or there is an accident of more major proportions, obviously your vet's advice must be sought quickly. If the animal is bleeding badly, apply a large wad of cotton wool, lint or the like on the wound to stem the bleeding, or apply a tourniquet but do not leave it so long that it cuts off the circulation. Keep the animal calm and quiet to avoid stress and shock. When moving a badly hurt dog, slide a coat or blanket carefully underneath the dog and lift each corner to avoid putting pressure on any hurt parts and thereby decreasing the chance of further stress. Be aware that the dog could act out of character and through pain and/or confusion, attempt to bite. It may be wise to gently fasten the mouth closed in severe cases.

A bite from a rodent can infect your dog with Leptospirosis among other diseases and this is why we use terriers for 'ratting' (not gundogs). Their instinct is to kill, whereas a gundog's instinct is to retrieve gently to you. This is another reason for keeping vaccinations valid. A bite from another dog or the like can cause problems, quite apart from the initial shock to you and your pet. Puncture wounds from dogs can be very deep and cause deep infections and abscesses, so, if in doubt after cleaning with a saline solution, consult your vet. Snake bites are possible in the UK although the adder is the only poisonous snake resident in this country. Apply a tourniquet to stop the venom circulating and seek professional help.

GENERAL CARE

The Weimaraner is a healthy breed that, on the whole, requires good animal husbandry to keep physically in fine form. As previously mentioned, regularly check ears, nails, anal glands and examine the dog for external parasites. An adult needs six-monthly worming with a product obtained from your vet, rather than an 'over the counter' preparation, which could be a false economy.

The coat of the Weimaraner is fine with no thick undercoat, so moulting is not a great problem. The hair is not as sharp as, for instance, white hair and therefore is less likely to attach itself to clothes, carpets etc. Grooming is important, but more for the circulation than hair removal (except when moulting). My father always told me that a good groom was better than a feed of corn for the condition of a horse, and this is applicable to your Weimaraner also. A rubber glove or specifically designed rubber mitten is ideal for grooming a Weimaraner. Make sure you use rubber and not a synthetic glove, as rubber draws the dead hair out. If you just use your hands, the natural oils in them also provide good gloss to the coat and the stroking action works to stimulate the circulation. Many folk find a chamois leather works to good effect also.

If you take your Weimaraner working or indeed for general exercise over moors or muddy fields, the mud on the coat is easily brushed off when dry, leaving the coat clean. Sometimes, however, a good bath may be necessary. As with most training, you need to start as you mean to go on. Bathing a 70 lb Weimaraner can be a harrowing procedure, with legs flying in all directions, so an occasional bath while still a youngster is useful to acclimatise your dog to the procedure. Always make sure your Weimaraner is dry and avoid draughts to prevent chills. Remember when you wash a dog, you wash out the natural protection oils, leaving the dog a little vulnerable. So not too often. It is funny how, out on a walk, a Weimaraner will happily jump into a foul, stagnant pond, creating the need for a bath and yet be totally alarmed at having to go into a warm, clean bath on returning home. When bathing Weimaraners be careful not to allow water into their ears, which can cause irritation, and do not let shampoo get into their eyes. If you are careful around their heads they will settle to a bath more easily. After shampooing, be sure to rinse thoroughly to avoid scurf and dandruff. A chamois leather is excellent for drying the dogs off and warming them up.

Teeth need care and, as with humans, decay or disease of the teeth or gums can cause general malady or worse. Crunchy, complete dry foods serve to clean teeth, as do bones and chews. One can buy dog toothpaste, but this is gimmicky – salt on a toothbrush will do just as good a job, but again, start early using a soft toothbrush. Any build-up of tartar may need removing, under anaesthetic, but the results will give teeth a better chance of remaining strong and healthy and keep your dog's breath smelling sweet.

Chapter Ten

WINNING KENNELS IN THE UNITED KINGDOM

Building on the sound foundation of the Monroe, Greyfilk, Ragstone and Hansom lines, with the help of imported dogs, mainly from the USA, the Weimaraner is now a very sound breed, which is quickly becoming the envy of other gundog breeds. This chapter aims to give the reader an insight into the way in which many of the significant breeders developed their lines and this breed into what it is today. To become a breeder of worth one must never become kennel blind and, while striving to succeed, must always have the welfare of the Weimaraner at heart.

MONROE

I instinctively gelled with Joan Matuszewska, known as Joan Mat, whenever I spoke with her, so straight and honest was her way, so I do regret therefore that she lived way down South and I live in Yorkshire, and busy lives meant I rarely saw this great lady. Joan had the great ability to look objectively at her dogs, know their faults and therefore improve with each mating. If a mating did not go forward, Joan was astute enough to realize where that coupling went wrong and not make the same mistake again.

Her initial breed was German Shepherd Dogs. In fact she exported, to Monroe in the USA, a GSD, and so the Monroe's affix was created and registered with The Kennel Club by Joan, becoming not only a very famous affix in Weimaraners but the foundation on which a great many contemporary affixes are built. It was while she was living at Romsey that Joan became friendly with Barbara Douglas-Redding (Wolfox), who also had GSDs. It was through Barbara that Joan acquired the Weimaraner, Manana Athene, who was first registered in Barbara's name and produced the first Show Champion in Barbara's Wolfox affix (Sh. Ch. Wolfox Silverglance). In the same litter was also the dog, Sh. Ch. Ace of Acomb. Athene was transferred to Joan and produced Joan's first Champion, in 1959, Sh. Ch. Monroe's Dynamic, who was the first Weimaraner to gain a BIS Open Show when he took the award at Hampshire Gundog Club Open Show in 1964. The second Champion was a Dynamic daughter, whelped in 1963, who became Sh. Ch. Monroe's Idyll.

1965 saw the birth of Sh. Ch. Monroe's Nexus, who was to sire some good dogs who are behind excellent stock today. A Nexus son was Joan Mat's famous Sh. Ch. Kympenna's Tristan. Sh. Ch. Monroe's O'Netti, owned by Nev Newton, was litter sister to Dorothy Chapman's Sh. Ch. Monroe's Nadine, who was the foundation bitch for the Heronshaw line. In Joan's last litter, her great friends Alistair and Janet Ford were delighted to be able to take 'pick' of litter. That dog became the record tenth Champion to be bred by a Weimaraner kennel. This record was broken by our Gunalt kennel in 1994 and it will remain to be seen if our kennel stands the test of time as Monroe's has. I sincerely hope we will. It was fitting that the Fords' Sh. Ch. Monroe's Assatis won

BOB at Crufts 1994, the first Monroe's to win this accolade.

Joan Mat also had a great interest in the Longhaired Weimaraner and when in 1973 a litter bred by Mr Seymour unexpectedly produced a longhaired puppy (both parents being shorthaired) this dog was acquired by Joan and registered as Mafia Man of Monroe's. Joan was admired by many and folk who knew her well had deep affection for her.

RAGSTONE

Gillian Burgoin already owned two Rhodesian Ridgebacks and she and her husband, Tony, were not about to increase their stock of dogs in a hurry. However, when the opportunity arose to view a litter of Weimaraners in 1963, they did so, on the strict understanding that they would view but not buy – so they bought Remus! He, in Gillian's personal view, is still the best-ever for type, colour,

Judge Joe Braddon pictured with Tony Burgoin and Ch. Ragstone Ritter (left) and Dick Finch with Sh. Ch. Hansom Symill Odette.

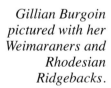

Gillian Burgoin pictured with her Weimaraners and Rhodesian Ridgebacks.

temperament and working ability, with the bonus element of passing on quality through the bitches he served. Ch. Ragstone Remus was a winner of 16 Challenge Certificates, the first Junior Warrant in the breed, and sire of seven Show Champions and Champions including Ch. Gunther of Ragstone.

One of their very first showing ventures with the puppy Remus was to Yorkshire Gundog Club show where the great, late, and much missed Mary Scott judged and where she told Gillian to rub her shoulder for luck. She did, and never looked back! Ragstone set many records in the breed – most since broken, which is only to be expected after such a long time. Some special ones included the final points Joe Braddon gave Remus in 1964 to gain the first Junior Warrant in the breed; the first Irish Green Star in Weimaraners went to Remus under judge Jean Beck – this was in 1965 at Tipperary. Remus's son, Ritter, won the Challenge Certificate at Crufts for a truly memorable record-breaking five consecutive years. Both Remus and Ritter gained their full title, as did the lovely "Spook", Ryuhlan, who, with Di Arrowsmith's Ragstone Rune and Wotan of Ragstone made it five full Champions plus several Show Champions for the Ragstone affix. Their one hundredth Challenge Certificate came at the LKA Championship Show in 1984. The name of 'Ragstone' is synonymous with Weimaraners and this Kennel has contributed more than the record of wins says through the many Ragstone dogs who are behind the successful kennels of today, ours included.

GREYFILK

Ken and Joan Fussell purchased their first Weimaraner, Manana Donna's Maxine, in 1963. This bitch whelped the first Greyfilk litter, by Monroe's Horsa, in 1964. Retained from the seven whelps were Joan's Sapphire and daughter Nicky's Topaz, who went on to win one CC and two RCC. Joan became frustrated at not gaining Sapphire's third CC, so asked Nicky to show her at Crufts. Too nervous to watch, Joan missed Nicky taking the Challenge Certificate, thus making the first Greyfilk champion – Sh. Ch. Greyfilk Sapphire. The Fussells always maintained Sapphire was the true foundation of the Greyfilks. In 1966 Monroe's Horsa was taken to the USA to live and so the Fussells used Wolfox Monroe's Hengist on Manana Donna's Maxine to produce

Sh. Ch. Greyfilk Knigthsman: Renowned for his beautiful colour and impeccable temperament.

Greyfilk Ambassador, who was the sire of Greyfilk Critic (who in turn sired Greyfilk Equerry ex Sh. Ch. Greyfilk Sapphire) and Greyfilk Caprice (dam of Carolyn Alston's foundation Ch. Giffords Lady) who put her stamp on the Greyfilk line. Greyfilk Equerry was the sire of Joan and Margaret Holmes' Sh. Ch. Greyfilk Granella, whose dam was Greyfilk Emmaclan Angelique. Equerry was also the sire of Marion Wardall's foundation bitch Sh. Ch. Phayreheidi Chelal of Ambersbury. Another daughter of Equerry was Greyfilk Ginza who, mated to Marion Wardall's record-breaking Sh. Ch. Gunther of Ragstone, produced Sh. Ch. Jehnvar of Greyfilk.

Bred by Mr Harper in 1974, Jehnvar of Greyfilk was originally owned by Joan Fussell. However, Joan let the young Jehnvar go to Mr Blofield and later a very overweight Jehnvar went on to the Absolams' where he became a great stud dog and was campaigned to his title of Show Champion. In 1976 the Fussells used Jehnvar on Greyfilk Haldana to produce the very famous Sh. Ch. Greyfilk Knightsman and sister Sh. Ch. Greyfilk Kirsty. I say famous: Knightsman was renowned for his superb silver grey colour and his impeccable temperament, and for his progeny who, while winning amazingly well themselves, were behind very good Weimaraners. After the death of her parents, Nicky has been keeping the Greyfilk line going.

EMMACLAN

Margaret Holmes first encountered Weimaraners at Crufts and later saw an article about this new exciting breed. After answering an advertisement in *Horse and Hounds*, the first Weimaraner joined the Holmes' household in 1966. This was Bevan Greta, a daughter of Derrybeg Argus. Unfortunately Greta only lived until she was nine months old, but she left a real hole in the lives of Margaret and her family. Another Weimaraner was sought, and Wildmoss Hesta, bred by Dave Modi and sister to Ch. Ragstone Remus, was bought. She produced Greyfilk Emmaclan Angelique who, as the name suggests, was bought from Margaret by Joan Fussell. Part of the deal was that Margaret should have a puppy back from Angelique's litter and in 1972 the puppy obtained from Angelique was Greyfilk Gallant. Margaret felt that showing was not for her and has over the years put her enegy into the administrative side of Weimaraners and is currently President of The Weimaraner Club of Great Britain.

WCGB President Margaret Holmes judging at Crufts with Sh. Ch. Linosa Lily Lace (left) and Sh. Ch. Gunalt Gaultier.

WESTGLADE

Gwen and Jack Sowersby bought their first Weimaraner in March 1963, from Sheila and Bunny Roberts, called Sylhill Holly. Mandy, as she was called, died in 1970 from bloat. Their next Weimaraner was Sweet Elsa, who was bred by a Mrs G. Nichol; her parents were Wolfox Grand Slam and Dangvord Deois. Jack and Gwen had another Weimaraner called Hansom Bunny Girl, born on November 14th 1965, out of Hansom Sylhill Odette, by Lamb's Sh. Ch. Cannyland Olympus Daedalus. Abbie, as she was called, was transferred to the Sowersbys from Bunny Roberts, her breeder, as he was unable to keep her. In 1973 Gwen and Jack returned to Singapore and Abbie went too, where she claimed her title of Singapore Champion. On her return to the UK her first show was Leeds in 1978. Abbie gained her first CC under Lily Turner. Then in April 1979 she died from bloat and at the time of her death she was in the first stages of labour, so not only did Jack and Gwen lose Abbie, they also lost three dog and seven bitch puppies.

On 21st April 1979 Gwen and Jack bought a puppy from Joan Matuszewska who was called Ch. Monroe's Ambition of Westglade; his pet name was Mr Harvey. He was a versatile working trial dog who gained his CDEx, UDEx and NDEx. He also gained his Gundog Certificate and his first CC at Crufts and was a full Champion by 1982. Mr Harvey won the title of Weimaraner of the Year for 1981-82 and won the Working Weimaraner Trophy in 1981. Several of his progeny gained working trial titles and one of his daughters, Beckstone Envoy, qualified for Crufts Obedience with her owner, Ann Cook. Mr Harvey was also a Hospital Pat Dog. Sadly on April 16th 1992 he died from bloat at the age of 13 years 2 months.

SCHONBLICK

Eileen and Bill Gates bought their first Weimaraner in 1965. Major, alias Watchant Targe, was bought from Eileen's brother from the only litter he bred, and began Eileen's love affair with the breed. Only shown briefly due to various reasons, one being lack of time – Eileen had three small children to raise – Major gained a CC and two RCCs and won very well. Over the years the Gates had four Weimaraners until Alison, their daughter, decided she would like to take an interest in showing, having previously only considered the dogs as pets. As a reward for passing her 'O' level examinations, Mum and Dad bought Alison her own puppy – of course, a Weimaraner. Ziggy arrived in the Gates' household in 1984 and although officially Alison's, she bonded with Eileen who campaigned this bitch to her title Sh. Ch. Silke of Schonblick, Eileen's first Champion. Eileen bred Elizabeth Bartram's Ch. Schonblick Chiff Chaff of Keldspring out of Silke by the great Sh. Ch. Kisdons Derring Do and also breeds and owns CC winners today. Eileen is currently very busy as Secretary of The Weimaraner Club of Great Britain.

Sh. Ch. Schonblick Chiff Chaff.

LINOSA

Realising that Alison had missed out on her puppy, Bill and Eileen booked a puppy from the Edminson's Sh. Ch. Kisdons Asti of Nevedith. All puppies from the litter died but, as fate would have it, at the same time a bitch puppy from the B litter of Kevin and Elaine Grewcock became available. Alison did click with this new puppy, called Christie, later to become Sh. Ch. Ryanstock Bramble, and the pair were an inseparable team, something which is very hard to describe, if you have never been there. Together they won 22 CCs, 8 RCCs, two Gundog Groups and three Reserve Gundog Groups at Championship level. Although no dog is perfect, I for one always admired this team: they really worked together. Christie had three litters, two by Sh. Ch. Hansom Portman of Gunalt and one to Sh. Ch. Flimmoric Fanclub. A daughter by Portman, Sh. Ch. Linosa Lilli Lace JW, also achieved great success, including 9 CCs, twice BOB at Crufts (1992 and 1993), 5 RCCs and BIS at Merseyside Gundog Club Championship Show, when I had the pleasure of being the breed judge and sending in this beautiful bitch through to the Group. Since her marriage to Andy Ackers, both Alison and Andy are involved in Wiemaraners.

CANNYLAD

John Lamb started in the breed in 1966 with a bitch puppy bought from Arthur Thirlwell, the sister to Hacket's record-breaking Balling, Cannylad Bimbo of Merse-side (in those days one could prefix one's affix whether or not the dog was bred by you). Bimbo and John attended a few shows and won a few prizes but as John puts it "she was not as good as her famous sister, but had a superb temperament and a proper silver grey colour". She was mated because she had so many terrible false pregnancies. The sire chosen was the Burgoins' Ch. Ragstone Remus. However, on arrival at Grantham for the 'grand union', John was informed that, as he puts it: "Remus had inadvertently pre-empted the day's activities by attending to one of Gillian's bitch Rhodesian Ridgebacks and paid little ardour in the direction of our bitch." So the young Ritter, the son of Remus, was used and the resulting litter contained Sh. Ch. Cannylad Olympus Daedalus, retained by John. He gained four Challenge Certificates and is behind many good dogs. Another brother from the litter gained his title. Owned by Mr Jones, he was Sh. Ch. Cannyland Olympus Artemis.

John also made Sh. Ch. Cannylad Dalenciaga le Dix into a Show Champion. A Daedalus daughter, this bitch was bred by Joan Mat and was litter sister to Sh. Ch. Monroe's Ubiquitous. Another famous daughter of Daddy Dog, as Daedalus was affectionately known, was Dick Finch's Sh. Ch. Hansom Hobby Hawk. Marjorie Richmond's Sh. Ch. Brundholme Bronella was another Champion offspring of this great dog, showing he could sire quality to many different lines.

AMBERSBURY

Marion Wardall acquired her first Weimaraner in 1968, a bitch, Marta of the Iken (Ch. Ragstone Remus ex Natasha of Abingdon), she being the only Weimaraner puppy available in the country at that time. She produced three litters, two to Ch. Ragstone Ritter and one to Sh. Ch. Gunter of Ragstone. From the two litters by Ritter came: their own Ambersbury Maestersinger; the foundation bitch for the Houblon prefix, Ambersbury Magdalena; Ambersbury Bandore, the first Weimaraner for the Ryanstock kennel; Zambian Ch. Ragstone Ritzun, owned by Captain and Mrs Evans; and Ambersbury Baryton, exported to Spain and later mated to Hollieseast Angelica, bred by the then Mrs Eve Kerslate (now Robinson).

In 1972 they bought in Phayreheidi Chelal of Ambersbury (Sh. Ch. Greyfilk Equerry ex Heidicopse Lisa), bred by Mrs Veasey, and Gunther of Ragstone (Ch. Ragstone Remus ex Dinna vom Morebach). Both became Show Champions, Chelal with four CCs and Gunther with 31 CCs, which was a long-time record for CCs won by a male Weimaraner. Chelal, mated to

Maestersinger, produced the Ambersbury D litter, with Ambersbury Delilah being exported to the USA. Her litter sister Dorabella, owned by Mr N. Ward Jones, was mated to Gunther and produced Zimbabwe Ch. Fatilla Romeo, owned by Mr Lee. Chelal mated to Gunther resulted in their own Ambersbury Engelstimme (winning two CCs), Ambersbury Friszka of Phayreheidi (one CC) and New Zealand Ch. Ambersbury Freeschutz, owned by Mr R.A. Drawbridge. Following a carefully planned breeding programme, Engelstimme was mated to Maestersinger producing Ambersbury Impromptu who, mated to Hawsvale Hermod (Gunther ex Hawsvale Zarin), provided them with Sh. Ch. Ambersbury Jazzman. He is the sire of Sh. Ch. Roxberg's Kamira (ex Kisdon's Fiction of Roxberg), a multiple CC winner, and of two other CC winning bitches, Ragstone Razzealea (ex Ragstone Wren) bred by Gillian Burgoin, and Merry Madrigal of Ambersbury (ex Sh. Ch. Ragstone Wromaine) bred by Steve Walton. Madrigal mated to her half-brother Ragstone Rommell (by Jazzman) resulted in the Ambersbury L litter, from which they have kept Ambersbury Lullaby. This will, unfortunately, be their last Weimaraner.

HANSOM
Dick Finch, a highly successful Dalmatian breeder, ran a well-respected boarding kennels and when Sylhill Odette had to be rehomed following the owners' divorce, 'Bunny' Roberts, the breeder, was advised by his vet, John Holmes, to put her into Dick's boarding kennels. Dick took to Odette and it was arranged that she could be retained by Dick on condition Bunny could choose the stud dog and have pick of litter. John Lamb's famous Sh. Ch. Cannylad Olympus Daedalus was chosen and the litter was whelped in 1971. Bunny Roberts' choice of puppy, Hansom Bunny Girl, was put into the care of Jack and Gwen Sowersby, and is described above in the Westglade entry. Bunny had just lost his wife at this time and was paralysed from the waist down due to a severe war wound, so was not able to look after a Weimaraner puppy.

Dick decided to show Odette and steered her to victory; she became Sh. Ch. Hansom Sylhill Odette, the winner of six CCs. Retained at Hansom, from the same litter as Bunny Girl, was one of my all-time favourites, Sh. Ch. Hansom Hobby Hawk. This bitch and Dick were, in my opinion, instrumental in putting Weimaraners on the map. Hobby was the first Championship Show Group

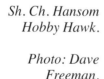

Sh. Ch. Hansom Hobby Hawk.

Photo: Dave Freeman.

winner, in 1974 at Birmingham Show where she finished Best Bitch in Show, an honour repeated at the same show in 1992 by her great-great-granddaughter Sh. Ch. Gunalt Obsession. Hobby was not only a great achiever but also a great producer. It was through her that the top kennels of today are producing quality, type and soundness, including Denise Mosey's Hobby daughter, Sh. Ch. Hansom Hirondelle. Josie Kneebone of Guernsey travelled to the mainland to obtain, campaign and make up Sh. Ch. Hansom Hospitality, a Hobby daughter. Hospitality's brother, our own Sh. Ch. Hansom Brandyman of Gunalt, won for us 19 CCs but, more than that, is behind so many of our top winners and is responsible for the soundness and temperament of which we are so proud here at Gunalt. His most famous Champion offspring must be our Sh. Ch. Hansom Portman of Gunalt who surpassed his grand-dam to be the first Weimaraner ever to win BIS at a Championship Show. Hobby was also the dam of Sh. Ch. Hansom Cordon Bleu, owned and shown by Dick in his indomitable way. Cordon Bleu was then mated to Sh. Ch. Jehnvar of Greyfilk, which produced the famous Sh. Ch. Hansom Misty Blue, the winner of 13 CCs and star of a pet food advert. Misty Blue is also the dam of Portman.

FT Ch. Wobrook of Fleetapple with owners Di and the late George Arrowsmith.

FLEETAPPLE

Di Arrowsmith and her sister, José Baddeley (famous for her Loudace Gordon Setters), were always involved in horses as youngsters, but their grandfather showed dogs, so it was a natural progression that the girls would go into dogs. George Arrowsmith liked rough shooting, so he and Di set about looking for a gundog to retrieve the shot game. Phil Drabble, neighbour and friend, had a GSP, so the Arrowsmiths set out to find one. Di met a lady waiting at the school gates with a strange grey dog and asked if this was some sort of German Pointer – German, yes, but a Weimaraner not a GSP. Seeing one advertised in the local paper for sale, they bought Cannylad Lady Hamilton of Fleetapple from John Lamb. She was an excellent working bitch and won reasonably well in the ring.

The Arrowsmiths met the Burgoins through showing and, when Gillian and Tony took Wotan of Ragstone back because his owners thought him 'dim and destructive', he was chosen as stud for Lady Hamilton because of his attributes. At a later date Di took Wotan on a temporary basis while Gillian's bitches were in season. He stayed and became Ch. Wotan of Ragstone and won the Gundog Group at East of England in 1978 – not bad for a dim and destructive dog! The second mating of the pair produced eight dogs and one bitch. Sandra Marshall acquired her Sh. Ch. Fleetapple Wilmar from this mating.

Di was fond of Wotan's sister, Ludmilla, and had a bitch from her second mating to Richtkanonier of Ragstone. Again Di made her into a full Champion, Ch. Ragstone Rune. Di took a stud puppy in 1979. Every morning Di was greeted by a 'brook' running across the kitchen floor, which is how Wobrook of Fleetapple got his name. He was taken as a shooting companion for George. However Di overheard some Weimaraner owners discussing the fact that Di knew nothing about training a dog for field trialling. She resolved to show them and did just that. Field Trial Champion Wobrook of Fleetapple is still the only Weimaraner to achieve this accolade. Di now runs field trial training classes very successfully, through her interest gained from George, a tribute to a great and gentle man.

DANGVORD
Alistair and Janet Ford's foundation bitch, Innisron Morgan's Mimic, was purchased in 1967. She was by Sh. Ch. Coninvale Paul of Acombdale ex Bilbrook Brunnhilde of Innisron, who was officially passed HD clear, but Morgan's Mimic's hips were terrible and still remain about the worst set of hip X-rays Alistair says he has seen in the breed. She gained one RCC and on one memorable day won the CC, with Ballina getting the RCC. Mated to Greyfilk Ambassador she produce Dangvord Bertis Bois. He got his first CC when about two-and-a-half and some three RCCs. At six-and-a-half he won his 2nd CC at SKC after an absence of showing of four years due to the Ford's personal commitments. After the death of Bertis Bois and then of Morgan's Mimic, Alistair began again. This time he purchased a bitch, Monroe's Ascendant, from Joan Matuszewska. Mated to Knightsman she produced Dangvord Renidia, owned by the Sakers, who went on to have 2 CCs.

In spite of various disasters and near misses, Janet and Alistair still felt that deep down there was nothing like a Weimaraner. So when they heard that Joan Mat had mated a bitch which had never been shown but which Alistair had often admired, as I said previously, they asked if they could choose the pick of litter. Although Alistair had to wait over 25 years to own a Show Champion, it was all the sweeter when it happened. Sh. Ch. Monroe's Assatis is his name and he had the honour of winning 2 CCs at Crufts, the second with BOB in 1995.

HAWSVALE & MERRYHELL
Val Hawes' first love among dogs was German Shepherd Dogs. When out walking a GSD bitch one day, a car drew up. Thinking the driver might require directions he moved over to the kerbside. "That's a nice bitch. What's her breeding?" said the driver. This chance encounter in August 1966 was to be the start of a friendship which grew and only ended with the death of Joan Matuszewska 29 years later. Val bought his wife, Betty, a Weimaraner puppy as a birthday present in July 1969. This palest of silver bitches was so pale that when viewed in the nest Val rudely remarked that she looked like a maggot which had just crept out into the light. Thus Maggi became the pet name of Monroe's Quicksilver (Sh. Ch. Monroe's Nexus ex Monroe's Waidman Jane) the foundation of the Merryhell Weimaraners.

After Val had some disappointments with his GSD breeding, Betty gave him Monroe's Repartee

(Sh. Ch. Monroe's Nexus ex Sh. Ch. Wolfox Nyria). The affix of Hawsvale was added later and Mini became the foundation bitch of the Hawsvale Weimaraners. Maggi won her first CC at the SKC show at Glasgow in May 1971. Mini's first litter in November 1971 was by her half-brother, Monroe's Supremo. This was the Hawsvale Z litter. Zarin was retained. This litter was followed by the A, C, E and G litters, all by Sh. Ch. Kympenna's Tristan. Named after drinks, Angostora was exported to Trinidad where she became a Caribbean Champion. Probably the most celebrated was Cherry Brandy. Exported to Holland, she not only became a Netherlands Champion, but a top brood bitch with Netherlands Champions and numerous other winners in each of her three litters to Monroe's Supremo. Gin Sling was exported to Czechoslovakia by way of Austria, where she became a top field trial bitch.

In the meantime Mini and Zarin had been joined by Bewohner of Hawsvale, Bev, (Monroe's Supremo ex Cannyland Olympus Hadria) and Uhlan Champelle of Hawsvale, Olga, (Ortega Opal Mint ex Gray Moonshadow of Duenna). The latter was obtained because she was a litter sister of the first known British Longhaired Weimaraner. From the F litter by Gunther, Fee was exported to Italy where she became an Italian Champion, Fuhrer was exported to the United Arab Emirates, while Furstin became a CC winner and the dam of Sh. Ch. Wivelees Wicked Charmer. Frolich also remained in the UK and in due course became dam of the leading Dutch sire, Onyx of H, who sired the Best in Show at the Dutch Weimaraner Club Show for four years in succession.

Olga was also bred to the longhaired Austrian import Dino von der Hagardburg. A shorthaired son, Impressario, became the sire of Hong Kong Champion H. Kay. From her M litter by Sh. Ch. Kympenna's Tristan, Merganser became the dam of the 1984 Weimaraner of the Year and Working Trial Weimaraner of the Year, Sh. Ch. Reeman Aurac CDEx UDEx WDEx. Nonpareil (Nonni), a full brother to Merganser from a later litter, was retained and featured in subsequent long and shorthaired breed ventures.

In parallel, but on a somewhat lesser scale, the Merryhell breeding programme was taking place. Maggi's first litter was by Monroe's Supremo, of whom Dainty and Dauntless were exported to Australia, and Decoy was exported to Trinidad. Here he obtained his CDX qualification at the age of seven months and went on to become a Caribbean Champion. Garland by Bewohner of Hawsvale was exported to the Austrian Breed Master, Hr Winfried Seidl, while litter-sister Grampus also went to Austria, where she became a Siegerin (Champion) and Field Trial winner.

FLIMMORIC

This is the affix of Carolyn Alston, chosen because it is an anagram of Microfilm, taken from the family business. In 1972 a friend of Carolyn's bought a Weimaraner puppy but then could not stand the puppy smell and gave her to Carolyn. That puppy, Ch. Giffords Lady, became the foundation of the kennel. Going back on the Greyfilk lines of Giffords Lady, Carolyn mated her to Sh. Ch. Jehnvar of Greyfilk and produced her Sh. Ch. Flimmoric Fieldday. An outstanding dog, he was always a gentleman, as well as a top winner. These qualities he passed on to his son, Sh. Ch. Flashman of Flimmoric, who was bred by Carolyn's great friend Marnie Marr. Flashman was a very successful dog who tragically died at the height of his career.

His death prompted two excursions to the USA and one to Canada to fulfil an ambition to buy in foreign blood. A bitch imported by Carolyn from Las Vegas, Lusco's Foreign Affair of Flimmoric, was shown sparingly before being mated to Int. Ch. Nanis Totally Awesome, an American dog, in Britain en route to New Zealand. From this unique English-bred litter of all-American lines nine puppies were born. A dog was retained and became Sh. Ch. Flimmoric Fanclub. A beautiful dog, with immaculate temperament, he won well in the ring, but it is through his stud work that he has become nationally famous. Top Stud all breeds in 1994, he is the sire of the present top CC winning male and through him, the grandsire of the record holder of CCs won. Fanclub has sired many Champions and Group winners. Although Carolyn has a small kennel – all Flimmoric dogs live in the home – she has maintained a consistent line of winners.

SHALINA

Although the affix is now owned jointly between Tina Cutting and Sue Bradley it originally belonged solely to Tina. Tina and Sue owned Weimaraners independently of one another for several years and did not know of each other's existence in spite of the small numbers of the breed in those days. This was due to the fact that Tina had an interest in showing and Sue was handling the dogs that her husband was shooting over.

Sue and Peter Bradley bought their first Weimaraner by mistake; they actually thought they were buying a GSP. Peter had taken up wildfowling but the English Springer Spaniels he was using for his other shooting were just not big enough. Clearly a bigger breed was called for and they had seen a couple of GSPs give a good account of themselves, so they set about trying to find one. They answered an advert in a shooting magazine which reading something like "Weimaraners, large German retriever".

Meanwhile Tina had been lucky enough to contact Joan Matuzewska and was awaiting the birth of a litter. Tina was quite taken with the Hungarian Vizsla and had been directed towards Louise Petrie-Hay, who at that time had both Weimaraners and Vizslas and had a partnership with Joan. Louise explained that it would be a very long wait for a Vizsla but not quite so long for a Weimaraner. All in all it is a wonder that either of them ended up with the breed!

This was all taking place around the late sixties and early seventies. Tina chose Monroe's Unity from the three bitches on offer because she was the biggest. The other two went on to become Sh. Ch. Monroe's Ubiquitous and Sh. Ch. Cannyland Dallencjaga le Dix. Eventually Tina mated Unity to Zak (for she had had an earlier litter to Sh. Ch. Greyfilk Equerry) and that litter contained Shalin Melody Man CDEx UDEx WDEx and Ch. Shalina Sky Diver. Sky Diver was a "bouncer" and at the age of ten months was looking for a new home. Quite by coincidence Sue was looking for a new dog and Margaret Holmes put Tina and Sue in touch with each other. Although by that time Sue had been to a few shows it was not really her scene and the rescue dog she was going to see would only be considered if he could demonstrate that he was willing to retrieve. Was he willing? You couldn't stop him picking things up! Sue had had him all of a week when he won a first prize in a puppy test of work, the second in the novice and the third in the open. Tina thought that he was well worth showing and so he went to his first Championship show a few weeks later and won the Junior class under Jimmy Cudworth, who later awarded him his third CC. After he had won his first CC, Sue entered him for his "qualifying certificate", which he gained with ease. One of the guns on the day was very impressed with the way the dog worked and suggested to Sue that she should Field Trial him. That man was Eddie Hales who, in Sue's opinion, is one of the best gundog trainers around, although she did not know that at the time.

Field trialling came easily to Sky Diver – he wanted to work. He was very fast and because of his wildfowling experience, an exceptional dog when it came to the water. He was the first Weimaraner to be placed at an Open Qualifying Field Trial. So in the space of about eighteen months, Sky Diver had a spectacular career, winning both in the Show Ring and flying the flag for Weimaraners in the field. He was also certified as having clear hips under the HD scheme, which was just changing over to the scoring system about then.

A few years earlier Sue had bought her first bitch from Mick and Liz Phillips of the Rujanta affix (prior to this all her Weimaraners had been males). Monroe's Unity had to be spayed. Tina wanted to continue her line and since this was impossible now via Unity, she decided to have a

*Monroe's Unity,
with Tina Cutting,
foundation of the
Shalina affix.*

*Photo: Dave
Freeman.*

pup from Sky Diver and the Rujanta bitch and of course she wanted her affix on it. It became easier to put the affix on the whole litter (in those days you could put your affix where you wanted, fore or aft of the name, whether you were the breeder or not). The arrangement continued for quite a while until in the end there were so many dogs owned by either Tina or Sue or sometimes both that even they became confused and one day filled in forms to put absolutely everything in joint names. Theirs is not just a partnership but also a close friendship and they now have the ninth generation on from Monroe's Unity.

RYANSTOCK
Kevin and Elaine Grewcock purchased their first Weimaraner in June 1972, a dog named Ambersbury Bandore (Ryan). Though only a companion, he was soon trained, and competed at Championship Level Novice Obedience. His first championship show was Manchester 1973 where he obtained a second in Junior Dog which at that time qualified him for Crufts and Blackpool. The Grewcocks were hooked. At 14 months old he was introduced to the shooting field, where he excelled. This proved to be the foundation of their requirement to produce sound, good-looking, dual-purpose Weimaraners. All their dogs of working age participate during the shooting season and Ryanstock-bred dogs join in at work on their shoot. What better foundation than such an all-rounder as Ryan. The Ryanstock affix was granted on September 1st 1980. The first bitch, obtained in 1981, was Monroe's Ash Lady of Ryanstock (April), shortly followed by a bitch who was Ryan's daughter, Miroku Balfreo of Ryanstock (Feebie). These two bitches were the foundation of all the Ryanstocks around today.

   Their first CCs were won with April in June 1985. This was quickly followed by their first Show Champion, Ryanstock Agnetha JW (Anya), crowned on 2nd August 1986. The winner of six CCs and five reserves, she was also a Reserve Gundog Group winner. She is still with them today in 1995 and is without doubt their favourite for looks, conformation and style. In 1987 Sh. Ch. Ryanstock Bramble JW obtained her title following an illustrious puppy career, owned and expertly handled by Miss Alison Gates, now Ackers. Bramble was the winner of 20 CCs and several Gundog Groups. The Ryanstock B litter produced Bramble, the show dog, Barabbas the working trials dog CDEx, UDEx, and the little-known Bracken who, at nine years, still works

*Alison Ackers
with her top
winning dogs.*

every week on their shoot throughout the season. Ryanstock have bred selectively, producing only six litters to date. From those they have provided 33 puppies who between them have the achieved five Junior Warrants, nine Stud Book numbers, and two Show Champions – others being RCC winners, and not forgetting the therapy dogs who also serve a useful role in society.

DENMO
Denise Mosey bought her first two Weimaraners in 1975, and they became Sh. Ch. Aislikng Tuathach and Sh. Ch. Hansom Hirondelle. She had her first litter out of Tuathach, followed six months later by Hirondelle's first litter. She always considered Hirondelle to be her foundation bitch and the one on which she wanted to base her future breeding programme. She has bred seven Show Champions and made a further two into Show Champions. Tuathach produced Sh. Ch. Denmo Debutante, but it was Hirondelle who went into the record books, becoming top Champion producing dam with six Champion offspring: her own Sh. Ch. Denmo Roadrunner (HD clear); Ch. Denmo Blueberry Muffin (foundation bitch for Fineshade); Sh. Ch. Raspberry Highball (foundation bitch for Sireva) and Sh. Ch. Denmo Prairie Oyster (HD clear, foundation bitch for Amtrack). All these bitches have produced Champions and Show Champions themselves. Then there was Sh. Ch. Denmo Sidecar (HD clear) and Sh. Ch. Denmo Broadway Melody. Denise prefers to have only three Weimaraners at one time and therefore, inevitably, found herself out of the ring for over 10 years without having bred a litter for several years.

She was back in the ring again in 1992 with her first longhair, Taxi (Pondridge Pioneer of Denmo), bought mainly as a pet because she had had a hankering for a longhair for some years, but she said if he turned out OK then she would show him. He has consistently won well and has noe become a Show Champion. He has always had a very strong natural working ability and finally, at the rather late age of three, Denise decided that he ought to be given the chance to work. So he introduced her to the field where he is working well, and they are learning together, him teaching her more than she is teaching him! He is a favourite and her constant companion.

1995 she introduced her new shorthair to the ring. She had no intention of getting a shorthair at that particular time. However, she saw this pup of a few days old at our kennel and was immediately drawn to her above all the others. She wanted her even more on realising that she went back to her old successful lines, being the grand-daughter on her sire's side and great grand-daughter on her dam's side of Ch. Kamsou M v B and Sh. Ch. Hansom Hobby Hawk (dam of Hirondelle). Gunalt Dame of Denmo, called Hovis (because she's better bred!), by Sh. Ch. Hansom Portman of Gunalt ex Sh. Ch. Gunalt Obsession, has started her show career winning well. She will also be worked in the field.

Denise Mosey with Gunalt Dame of Denmo (left) and Sh. C h. Pondridge Pioneer of Denmo.

Photo: Dave

KISDONS

The foundation bitch for Neil and Pam Edminson, Ch. Petraqua Wagtail, was born in 1975 and although bred by Mrs Davis, was of all Monroe breeding. They met and became friendly with Nev Newton, who later handled Wagtail to win her title. Together they decided to mate Wagtail to the Fussells' great Sh. Ch. Greyfilk Knightsman. From the resulting litter, two were retained by Pam. Sh. Ch. Kisdon's Artist gained 3 CCs while still a puppy, gaining his qualifying CC at 19 months, and in 1982 he was exported to New Zealand. His sister, owned and campaigned by Pam, became Sh. Ch. Kisdon's Asti of Nevedith, the winner of 29 CCs and 3 Reserve Group wins at Championship Show level and renowned for her super type and movement. A third champion from this litter belonged to Lt. Cdr. J. Bond RN, Sh. Ch. Kisdon's Arabella.

Neil and Pam mated Asti to the Burgoins' great dog Ch. Ragstone Ryuhlan and retained Sh. Ch. Kisdon's Derring-Do. Born in 1982 Derry not only won well in the ring but went on to sire 12 Show Champion and Champion offspring and one New Zealand Show Champion. Derry generally passed on his beautiful silver-grey colour, and the thing I remember him for was his lovely temperament, always happy, always playing the clown, a great character. Derry was the sire of many Varstock winners. Paul Owens mated Honky Tonk Lady to Derry and produced three

Pam Edminson with the famous Sh. Ch. Kisdons Asti Of Nevedith.

Champions and Show Champions from that litter. Eileen Gates mated Sh. Ch. Silke of Schonblick to Derry to produce the super working dog Ch. Schonblick Chiff Chaff of Kelspring, owned by E. Bartram. The Burgoins bred Sh. Ch. Ragstone Wromaine by Derry. Mary Brennan successfully used Derry on her Sh. Ch. Denmo Prairie Oyster to produce Sh. Ch. Amtrak Amoreuse. Kevin and Elaine Grewcock showed their Sh. Ch. Ryanstock Agnetha, a lovely bitch of perfect silver grey, again by Derry. I say, with pride, that the first to use this good stud dog was us – we produced Sh. Ch. Gunalt Gildoran by Derry. The Kisdons affix did much winning in the early 80s, and produced foundations for other kennels.

VERRAMI
Verrami is the affix of Veronica Clark and daughter, Rachel Barney, who is married to Julian Barney of the famous Cilleine Cocker Spaniels. They started in Weimaraners in 1976 having been persuaded by Joan Mat that a rescue dog would be suitable for them. They collected Gerda of High Garrett for a two-week trial and she stayed! Gerda was built like a tank, medium-size and totally bomb-proof, and her only hate was being alone in the house. They had not considered breeding, so they took Gretta to the vet's to discuss spaying her. Their vet was John Holmes! He suggested they mate her to his young homebred dog Clackhill Cristian. This mating produced five puppies. John had pick of litter and this bitch was sold to Dot Bushby who wanted a companion to her show dog Miranda Eliza. Dot did show the puppy and she became Sh. Ch. Verrami Aphrodite. Veronica and Rachel kept Verrami Abbaca who won 1 CC and a C of M at a field trial.

Due to a change in Dot's situation, Aphrodite came back to them in 1983. She eventually produced her only litter of one bitch and three dogs to Ch. Ragstone Ryanlan in 1985. The bitch, Verrami Joint Effort, went to Sue and Ashley Simmons on the understanding that Veronica and Rachel would have a puppy back when she had a litter, but Joint Effort was back with them when aged nine months. She won her first CC and BOB at 16 months and was eventually made up and field trialled to full Champion. From her three litters, they kept Verrami Double Take who has become their third linebred Champion, an achievement few kennels have attained.

GUNALT

We were already reasonably successfully showing English Setters when we finally decided on a second gundog breed to own and show. After careful deliberation in 1976 a short list of GSP, Hungarian Viszla or Weimaraner was drawn up. I was happy with either of the former but wasn't keen on the grey things with yellow eyes! Perhaps this sums up who is boss at Gunalt! Vimana Viveca of Gunalt came to Gunalt from Fiona Dow in Scotland. I always say that she could be dropped from a great height and still stand square, so sound was this little bitch with the big character. Black and white, fearless, yet always fair, you would have thought her Yorkshire-born in personality! Being involved firsthand in the breed, we studied in depth the Weimaraners we liked. Dick Finch was approached and a deal, consisting of money, a bag of home grown potatoes to Dick, and a dog puppy and bottle of red wine to us, was done.

Sh. Ch. Hansom Brandyman of Gunalt produced many big winners, Sh. Ch. Hansom Portman of Gunalt came to us as a stud puppy when Dick used Brandyman and, handled by me, became the

Sh. Ch. Hansom Brandyman of Gunalt with Patsy Hollings, and daughter Sh. Ch. Gunalt Anais Anais with Stephen Hollings, winning the double at the East of England.

Karen Robinson handling her male recordholder Irish Ch. and Sh. Ch. Gunalt Harris Tweed.

first all breed BIS winner at Championship level. He also won four Groups at Championship level. Brandyman was also mated to Viveca to produce Sh. Ch. Gunalt Anais Anais (29 CCs). Anais in turn was mated to Ch. Czolkin's Platinum Cirrus (an outcross) to produce another Group winner, Sh. Ch. Gunalt Cacherel and his sister, the Wards' Sh. Ch. Gunalt Armani. After much thought Cacharel was put back to Anais to produce Gunalt Joy. This joint record top brood bitch in breed has, to date, produced three Group winners, in her Champion and Show Champion progeny: our Sh. Ch. Gunalt Obsession, Karen Robinson's Sh. Ch. Gunalt Harris Tweed (now top CC winning male and sire of top CC winning Weimaraner), and Steve and Karen Redman's Sh. Ch. Gunalt Global – plus Ward and Turner's Sh. Ch. Gunalt Posh Enough for Gamepoint, a Reserve Group winner, all by the successful stud and show dog Alston's Sh. Ch. Flimmoric Fanclub.

Joy, mated to a Fanclub son, Khamsynn Cardinal Synn, has produced Longbottom's Sh. Ch. Gunalt Hedonist and Jackson's Sh. Ch. Gunalt Tart. Joy was Top Brood All Breeds and Runner Up for two years.

When one considers that in excess of fifteen thousand dogs are exhibited at Championship Shows in the UK, this is a remarkable achievement. With 14 Gunalt-bred Champions and Show Champions, this kennel holds the record of the most champion Weimaraners produced from one kennel, and is the Kennel which has really familiarised the breed to the dog show fraternity, with its record produced top winners. We have also bred champions in South Africa, Barbados and Ireland. We also run all canines together – quite a unique sight.

FINESHADE
Jane George bought a Weimaraner dog as a 'pet'. On a visit to the USA with her husband, Jane looked more closely at this wonderful breed and decided to bring home Ch. Kamsou Moonraker von Bismarck from the Kamsou Kennels in 1976. A wise choice. Moonraker had a profound effect on the breed in Britain. The sire of ten Champions and Show Champions including one in New Zealand, this dog was the ultimate gentleman. His progeny inherited his temperament and beautiful sound construction. Progeny produced from the good English affixes coupled with this dog have given current top kennels their good foundations. Jane later took a daughter from a mating of Denise Mosey's Sh. Ch. Hansom Hirondelle, who became Ch. Denmo Blueberry Muffin, an excellent 'picking up' dog. Jane agreed to campaign Tank while he was in England during transit to Australia. During his six-month stay with Jane he gained his title and ultimately became English, Australian and New Zealand Sh. Ch. Arimar's Rolf vd Reiteralm, owned by the Mayhews in New Zealand. Jane bred Penny Pickstone's Ch. Fineshade Full Flush, a true working Weimaraner, and Gordon Shaw's Sh. Ch. Fineshade Magical Mystery.

CLEIMAR
Marnie always goes under her maiden name of Marr in the dog game although she has been married to Chris Henkey for a long time now. In 1976 Marnie approached Carolyn Alston with a view to purchasing a Weimaraner as a pet. Carolyn's choice, and encouragement to show, gave Marnie the incentive and enthusiasm to make her pet bitch into Sh. Ch. Wineleas Wicked Charmer. Wicked Charmer, a bitch I always admired, was bred by Mrs Brown (but of all Hawsvale breeding) in 1976. Mated to Carolyn's Sh. Ch. Flimmoric Fanclub both times, Wicked Charmer produced Carolyn's Sh. Ch. Flashman of Flimmoric in 1980, although Marnie omitted to include her affix on this dog. Marnie had Flimmoric Fairdinkum from Carolyn and won 1 CC and 7 RCCs, a bitch who spoilt her chances by playing the fool. Fairdinkum produced Siglende Smith's Sh. Ch. Cleimar Country Cobbler and the Jupps' Sh. Ch. Cleimar Elegant of Czolkins. Marnie also bred Nor. Ch. Cleimar Gracious Gerti.

Sh. Ch. Wivelees Wicked Charmer, handled by Marnie Marr.

RISINGLARK

Pam Thompson's addiction to Weimaraners started in the 50s. A pair were in her employer's kennel of working gundogs. They must have been the first or second generation bred in the UK. It was in the early 70s that she bought her first Weimaraner, a bitch registered as Heatherdam Phantom, by Belazieth Silver Ace ex Inniston Aphrodite. She would point and flush larks which rose straight up – hence Risinglark! Pam trained her and qualified her CDEx, UDEx before mating her to Val O'Keefe's dog Grinshill Malphaquet of Castlegarnstone CDEx UDEx WDEx. She produced one bitch, Risinglark Tomboy, who was mated to Cyril Dunk's dog Sh. Ch. Abbeystag Oceanmist. From that litter Pam's husband Eric got his way and they kept a male, Risinglark Tarka. He won 1 RCC. Liz and Mick Phillips mated a bitch, Vanwilkie Naughty Nancy, a working bitch of the type Pam admired, to Ch. Fossana Quartz and Pam had the choice of bitches. That was her lucky day, for thirteen and a half years on, Ch. Ruganta Game Plucker is still with her. She picked up her Junior Warrant, 7 CCs and 4 RCCs. She produced and reared, without any problems, three litters. The first, to R. Tarka, produced Lyn Turtle's R. Select who gained a RCC. Her second litter was to her uncle, Vanwilkie Nearly Napoleon, owned and bred by Costas and Vanessa Wilkinson. From this litter came several good winners – Pauline Brooke's R. The Rainmaker at Omerod JW 1 RCC, Garry and Mandy Woodham's R. Rainplover 1 RCC, and Pam retained R. Raincheck who won 1CC 1 RCC before an injury put paid to his show career. She also retained a bitch R. Rainbow, who is beautifully constructed, and a good worker but is not a showy bitch, whom she mated her to Sh. Ch. Gunalt Harris Tweed and got Sh. Ch. R. Notorious who was Top Weimaraner Puppy 1992. He also won his JW and to date has 4CCs and 4 RCCs and was Group 2 winner Paignton Ch. Show 1995. For her third litter Ch. Game Plucker was mated to Sh. Ch. Czersieger Clever Clown and Pam was lucky enough to get an excellent bitch, R. Old Ruby. She has proved a good producer also and her first litter to R. Notorious produced a lovely bitch, R. Matchless, who won Best Puppy at WCGB Ch. Show 1993. She had an argument with a tractor and that put an end to her show career. Pam excels in a very good bitch line.

VARSTOCK

This is the affix of Keith and Margaret Absolam. Ch. Lodgewater Amber, a beautiful bitch, started the Absolams off in 1977. Amber was twice mated to Sh. Ch. Kisdon's Derring-Do. From the first litter 'Moggsie' Brassett had Varstock Voodoo of Leifland to join her Sh. Ch. Houldon Euryalus. Voodoo won 2 CCs before Moggsie was tragically killed in a car accident. Voodoo returned to the Absolams and was consequently 'made up' into a Show Champion. From the second (repeat) mating came Ch. Varstock Voyager of Roxburgh and Sh. Ch. Varstock Vicerine of Aquila. In 1979, as has been mentioned before, the four-year-old Jehnvar of Greyfilk came to the Absolams as a 'rescue', grossly overweight. It is all credit to Keith and Margaret that they worked with him to the extent that he later gained 4 CCs with Keith handling, thus becoming Sh. Ch. Jehnvar of Greyfilk.

AMTRAK

When Mary Brennan started showing Weimaraners in earnest and then bred her first litter, Amtrak seemed to be the appropriate affix, the AM being the first two letters of her bitch's name, Amie, and half her pedigree being an American line. She had had two other affixes previously, one in Poodles and one in Dobermans. She had always enjoyed being around dogs, so upon leaving school, went to Bellmead Training Kennels, which is now of course an overspill for Battersea Dogs' Home. From there she was lucky enough to gain further valuable experience at the Panfield Boxer Kennel. After years of successfully showing and breeding Poodles she got married, and in 1969 she and her husband decided to emigrate to Rhodesia. She had her first contact with a Weimaraner while they were there, not at the shows but at the local emporium. 'Hasso' was an impressive male who had the run of the small town but ignored everything and everyone with his typically aloof attitude. He made a lasting impression on Mary who was always frustrated when he refused to let her fuss him. They came back to the UK and, with a young family, showing was put on a back burner.

In 1977 they saw an advert in the local press for Weimaraner pups and the old hankering returned. They purchased a bitch from this litter out of Sh. Ch. Brundholme Bronella by B. Banacheck with a view to getting back into showing. Now really smitten with the grey beauties, they decided to purchase another bitch and in 1979 bought Denmo Prairie Oyster from Denise Mosey. Coming from a repeat mating of Sh. Ch. Hansom Hirondelle to Ch. Moonraker von Bismarck, she, like two of her litter mates and three out of the previous litter, gained her title. This was in 1983 and in the same year she was mated to Sh. Ch. Kisdons Derring-Do. This gave them their own Sh. Ch. Amtrak Amoreuse and although she did tremendously well in the ring she never really reproduced her own superb quality. However, as luck would have it, Amtrak Amethyst was returned to Mary in 1988 and she succeeded where her sister had failed, and her mating to Sh. Ch. Hansom Portman of Gunalt produced Sh. Ch. Amtrak Ameros of Ormerod, owned by Pauline Brooks. Sh. Ch. Denmo Prairie Oyster's final litter was by Sh. Ch. Czersieger Clever Clown and out of that came A. Amadiamond 2 CCs and 2 RCCs and A. Amajavelin 2 CCs 2 RCCs. Amethyst's final litter, by Savril Lucky the Reverant (used because his dam's line went back to A. Amalance, brother of Amoreuse and Amethyst), gave them their current show bitch Amtrak Amangelica 1 CC, 1 RCC. Her recent litter, to Sh. Ch. Gunalt Hedonist, looks promising but only time will tell.

SIREVA

Gil Averis bought her first Weimaraner from Denise Mosey (Denmo) in 1979, and soon decided to have a go at this showing game. After her first Championship show and first win, she was well and truly hooked and Emma gained her title to become Sh. Ch. Denmo Raspberry Highball. Her first litter, to Sh. Ch. Ragstone Ryuhlan, produced Sireva Skylark, a CC and Junior Warrant winner. A fan of Sh. Ch. Kisdon's Asti of Nevedith, Gil bought her grandson, who became Sh. Ch. Kisdon's Fagan of Sireva who went on to win 10 CCs and the Gundog Group at Bournemouth. Fagan was

A group of Sireva Weimaraners.

Photo: C. Rayner.

the grandfather of Gil's next champion, Sh. Ch. Benpark Strange Magic of Sireva, bred by Ann Thorpe of all Sireva breeding. Sireva Sideshow also won a CC. Gil's next champion was Sh. Ch. S. Sapphire out of a Fagan/Highball daughter by a Fagan son.

Fagan was mated to Strange Magic, a father/grand-daughter mating, to produce Sh. Ch. Sireva Silk. Her CC winning offspring include S. Phancue (2 CCs), S. Phanny Hill at Foulby (A. Williams), S. Syndicate of Khamsyn (Mr & Mrs Rutland) and S. Sansovino (Mrs Bowley). Sapphire, when mated to the top producing sire Sh. Ch. Flimmoric Fanclub, in turn produced Sh. Ch. Sireva Sackadallion with Lowerdon, owned in partnershp with Mrs Sandra Marshall. Sackadallion's sister was then mated to Khamsyn Cardinal Synn and produced the seventh Champion, Sh. Ch. Sireva Sahne, who won BIS at the National Gundog Association Championship Show. Other CC winners from this kennel are Sireva Sea Breeze, Sireva Show Stopper and, of course, Mr and Mrs Rayner's Sh. Ch. Sireva Montana (Fagan ex Raspberry Highball), a reserve Group winner.

GAMEPOINT

Julie and Paul Turner bought their first Weimaraner in 1979 from Richard and Helena Jupp. The initial idea of Obedience trialling a Weimaraner by Julie was dismissed in favour of showing and working the dog to the gun. This aspect was encouraged by the Jupps. Two male puppies were selected by Joan Fussell and Margaret Holmes for Julie to choose between. Julie, as she says "decided on the less 'gobby' male", a decision I do laugh at, as quiet wasn't much in Quince's vocabulary, ever. Quince was a once-in-a-lifetime dog, who gave Julie ten years of fun and success in the ring and field. Through him they visited several Weimaraner breeders in the USA, attended the 1984 Nationals in Washington and imported a USA-bred male. Quince was Weimaraner of the year in 1980. He quickly won 2 CCs in 1981 but then managed to mistime jumping a gate when out working, got caught on the top and suffered back problems for several months. During his second full season in field trials, he won two Novice trials and was placed several times in spite of,

ABOVE: Sh. Ch. Gunalt Posh Enough for Gamepoint handled by Jacqui Ward, owned in partnership with Julie Turner.

LEFT: Julie Turner with Ch. Czolkins Platinum Cirrus: The first Field Trial-winning Champion in the breed.

as Julie says, having a novice owner who also happened to be pregnant at the time! He achieved his third CC in 1983 and became Champion Czolkins Platinum Cirrus – the first field trial winning Champion in the breed. Julie and Paul firmly set their sights on making him into a dual Champion but his cleverness was his downfall and he became very unsteady on runners in the advanced stakes. He knew when a bird came down and if it was a runner or not and, although rock-steady if it was dead, a runner to him was something you did not hang around for! He was a true rough-shooter's dog.

In spite of his successes, Quince was not extensively used at stud, but his chance to shine did arrive when he was six years old. Julie says she was gobsmacked when we telephoned her asking if we could use Quince on our outstanding bitch Sh. Ch. Gunalt Anais Anais. This was to be her first litter. Nine puppies resulted and two years later, two became Show Champions, Sh. Ch. Gunalt Cacharel (Harry) and Sh. Ch. Gunalt Armani. Sadly, Armani was unable to be bred from as she suffered a pyometra and had to be spayed, but Harry, in his short stud career, produced several Show Champions and, most significant of all, when bred to his mother, produced Gunalt Joy, winning once, runner-up two years running in the All-Breed Brood Bitch of the Year award, an incredible achievement.

Harry died while still a young dog, a very great loss, and Quince, although he made it to ten, died from prostate cancer. His last litter was born when he was only six because of this problem. Julie, through her involvement with US-bred stock, has managed to combine these lines with that of Quince and this is what their kennel is founded upon today. They have his daughter, granddaughter and great-granddaughter, the latter being Sh. Ch. Gunalt Posh Enough for Gamepoint (Connie), owned in partnership with Jacqui Ward of Mianja kennels. Julie is a firm believer in the benefits of using imported stock wisely.

TASAIRGID

Pronounced Tash-err-i-kit, this affix is a corruption of the Scottish Gaelic for 'Grey Ghost', owned by the Fairlies. After many years in Bloodhounds, in 1978 they acquired Gunalt Winter Will o' the Wisp. The show bug had bitten and they wanted a daughter of Sh. Ch. Greyfilk Knightsman, out of working lines for ability and strong instinct. The Hardmans' Bredebeck lines fitted the bill. Bredebeck Ilka arrived. She became Sh. Ch. Bredebeck Ilka, JW Best of Breed Crufts 1984, 9 CCs, 13 Res CCs. She had three litters producing CC winners in each: Sh. Ch. Tasairgid Deep Secret (sired by Aylmarch Aldous of Tasairgid); Ch. Tasairgid Talked About (sired by Ch. Ragstone Ryuhlan); and Dog CC Tasairgid Prime Candidate (sired by Am. Imp. Colsid ex Yankee at Gamepoint). In turn Tasairgid Prime Candidate's sister, Tasairgid Grade A-Plus, mated to his son, Savril Lucky the Reverant, produced Sh. Ch. Tasairgid Ultra Easy and, in Sweden, Tasairgid Certain Flair has won 10 CACIBs and Obedience qualification.

Through the 1980s, the general improvement in Weimaraner temperament, quality and construction brought about by the influence of the few American imports had so impressed them that they decided to go to see the US scene for themselves. Having previously been unable to use Int. Ch. Nani's Totally Awesome at stud during his short stay before he left the UK for Australia, Nani's seemed the perfect starting point and to date they have imported Am. Ch. Nani's Whistle in the Wind and now Am. Ch. Nani's Class Clown at Tasairgid. Bredebeck Ilka remains a vital part of their programme in the shape of her great-granddaughter, Tasairgid Hot Property. They have no wish to lose the foundation, but rather to build and extend it using a combination of lasting traditional UK and US bloodlines with proven good hips and eyes. They are proud that, after 17 years, they remain the only kennel in Scotland to have maintained a consistent record of producing Champions.

MIANJA

Sh. Ch. Kentoo Benjamin was the first Weimaraner for Mick and Jacqui Ward. Whelped in 1982 Ben never won a first prize until he was 18 months. He then went on to win 26 CCs – who says novices never win! He was campaigned primarily by Mick, but Jacqui nevertheless went to many shows, sitting in the background learning her trade. Although Ben and Mick had a special relationship, Jacqui showed their second Weimaraner, Silver Grey Lady, who won well gaining a

Sh. Ch. Kentoo Benjamin: Winner of 25CCs. Owned by Mick and Jacqui Ward.

Photo: C. Rayner.

RCC and Junior Warrant. Following an injury which curtailed her showing, Lady was mated on veterinary advice. Sh. Ch. Hansom Brandyman of Gunalt was the chosen sire and from this a dog was retained. Shown by Jacqui he became Sh. Ch. Hot Brandy – 'H'. Both Ben and 'H' had the honour of gaining BOB at Crufts and of being shortlisted in the Group at same.

Following the dogs the Wards bought a bitch puppy from us. On the theme of perfume (the dam being Sh. Ch. Gunalt Anais Anais) the Wards chose the name Armarni because "we have our Ben, our H and now Ar-marni". She became Sh. Ch. Gunalt Armarni. Unfortunately she had to be spayed so no puppies were bred. The Wards love showing and working their Weimaraners and are famous in their hometown of Morley, as Mick regularly walks through the town with six Weimaraners on leads, yet they have no great desire to breed and do so very infrequently. Jacqui regularly attends shows with me and is an invaluable aid and friend, often showing the Gunalt stock.

ANSONA

Having had Border Collies as a family dog, Trish Grimes was asked, what breed would she have if she had a dog of her own? After a short think, she said a Weimaraner. What's one of those? was the reply. A few weeks later the same person produced one for her birthday present. That was in 1986 and Beth became the foundation of the Ansona kennel. Beth was successful in the show ring, gaining her show title and 1 Res Group and then in 1991 she gained a C of M at her first field trial to become Ch. Joanscroft Bassoon Bertha. She was mated to Sh. Ch. Hansom Portman of Gunalt and produced two ticket winners; one of them went on to become Sh. Ch. Ansona Charisma. Her second litter was to Sh. Ch. Gunalt Harris Tweed. This produced Ir. Sh. Ch. Ansona Kreighoff of Huntly and Sh. Ch. Ansona Purdey (37 CCs – breed record), BIS at Bath Championship Show 1995 (only the second Weimaraner ever to achieve this), 9 Groups and 7 Res Groups. Beth also

Record CC winning Sh. Ch. Ansona Purdey, handled by Gordon Haran. Purdey is owned by Jack and Sandra Ross and was bred by Trish Grimes.

Photo: C. Rayner.

produced Ansona Beretta and Ansona Carrera, both gained a number of awards at shows and are worked regularly on their shoot, having a number of working test awards. Charisma was also mated to Harris and produced Ansona Murphy, 1 CC, 7 Res CCs. As well as the Ansona Weimaraners they also have Zeus (Savril Lucky Strike) although not a show dog. Zeus has certainly made his mark in the working team: he is worked on fur and feather, and used for stalking, but is at his best retrieving foxes. He has retrieved over 900 so far and his party piece is to jump into the back of the truck with them.

KHAMSYNN

Adrian and Lesley Rutland started showing Pointers, and their first Weimaraner was Forever Amber. She produced their first CC winner when mated to Sh. Ch. Hansom Brandyman of Gunalt – Khamsynn Kaliban JW, born 1984. Amber was mated to Ch. Tasairgid Talked About in 1986 to produce Khamsynn Khali who gained 2 RCCs. A third litter, to Sh. Ch. Flimmoric Fanclub, produced the CC winning Khamsynn Crazy Capers. Khali was then mated to Khamsynn Cardinal Synn which produced their first Show Champion in Sh. Ch. Khamsynn Quasar. Khamsynn Cardinal Synn was used on our Gunalt Joy and produced two champion offspring. Gil Averis also used this dog to produce a Champion. The Rutlands are a small, forward-thinking kennel steadily producing sound stock.

Chapter Eleven

THE WEIMARANER WORLDWIDE

The first British Weimaraners were imported into Australia in 1955 when Major Petty sent four Strawbridge – two of each sex. At the same time an import was also introduced from the USA but this dog tragically died in a road accident after siring only one litter. Then an American student took his pet Weimaraner to Australia with him. This dog, Fritz von Singen, was used at stud, mainly on a British import, Halsall Brown Pheasant. These first Weimaraners were the foundation of the breed in Australia. Today the Weimaraner is flourishing there and the present imports, mainly from the USA, have assisted in providing the country with sound quality Weimaraners.

GHOSTWIND
The Ghostwind kennel of Sue Shrigley, which she started in 1973, is one of the most famous Australian kennels and was based on stock which were direct descendants of Ch. Fritz von Singen and Ch. Halsall Brown Pheasant. Since then Sue has bred more than 50 Champions in Australia and overseas. Ghostwind is behind many kennels in Australia and New Zealand including the Weissenberg kennel of Kathy White in New Zealand, Kathy's foundation bitch being Ch. Ghostwind Shades of Grey who went to her as a mature animal after producing good dogs for Sue Shrigley. Sue has used English and American bred stock to maintain her top kennel, including Sh. Ch. Kisdons Artist and, from the USA, a sister to Am. Ch. Nani's Totally Awesome. She also campaigned Dianne Thomas's Aust. NZ Ch. Rifleman Poacher's Moon while he resided in Australia. Richard and Helena Jupp have imported a Ghostwind's bitch into their kennel in the UK.

BROMHUND
John and Rosemary Mayhew bought their first Weimaraner in 1972 and were won over by his brave, affectionate and smart personality. They were encouraged by other gundog fanciers to pursue the working attributes of the breed and had a lot of success, which led them to buy their second Weimaraner. The breeder of this bitch encouraged them to show and since then they have imported two dogs from the USA and one from Germany, exported dogs to seven countries, and bred 66 Champions, including the breed's only Grand Champion.

   Their third Weimaraner was a lovely bitch by the name of Ch. Whimani Grey Haze CDX CM. John travelled to America in 1978 and came back with the impression they were 30 years ahead in the breed's development, which, considering the history and the number of Weimaraners that they got from Germany and Austria after the War, is no wonder. They selected Eng. NZ Aust. Ch. Arimar's Rolf vd Reiteralm (Tank) who sired 62 Champions, dual Champions both in the field and retrieving, and many titled dogs in Obedience, with highest qualified gundog in the UK and the

Aust. NZ Ch. Bromhund Ellice winning BIS at the Weimaraner Club of Auckland under British specialist Gillian Burgoin.

highest qualified Weimaraner in Australia. His legacy lives on, with his grandchildren taking most of the big wins at major shows today and winners in the field.

While Tank was in the UK with Mrs Jane George (Fineshade), John and Rosemary visited and witnessed him get his final 2 CCs under gundog specialists. They also visited Germany and were impressed with the dogs there, especially their working ability, heads and colour. So much so that they imported the dog Salto vom Zehnthof and, though he lived only six years, the majority of their bitches have him in their pedigree. To complement 'Tank' they were offered the bitch, Nani's Helga for Bromhund, from the well-known kennel in the States. Being a Longhair she was unable to be shown there and as Bromhun had been the first kennel to have bred a litter of longhairs, John and Rosemary were thrilled at the offer and welcomed her with open arms, which again proved a winner as she produced ten champions with many BIS progeny as well as setting up another gene pool for the longhairs.

Their aim is to continue to produce Y's, as they call them, with good movement, sound temperaments, the ability to be trained and pleasing to the eye. They have been able to travel to many parts of the world looking at the breed, and so have obtained a good perspective on how it is progressing, and they feel it is in very good shape – and will continue to be if working ability is not forgotten when breeding the next generation.

GRAUHUND

Carol Wright was at Obedience in 1972 with her crossbred and saw a Weimaraner. She went home and said to her husband that she just had to have one. Naturally he wanted to know what it was she wanted so badly but she says she couldn't even pronounce Weimaraner, all she could tell him was that it sounded like wineasomething. Then she had the opportunity to purchase a 10 month old male. He was totally untrained including housetraining and any dog that lives in their household comes inside. She took him to Obedience and he got his CD title. Then she started showing him

*Five generations of
Grauhund
Weimaraners:
(from left to right)
Grauhund Total
Recall, Ch. G.
Midas Touch,
Ch. G. It 'N' Abit,
Ch. G. Nite Moves,
Ch. G. Deyarna,
aged fifteen.*

and he became Ch. Baunduv Miccah CD. In 1973 Miccah's breeder used him at stud and Carol was given her first bitch. She was titled at 11 months of age and she became Ch. Baunduv Zelda, the foundation bitch for Grauhund Kennels. She produced three Champions from three litters, the most famous being Ch. Grauhund Bold as Brass, who was a multiple Best in Group winner and won six Royal CCs and multiple Specialty wins, which at that time was quite a record. He was sired by English import Ch. Monroes Zebedee. The litter brother Grauhund Buccaneer was only the second Weimaraner in the country to obtain his AOC (Australian Obedience Champion) title. Unfortunately he was never shown, as the owner sterilized him. Carol kept a bitch from Zelda's first litter who eventually became Ch. Grauhund Jindina CD. She produced five champions who were all multiple Best in Group winners.

Carol mated Jindi to Monroe's Zebedee and kept a bitch who did a great deal of winning in the ring. She obtained her Championship title at 11 months of age and became Ch. Grauhund Deyarna. She was not a great brood bitch, only having two surviving litters which consisted of four puppies in total. Two of these were Champions. For her second litter she was mated to the American import Am. Ch. Deerpaths Charlemagne. She had only one puppy, who was superb. She too was titled at 11 months and became Ch. Grauhund It'N'Abit. She was a magnificent brood bitch, producing 10 Champions from three litters. Her first litter (L litter) produced one of Australia's top winning Weimaraners, Ch. Grauhund Lord O'The Rings. He was Best in Show winner and multiple Speciality winner, and his most prestigious win was at Melbourne Royal in 1991 when he won Best Exhibit in Group under Weimaraner specialist judge Mrs Barbara Heller from the USA. This mating was repeated (M litter) and produced two Champions who were both multiple group winners. Carol kept a male from this litter who became Ch. Grauhund Midas Touch.

In 1989 Carol was corresponding with Judy Colan of Colsidex Kennels in the USA and agreed to purchase some frozen semen from her top dog Am. Ch. Colsidex Nani's Reprint. The semen was sent in late 1989 but was lost in transit. After many days of searching and sleepless nights it was found in the North of Australia. Fortunately it was not harmed. This was inseminated into Tia and nine puppies were born, six bitches and three dogs – a superb litter, which produced five Champions, all of which are multiple Best in Show, Specialty and Royal winners, the most famous being Ch. Grauhund Nite Moves (AI) who Carol kept. This bitch created history when she won Best in Show at the Sydney Royal Show in 1993 at two years of age, beating overall some 5,000 dogs. She has won multiple Best in Shows at Weimaraner Specialties, gundog Specialties and to date is the only Weimaraner to win three Best in Groups at Royal shows. Of her brothers, New Man in Town has produced nine Champions, Nacotia Reprint four Champions, and sister Nikkitah three Champions. To date Grauhund has produced 20 Champions and many top winning stock.

WALDWIESE

Lois Richter's Waldwiese Kennel was registered in 1977 and the foundation bitch was Ch. Greywood Silver Glory CD (Ch. Riverdrive Sandroxk Rex CD ex Susilau Pearl). Known as Heidi, she was the equal-first Weimaraner to win Best Exhibit in Show in South Australia. Another Weimaraner won BIS on the same day 700 kms away. Heidi was mated to Ch. Greymar Corey to produce one Show Champion and one CDX offspring. She was twice mated to Ch Monroe's Zebedee (UK Import) from which came B and C litters, producing two Champions, Bianka and Classic, and one CD title, Clemency. Classic (Sheena) was retained by the breeder and proved to be an outstanding brood bitch, producing four litters. From those litters came Ch. Dimity, Desert Fox CD, CDX, Dior CD, CDX (sire Grauming Asher), Ch. Earl Grey CD CDX ET, Ch. Evita (sire Ch. Bromhund Waldemer CD), Ferne CD, CDX, TD, Fidget CD (sire Ch. Poshvwei Man About Town). Gypsey Rose CD, CDX, TD and Ch. Ginja Jones ET CD CDX TD TDX (sire Ch. Lindridge Wakefield).

Aust. Ch. Waldwiese Ginja Jones CDX, TDX ET.

Ginja has been an outstanding example of the breed in South Australia, winning many In Group and In Show awards. In 1993 Ginja took out the Gundog Club of SA Top Showing Gundog Bitch, Top Obedience Bitch, Top Open Gundog and Top Tracking Bitch trophies and, in that same year, won the SA Weimaraner Club trophy for Top Showing Weimaraner and The Dual Purpose Bitch Trophy for achievements in Showing, Tracking and Obedience. At six-and-a-half years of age she won Best of Breed at the 1994 Adelaide Royal and shortly after a Runner Up Best In Show (All breeds) and then, a month after her seventh birthday, she won Best Bitch and Runner Up Best in Show at the South Australian Weimaraner 1995 Specialty.

BRITFELD

Owned by Kevin and Sally Johnston, this is a young breeding kennel which began in 1983. When they purchased their first Weimaraner, little did they know that Duchess, as she was known, was destined to be Australian Champion Cauldon Sommer Frau CDX and a wonderful shooting companion for Kevin. Duchess produced their A, B and C litters. The A litter was a disappointing one. Since then the Johnstons have not allowed themselves to be influenced by others, but have used their own instincts to choose the future sires with care and have gone from strength to strength. Now they can proudly boast of 16 Australian Champions, seven CD titled dogs, one CDX title, one UD title and one Retrieving Trial QC award. They are the proud breeders of Tasmania's most successfully shown Weimaraner, Ch. Britfeld Havoc Express. Known as Hannah, she has won three RUBIS awards, two of which were at Championship level. In Queensland Ch. Britfeld Precision Made gained his show title at ten months of age. On the way to this title he was awarded a BIG from Puppy class at All Breeds Championship level. These are just two of their many successful Weimaraners.

They imported frozen semen from Am. Ch. Wismars Jack Daniels (USA) and are very happy with their three beautiful AI puppies. They have also exported Britfeld Original Choice to Gerda and Wim Halff-Van Boven in Holland, Britveld Light Fantastic to Mr Ho in

Aust Ch. Britfield Havoc Express.

Hong Kong, and frozen semen, from their beautiful American-blooded dog Aust. Ch. Bromhund American Express, to Norway. The first litter whelped in Norway from Ziggy's semen for Eva Pedersen's Hella Kennels comprised one shorthaired male, two longhair bitches and three shorthair bitches. Hella's Floyd has done exceptionally well with BIS puppy show – this is the first time a Weimaraner has taken out such a high award in Norway – while his sister Hella's Fantasy has won Reserve BIS. The Johnstons look forward to a promising future at Britfeld with their two young ladies, Britfeld Poetry In Motion and Britfeld Quake and Shake AI, more semen importation and the use of some great bloodlines available in Australia and New Zealand.

SILVASHEEN

Silvasheen Kennels, owned by Chris and Dianne Brown of Morwell, Victoria emerged in 1983. Both are keen shooters and Dianne purchased a puppy for Chris as his shooting companion. This was Greybeau Archilles who arrived in December 1980. A year later Greylag Silva Warena joined the kennel. Both were very strongly English bred. In 1983 a friendship was formed with Carol Wright of Grauhund Kennels and the Browns purchased Grauhund Hi Calypso (Sh. Ch. Monroe's Zebedee (Imp UK) ex Ch. Grauhund Jindina CD). Hi Calypso became the Kennel's true foundation. She produced Ch. Silvasheen Coffee Kisses, who in turn produced two Champions from her only litter, sired by Ch. Grauhund New Man in Town (AI). These are the Browns' Ch. Silvasheen Iced Coffee and Mary Clarke's Ch. Silvasheen Capuccino Kid, both of whom are multi-class in show winners. In 1995, Iced Coffee was mated to Ch. Divani Loads A Trouble (AI) (S. Am. Ch. Nani's Bahta Packa Trouble ex Ch. Divani Enter Thstar). They have retained the puppy bitch Sivlasheen L'Bit Dangerus. The Browns have always been keen on English lines, so semen from our Sh. Ch. Hansom Portman of Gunalt will be exported to Australia in 1995 to add that 'Dash of British' so admired over the years.

CLAYCO

Clayco Kennels is the prefix of Simon and Karen Mills. One Weimaraner was Aust. Ch. Quilan

Baskerville who was a runner-up Best of Breed Weimaraner Club Specialty winner. This led them to purchase their first bitch, Ch. Furstlich Abbey Road (Am. Ch. Deerpaths Charlemagne Imp. USA ex Bromhund Sylvia Rose CD). She won Best Gundog in Group at the Melbourne Royal Show, beating over 1000 gundogs. She was the first Weimaraner to achieve this award. From this bitch's line they produced Ch. Clayco Toronto Bluejay (Ch. & Eng. Sh. & NZ Ch. Arimars Rolf VD Reiteralm Imp. USA ex Ch. Furstlich Abbey Road CD) who is a BOB Weimaraner Club Speciality winner and runner-up BOB Weimaraner Club Specialty winner. During this time they acquired Ch. Bromhund Galaxie (Eng. NZ Aust. Ch. Arimar's Rolf vd Reiteralm, Imp. USA ex Nani's Helga for Bromhund Imp. USA), who is one of Australia's leading Weimaraners with 17 Best in Shows. At all-breeds Championship shows he had 16 to his credit, number 17 was to be his last show at New South Wales Weimaraner Club Speciality under Mrs H. Parkinson (England). He was retired at six years of age. As a sire he produced 18 Champions, one of these being Ch. Talfryn Desert Jewel (Ch. Bromhund Galaxie ex Ch. Silknsilver Wild Gypsy) who is a Sydney Royal CC Winner.

This bitch went on to be an excellent producer with Ch. Clayco Boston Celtic, a multiple Best in Show winner, and Clayco Desert Dream, opposite sex puppy in Group, Brisbane Royal (1995), also Runner Up in Show at the Queensland Weimaraner Club Open Show (1995). In 1991 Clayco kennels obtained Ch. Grauhund Nikkitah (AI) (Am. Ch. Colsidex Nani's Reprint USA ex Ch. Grauhund It'N'Abit) who is jointly owned with Grauhund Kennels. She is a major winner in Australia with two Best in Shows at Weimaraner Specialties. This bitch has produced one litter to Ch. Bromhund Galaxie; from this four dogs have gained championship titles: Ch. Clayco Hot Chilli Woman, Ch. Hot August Nite, Ch. Clayco Damn Hot – this dog has gone on to produce several litters to leading kennels – and Ch. Clayco Totally Hot, who is a major winner at Weimaraner Specialties. Weimaraners at Clayco are often worked in the field and are shot over. Ch Clayco Seattle Seahawk, owned by R. and R. Curphey, runs in nonslip field trials and displays excellent natural hunting ability. A first for Australian Weimaraners is Ch. Clayco Toronto Bluejay being selected as a detector dog for the Australian Quarantine Inspection Service. She is used to detect items of quarantine concern coming into Australia. These include fruit, meat, plant foliage, eggs, birds, reptiles and bees.

*Aust. Ch.
Aceweis Laser
Beam.*

BESKO

Ian and Colleen Besanko of South Australia are great field trailling enthusiasts, having bred seven retrieving trial winners. From their first litter of Weimaraners they produced two Champions and three retrieving trial winners. Australian Ch. Besko Silver Baron RRD has won a great deal both working and in the show ring, winning BOB at the Adelaide Royal. He has competed in and 'finished' two SA State championships and competed in the 1988 Nationals Retrieving trials. He is the only SA Weimaraner to achieve this standard. In their opinion their greatest Weimaraner is Aust. Ch. Besko Silver Rose, CD. A BIS winner all-breeds, when winning the Adelaide Royal Challenge she was graded Excellent by German expert Dr Petri. She has also produced winners in the show ring, Obedience and retrieving trials.

ACEWEIS

Jill Townley, having been in the breed less than eight years, has already bred four Champions, one, from a litter out of Aust. Ch. Besko Vienna Charm, being Aust. Ch. Aceweis Traditional Charm. Out of Aust. Ch. Ghostwind Southern Comfit by Aust. Ch. Divani Loads A Trouble, she bred Aust. Ch. Aceweis Ice Krystal and Ch. Aceweis Lazer Beam, who is a BIS winner and won the CC at the Royal, plus numerous BIG wins. Jill recently used NZ & Aust. Ch. Rifleman Poacher's Moon, while he was in Australia being campaigned by Sue Shrigley, on her Aust. Ch. Ice Krystal, and their youngsters are already taking Best Puppy in Group awards, so look destined to a future at the top. Jill also has bred Aceweis Suthern Typhoon CDX, TDX, a longhaired dog, the first and only, to date, to gain a tracking title in Australia.

Left to right: Aust. Ch. Besko Silver Rose CD, Aust. Ch. Besko Silver Baron RRD, Aust. Ch. Besko Yartune CD.

ATAWAY

Ataway came into being in 1975 when Dianne Thomas bought Klipper – Ch. Puke Ataway. But it was another three years before she took the Ataway name, having shown and bred GSDs under another affix; and it is only for the last two years that Weimaraners have been the sole breed in the household. Prior to that her Weimaraners have lived, worked, played and shown alongside the

Aust. NZ Grand Champion Rifleman Poacher's Moon.

GSD, the English Setter, the Boxer, the Curly Coated Retriever, the Pointer and the German Shorthaired Pointer. But it is to the Weimaraner that she has always returned. Basically she has dogs because she enjoys living with them. She admires the look of the Weimaraner, but it is the complete animal that really suits her. She says that they provide her routine, her exercise, her entertainment and her therapy. Klipper won 184 CCs, five BOB out of eight at National Dog Show, 26 Group awards, and was always placed in any field trials entered.

After Klipper's untimely death, Dianne could not face another Weimaraner for a few years. Then she was given one of his grandsons which reactivated her interest in showing. She subsequently bought a bitch that was sadly lost through sickness at a young age. By then Poacher had just joined the family. Little did she know then that Aust. NZ Grand Ch. Rifleman Poacher's Moon, to give him his full title, was to thrust her into the political arena of the showring. Poacher currently holds some 180 CCs, having been awarded over 1200 Group and In Show awards, including two Best in Show (all breeds), four Reserve in Show (all breeds) and Best in Show at three Specialty Shows. But it is said that the mark of a good dog lies with his progeny. Poacher's first litter resulted in four Group and In Show winners: Ch. Bruchholz Top Dollar, Ch. Bruchholz Megabucks, Ch. Ataway Poacher's Reward and Ch. Ataway Poacher's Return. Ataway has continued with the two multi-group and In Show winnng daughters from subsequent litters, Ch. Ataway Poacher's Tribute and Ataway Poacher's Profile. More recently, Poacher's progeny are taking Group and In Show puppy awards in two states of Australia.

Dianne feels that the gene pool of the Weimaraner has not grown in step with the popularity of this relatively new breed in Australasia. Consequently, she has introduced Gunalt Sandown to the family. Sandown is now a NZ Champion and has sired his first litter ex Ataway Poachers Profile, born July 1995. This is looking promising – two puppies have been retained and at his first show the dog puppy took Best Baby Puppy, then went on to win the CC while still a pup.

WEISSENBERG

Kathy White's original breed was the Afghan Hound but she changed to Weimaraners in 1979, obtaining Sasha whose bloodlines went back to Ragstone. Sasha grew too big to show but had pleasing conformation. Kathy mated her and kept a bitch which she titled and from there 'got the show bug'. She decided she needed to go to Australia if she wanted to do any big winning and breeding – which is not the case now, as New Zealand stock matches that anywhere. In 1983, after looking at many kennels, she purchased, as previously mentioned, the proven brood bitch Aust. NZ Ch. Ghostwind Shades O'Grey, in whelp to her sire. From the subsequent litter four gained their title and Bruen (the dog she kept) also gained his first step in Obedience – Companion Dog Title. In 1984 Shades was mated to Eng. Sh. Ch. Kisdons Artist who had just arrived in New Zealand. Kenna resulted from this mating (Aust. NZ Ch. Weissenberg Kenna Kween) and became one of the top consistently winning bitches.

Kathy moved to Sydney, Australia with Bruen, Kenna and Shades in 1985 and soon after her arrival Bruen took Best of Breed at the Sydney Royal Show and Kenna the Bitch CC at 10 months. Bruen went on to take a Best in Show All Breeds with many Group wins along the way, gaining his title in four shows (four weeks). Kenna's successes have been impressive. She took out almost every major show CC she entered, with three Royal Specialty wins. Hardly a weekend went by without her taking a Group win. They returned to New Zealand early 1987. Kenna then went on to take the National Dog Show CC for the next four years and many Group and Reserve in Show All Breeds and Specialty along the way, but her peak was in Australia. Kenna's progeny have also done well. Kathy campaigned Ch. Weissenberg Ureka Joe to his title. Ch. Weissenberg Kenna's Mist was also very successful. Ch. Weissenberg Kenna's Girl has followed in her mother's footsteps, achieving the Ultimate All Breeds Best in Show. Trix is now four and still consistently taking these awards and currently leads the Northern Weimaraner Points score for Show Weimaraner of the year.

CARNMELLIS

Carnmellis Weimaraners is owned by Pip Simmons who lives just north of Hamilton. In 1982 she purchased, as a pet, Lady Tikka of Nimbus. Her experience in eventing and showing horses, and encouragement from other dog showing people, led her into showing her, where she gained her Championship status. Late in 1983 she chose Carnmellis as the kennel name which, as she discovered some five years later, is a village in Cornwall where her father's ancestors came from. Tikka was mated to Ch. Awhitu Dal Fritz and provided Carnmellis with its first home-bred Champion, Carnmellis Acclaim, who went on to win many group placings.

In 1987 Pip purchased Australian Champion Bromhund Ellice (Gretel) (Am. Aust. Ch. Deerpath Charlemagne ex Bromhund Penelope) who arrived in whelp. From this litter, Carnmellis Endless Love was shown to her championship title and has since produced show-winning stock under the Fynepoint prefix. Two of Endless Love's sisters have produced longhaired Weimaraners. In April 1988 Gretel won the bitch challenge and BOB. In April of this year, Dick Finch (UK) judged a Weimaraner Open Show: Gretel went Reserve Bitch. In June 1988, Dr Werner Petri (Germany) judged the Weimaraner Championship Show. Gretel went Reserve in Show. Following a field trial that the Club put on for Dr Petri, he stated that of all the dogs that he had seen worked on the day, he would like to take Gretel home to train, as she exhibited so much natural working ability, although handicapped by her handler. At the Weimaraner Club Championship Show, judged by Gillian Burgoin, Ragstone (UK) Gretel went Best in Show. Gretel obtained her New Zealand Championship status and won numerous Best of Group wins.

For her next litter Gretel was mated to Am. NZ Ch. Nani's Totally Awesome (Imp. USA) and from this mating Carnmellis Future Charm was shown to his Championship title. In 1990 Gretel won her first All Breeds Best in Show, being the first Weimaraner in New Zealand to do this. In 1991 she won a further two more All Breed Best in Show wins and following this ended up with the title of Aust. NZ Grand Champion Bromhund Ellice. (To have this title a dog or bitch has to have 50 challenges and 3 All Breeds Best in Show Wins under three separate judges.) In January 1993 Gretel was handled by the well-known GSP handler Mac McArthur to attain her Qualifying Certificate in Pointer/Setter field trials.

The future of Carnmellis looks very promising with four Champion progeny from Gretel's last litter, these being Ch. Carnmellis Loads A Fun, Ch. Carnmellis Loads A Hope, Ch. Carnmellis Loads A Joy and Aust. Ch. Carnmellis Loads A Class, owned by Graeme and Ingrid Gilbert. Ch. Carnmellis Masterpiece (sired by Ch. Carnmellis Loads A Fun) is proving his worth in the show ring. As well as showing shorthaired Weimaraners, Pip has for the last three years found it very challenging showing Carnmellis Innovation, who is a longhair. She has done extremely well in the show ring having won a Puppy Sweepstake at an All Breeds Show; in 1993 she went Reserve in Show under Judy Colan; she has had a Best of Group win and a Reserve of Group win; and at the end of 1995 requires one more challenge to finish off her title. At the end of the 1995 year, Gretel is still the only Weimaraner to carry the Grand Champion title.

ANNVID
Annvid Weimaraners are owned by David and Anne Porter in South Auckland. They are relative newcomers to the breed, having owned Weimaraners for only eight years. The original foundation stock for the line were litter mates, NZ Ch. Kurowai Soldier Blue and NZ Ch. Kurowai Blue Belle. The bitch was put to Aust. NZ Ch. Ghostwind Star Prince CD; this produced NZ Ch. Annvid First Edition (dog) and NZ Ch. Annvid Spirit of Omana (bitch), who both gave a great deal of fun and enjoyment in the show ring. The dog did a lot of winning at group and show level.

NZ Ch. Argental Jeremy Fisher.

On careful reflection it was decided that these lines were not really going to give the style of Weimaraner that David and Anne really liked. With a distinct type firmly set in their minds, new stock was imported from Tasmania, NZ Ch. Argental Jeremy Fisher (AI) (Am. Can. Ch. Hoot Hollows Peter Rabbit ex Aust. Ch. Divani Fortunes A'Lady). To complement this line a bitch, Truestone Flight O'Fancy, known as Fleur, was also acquired. Her grandfather was Weissenberg Fire 'n' Ice (LH) and her great-great grandfather Am. NZ Ch. Nani's Totally Awesome (Imp. USA). Both lines lead back to Am. Ch. Colsidex Standing Ovation.

Both animals are doing well in the show ring, with group awards to their names. Jeremy Fisher, known as Webb, earned his New Zealand title at fourteen months. Webb's first stud produced a litter of ten, from which Weissenberg Just Jeremy (Drew) was retained. Now just 12 months old, Drew has several all-breed Puppy in Group awards and also a Puppy in Show to his name. A subsequent Webb/Fleur mating has produced another promising bitch, Annvid Golden Dream, now being shown with success by Chris Thompson of Truestone Kennels, to date having taken one all-breed Baby Puppy in Show, three specialist Breed Show Baby Puppy in Show and several all breed Baby Puppy in Group awards. The Porters look forward to seeing this new line, bearing the Annvid prefix, develop over the coming years.

Chapter Twelve

THE WEIMARANER IN NORTH AMERICA

By Judy Colan

In the 27 year period from 1943, when the first Weimaraner was exhibited at an American dog show, through 1970, only nine Weimaraners had achieved the ultimate goal of breeders and exhibitors world-wide – an All Breed Best In Show. Of these nine, only four were multiple Best In Show winners. Among these four were two dogs who were to have a lasting influence on the breed: Ch. Val Knight Ranck and Ch. Shadowmar Barthaus Dorilio. Both of these dogs are behind most of the Top Winners and Top Producers of today. The 1970s through the 1990s were exciting years for Weimaraners. An astonishing number, 39, won Best In Show awards during this period.

As a breeder, I look back and see the impact certain dogs and bitches have had on the breed in the show ring and as top producers. Some dogs were prepotent producers and passed this ability on to their offspring. These dogs have endured the test of time and can be found in the background of most of the Weimaraners of today. Most notable are: Ch. Val Knight Ranck, Ch. Shadowmar Barthaus Dorilio, Ch. Maxmillian v.d. Reiteralm, Ch. Ronamax Rajah v.d. Reiteralm, Ch. Doug's Dauntless von Dor and Ch. Colsidex Standing Ovation. These names are seen over and over again when looking at pedigrees of today's winners and producers.

*Ch.
Shadowmar
Barthaus
Dorilio.*

*Photo:
Evelyn M.*

Ch. Colsidex Standing Ovation.
Photo: Chuck and Sandy Tatham.

Ch. Seneca's Medicine Man.
Photo: Evelyn M. Shafer.

AN ANALYSIS OF THE TOP DOGS

The Weimaraner Club of America maintains a Bench Register of Merit (BROM) which is based on the accomplishments of a sire or a dam's offspring as well as the number of Champions they have produced.

WEIMARANER CLUB OF AMERICA BENCH REGISTER OF MERIT
Top Ten All Time Top Producing Sires and Dams
Standings as of 9/30/95

SIRES	BROM Points	Number of Champions
1. Ch. Colsidex Standing Ovation	3915	146
Ch. Seneca's Medicine Man – Ch. Colsidex Dauntless Applause		
2. Ch. Valmar Smokey City Ultra Easy	2706	127
Ch. Smokey City Easy Does It – Ch. Valmar's Serenade V Wustenwind		
3. Ch. Ronamax Rajah v.d. Reiteralm	2345	118
Ch. Maxmillian von der Reiteralm – Ch. Norman's Rona v.d. Reiteralm		
4. Ch. Greywinds Jack Frost	1563	59
Ch. Colsidex Standing Ovation – Ch. Greywinds Ashley Frost		
5. Ch. Sir Eric Von Sieben	1401	44
Ch. Dougs Dauntless von Dor – Ch. Chaskars Suddenly It's Rainy		
6. Ch. Maximillian Von Der Reiteralm	1377	62
Ch. Val Knight Ranck – Ch. Bella von Der Reiteralm		

SIRES	BROM Points	Number of Champions
7. Ch. Valmar's Jazzman	1343	75
Ch. Valmar's Chancellor V Starbuck – Ch. Valmar's Elke Schwenden		
8. Ch. Seneca's Medicine Man	1374	27
Ch. Durmar's Karl – Ch. Eilatans Karlrise Seneca		
9. Ch. Doug's Dauntless von Dor	1178	52
Ch. Shadowmar Barthaus Dorilio – Norman's Nuther Nina		
10. Ch. Colsidex Nani Reprint	1132	51
Ch. Colsidex Standing Ovation – Ch. Nani's Cobbie Cuddler		

DAMS	BROM Points	Number of Champions
1. Ch. Valmar's Serenade V Wustenwind	885	9
Ch. Valmar's Jazzman – Ch. Arimar's Majestic Moriah		
2. Ch. Norman's Frostyroy Colleen	673	13
Ch. Greywinds Jack Frost – Ch. Doblens Serene Sunrise		
3. Ch. Norman's Rona v.d. Reiteralm	656	20
Ch. Graves Rouge – Shadowmar Valentress		
4. Ch. Harline's Hurrah	565	10
Ch. Colsidex Standing Ovation – Ch. Dofo's Cristel v Hoot Hollow		
5. Ch. Rona's Sea Sprite v.d. Reiteralm	559	6
Ch. Vals Viking v.d. Reiteralm – Ch. Normans Rona v.d. Reiteralm		
6. Ch. Silversmith Omni V Reiteralm	550	14
Ch. Reiteralm's Rio Fonte Saudade – Ch. Robins Song v.d. Reiteralm		
7. Ch. Norman's Easybrae Katie	545	6
Ch. Valmar Smokey City Ultra Easy – Ch. Norman's Frostyroy Colleen		
8. Ch. Colsidex Dauntless Applause	535	12
Ch. Doug's Dauntless von Dor – Shadowmar Winema v Elken		
9. Ch. Weimar Castles Jabetwheel	504	6
Ch. WC's Thunderwheel of Marquez – Ch. Duskins Princess Shellie		
10. Ch. Smokey City Jedda Arokat	474	16
Ch. Arokats Legionnaire – Ch. Smokey Citys Split Decision		

Ch. Colsidex Nani's Reprint.
Photo: John L. Asbey.

Ch. Smokey City Jedda Arokat.

It is here on the BROM list that you can see the contribution to the breed made by Ch. Seneca's Medicine Man (Ch. Gronbach's Aladdin–Ch. Eilatans Karlrise Seneca). He was known as Doc. His owners, Bill and Liza Hammond, had an unfortunate experience when a bitch, shipped to them for breeding, succumbed to bloat. After this, they would not keep any bitches and only bitches who were brought by their owners were bred to Doc. This limited his use as a stud dog but, despite this, he is the #8 All Time Top Producing BROM sire with only 27 Champions. Of these 27 Champions, three were Best In Show winners: Ch. Springdale's Rhea v.d. Reiteralm, her litter brother Ch. Chataways Charlie v.d. Reiteralm, and Ch. Colsidex Standing Ovation, who is also the #1 BROM sire.

In 1969, Ch. Doug's Dauntless von Dor (Ch. Shadowmar Barthaus Dorilio-Norman's Nuther Nina) bred by Doug Kline, owned by Frank and Gail Sousa, dominated the breed in the show ring and was a top contender in the Sporting Group ring. Daunt, a Dorilio son, was also a Val Knight Ranck great-grandson. Although never achieving the elusive Best in Show win, Daunt left a legacy of top producing, top winning offspring, siring 52 Champions, which included two Best In Show winners. Several Daunt sons were top producers but, most remarkable was the ability of his daughters to produce. 11 daughters are on the BROM list, more than for any other sire.

Early in the 1970s Ch. Ronamax Rajah v.d. Reiteralm (Ch. Maxmillian v.d. Reiteralm–Ch. Norman's Rona v.d. Reiteralm), bred and owned by Virginia Alexander and handled by Stan Flowers, initiated the revolution of Weimaraners as Sporting Group and Best In Show winners. Rajah, a four-time Best In Show winner, proved himself an outstanding sire as well. He was the sire of 116 Champions. Rajah's sire, Ch. Maxmillian v.d. Reiteralm, was a Val Knight Ranck son and a top producer himself, siring 66 Champions. His dam, Ch. Normans Rona v.d. Reiteralm, was also a top producer, the dam of an unheard of 20 Champions. She too was a Val Knight Ranck granddaughter through her dam, Shadowmar Valentress.

Ch. Sir Eric von Sieben (Ch. Dougs Dauntless von Dor – Ch. Chaskars Suddenly It's Rainy), bred and owned by Helene Burkholder, was another Best In Show winner that has had a lasting impact on the breed. He was the sire of the Top Producing litter mates, Ch. Reiteralms Rio Fonte Saudade and Ch. Anns Magic v.d. Reiteralm out of a Rajah daughter, the Best In Show winning

Ch. The Rajahs Magic v.d. Reiteralm. His daughter, Ch. Valmars Pollyanna out of Ch. Valmars Serenade v Wustenwind, was a multiple Best In Show winner and a Top Producer.

In 1974 breed history was made when a beautiful little bitch, Ch. Springdale Rhea v.d. Reiteralm (Ch. Seneca's Medicine Man–Ch. Rona's Sea Sprite v.d. Reiteralm), bred by Gayle Eckenrode and owned by Sue Orth, went Best In Show. Rhea was the first bitch to attain this honor and proceeded to win a total of three Best In Shows. Rhea's litter brother, Ch. Chat-A-Wey Charlie, was also a Best In Show winner and, again, breed history was made, for these two dogs were the first litter-mates to win Best In Show. Rhea was a born show dog and was proof of the saying, 'good things come in small packages'. Here was a Weimaraner that stood out in the Sporting Group with her showmanship, ring presence, and ground covering movement. Rhea paved the way for future Best In Show winners.

At Rhea's last show, Westminster Kennel Club in 1976, a young dog, Ch. Colsidex Standing Ovation (Ch. Seneca's Medicine Man-Ch. Colsidex Dauntless Applause), was pulled out by the judge and these two, half-brother and half-sister, battled it out for over 30 minutes. Gaiting and stacking over and over again to a packed ringside audience, they performed to perfection. Finally, the judge gave the nod to Rhea for Best of Breed and to Ovation for Best Opposite Sex.

Ch. Colsidex Standing Ovation went on to be a consistent winner, winning three Best In Shows, handled by his breeder and owner – me! He was a prepotent sire, passing on his reaching, driving gait and his style and elegance. He sired three Best In Show winners and is not only the Breed's #1 all-time top producing sire, but sired more Futurity and Maturity winners than any other sire and also produced more BROM offspring than any other sire, namely 23. There is hardly an American pedigree that does not go back to Ovation. Ovation's dam, Ch. Colsidex Dauntless Applause (Ch. Doug's Dauntless von Dor–Shadowmar Winema von Elken), which I bred and owned, was also an outstanding producer. The dam of 12 Champions, she holds the record in bitches for producing the most BROM offspring – six.

An outstanding bitch, Ch. The Rajahs Magic v.d. Reiteralm (Ch. Ronamax Rajah v.d. Rieteralm–Ch. Brandys Blizz v.d. Reiteralm), known as Yellow Bird, bred and owned by Virginia Alexander, came on the scene shortly after Ovation began his career in the ring. Here were two of

Ch. Valmars Pollyanna.

Ch. Nani's Visa v.d. Reiteralm.

Ch. Nani's Hawaiian Punch.
Booth Photography.

Ch. W.F. Mattrace Harline Roquelle.
Photo: Missy Yuhl.

Ch. Harline's W.F. Rockafeller.
Photo: Don Petrulis.

Ch. Valmar Serenade v Wustenwind.

the finest Weimaraners the breed had seen battling it out for the #1 spot. One year Ovation was #1 and Yellow Bird #2, the next it was Yellow Bird #1 and Ovation #2. Again, here was the intertwining of those influential dogs, Ch. Val Knight Ranck, Ch. Shadowmar Barthaus Dorilio, Ch. Doug's Dauntless von Dor, Ch. Ronamax Rajah v.d. Reiteralm and Ch Seneca's Medicine Man. Yellow Bird was bred to a Dauntless son, Ch. Sir Eric von Sieben, and produced two influential BROM sires, Ch. Anns Magic v.d. Reiteralm and Ch. Reiteralms Rio Fonte Saudade.

Another outstanding bitch hit the show scene in the early 1980s. Ch. Nani's Visa v.d. Reiteralm (Ch. Reiteralms Rio Fonte Saudade–Ch. Nani's Soul Sister), bred and owned by Christine Medeiros, made breed history by being the youngest Weimaraner to go Best In Show, at nine months of age, from the puppy class. Visa continued her winning ways and won a total of five

Ch. Greywinds Jack Frost.

Ch. Nani's Cobbie Cuddler.
Booth Photography.

Best In Shows. She was bred to Best In Show winner Ch. Colsidex Standing Ovation and proved herself an outstanding producer. She is the dam of nine Champions, which include a Best In Show winner, Ch. Nani's Hawaiian Punch, BROM, two Futurity winners and one Maturity winner.

Ovation's first Best In Show winner was Ch. Harline's Ballet (Ch. Colsidex Standing Ovation – Ch. Dofo's Cristel v Hoot Hollow) bred and owned by Alan and Susan Line. Ballet was shown for 18 months and won two Best In Shows. Her sister, Ch. Harline's Hurrah, proved to be an outstanding producer. She was bred to her half-brother, an Ovation son, Ch. Nani's Scirroco of Mattrase (Ch. Colsidex Standing Ovation – Ch. Nani's Cobbie Cuddler), owned by Jack and Vicki Roye, and produced 10 Champions which included two multiple Best in Show winners, Ch. Harline's W.F. Rockefeller and Ch. W.F. Mattraces Harline Roquelle. These litter-mates dominated the show ring for several years. In 1991 Rockefeller was #2 and Roquelle #3.

Another bitch who proved herself in the show ring and in the whelping box was Ch. Valmar's Pollyanna (Ch. Sir Eric von Sieben – Ch. Valmar's Serenade V Wustenwind). Bred, owned and handled by Joan Valdez, Polly was a multiple Best In Show winner, #1 Weimaraner and #3 Sporting dog. If that wasn't enough, Polly took time out have puppies and produced 10 Champions, which include a Dual Champion. Then she came back at six-and-a-half years old and won the largest National Specialty in the history of the breed!

Polly's dam, Ch. Valmar's Serenade V Wustenwind (Ch. Valmars Jazzman – Ch. Arimars Majestic Moriah) is every breeder's dream for a brood bitch. She is the dam of nine Champions, which include two Best In Show winners, Polly and Ch. Valmar's Smoky City Ultra Easy (Ch. Smokey City Easy Does It – Ch. Valmar's Serenade V Wustenwind). Both Polly and Easy were ranked #1 Weimaraner.

In the mid 1980's Ch. Greywind's Jack Frost (Ch. Colsidex Standing Ovation – Ch Greywinds Ashley Frost) dominated the show ring. Brae was breeder and owner handled by Ellen Grevatt. He was a three time Best In Show winner and was ranked #1 Weimaraner in 1986 and 1987. He is the sire of 59 Champions, which include two Best In Show winners – Ch. Wolfstadt's First Frost and the record-breaking Ch. Norman's Greywind Phoebe Snow, who was also ranked #1 Weimaraner for two years.

Ch. Norman's Smokey City Heat Wave.

Ch. Norman's Greywind Phoebe Snow.
Photo: John L. Ashbey.

Another bitch who proved herself an outstanding producer was Ch. Nani's Cobbie Cuddler (Ch. Nani's Master Charge – Ch. Nani's Cascade v.d. Reiteralm). Cuddles, bred and owned by Chris Medeiros-Grisell, was bred to Ch. Colsidex Standing Ovation. Fifteen Champions were the result of this match. Of these fifteen, four distinguished themselves as Top Producers: Ch. Nani's Kona Gust, Ch. Nani's Scirroco of Mattrace, Ch. Nani's Totally Awesome and Ch. Colsidex Nani Reprint. With the exception of Awesome, who was sold to New Zealand as a young dog, all of these dogs sired Best In Show winners.

Ch. Colsidex Nani Reprint (Ch. Colsidex Standing Ovation – Ch. Nani's Cobbie Cuddler), bred by Christine Medeiros and me, and owned by me, was a multiple Specialty winner and Group winner and Top Ten Weimaraner. He sired 51 Champions, which include 17 Futurity and Maturity winners and a Best In Show winner. The only dog to produce more Futurity and Maturity winners was his sire, Ovation, who produced nineteen. In the late 1980s Ch. Valmar Smokey City Ultra Easy (Ch. Smokey City Easy Does It – Ch. Valmar's Serenade V Wustenwind), bred by Joan Valdez and owned by Tom Wilson, began making his mark in the show ring and as a top producer. Easy was on the Top Ten for two years and has proven to be an outstanding sire, with 127 Champions to his credit. As the 1980s drew to a close, the pedigrees of the Top Winning and Top Producing dogs still echoed the names of those influential sires: Ch. Colsidex Standing Ovation, Ch. Doug's Dauntless von Dor, Ch. Ronamax Rajah v.d. Reiteralm, Ch. Seneca's Medicine Man, and Ch. Val Knight Ranck. Amazing to realize that just a few dogs could have such a profound effect and lasting effect on the breed!

In 1991, Ch. Norman's Smokey City Heat Wave (Ch. Valmar Smokey City Ultra Easy–Ch Norman's Frostyroy Colleen), bred by Norman LeBoeuf and owned by Tom Wilson, was #1 Weimaraner. Allie, as she is called, was a multiple Specialty winner, including the National Specialty and Group winner. Like her great-great-great-grandfather, Ch. Doug's Dauntless von Dor, Allie never achieved a Best In Show win but not for lack of quality. A beautiful bitch, she was deserving of this prestigious win. Allie is just beginning to make her mark as a brood bitch. In the mid 1990s two outstanding bitches came on the scene, Ch. Greymists Silver Cloud (Ch. Silversmith Easy Payment Plan–Ch. Sunmist Silver Shadow), bred and owned by Roger and

Ch. Greymists Silver Cloud.

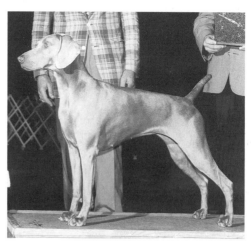

Ch. Arias Allegra of Colsidex.

Jeanne Shelby, and Ch. Greywinds Phoebe Snow (Ch. Greywinds Jack Frost–Ch. Norman's Easybrae Katie), bred by Norman LeBoeuf and owned by Ellen Grevatt and Mrs. Jack Billhardt. Both of these bitches dominated the show ring, each making breed history. Ch. Greywinds Phoebe Snow was #1 Weimaraner in 1993 and 1994 and broke the record for Best In Show wins, held by Ch. Val Knight Ranck, winning 14 Best In Shows. Ch. Greymists Silver Cloud won the National Specialty three times, was #1 Weimaraner in 1995 and ended her career by breaking Phoebe's record of 14 Best in Shows by winning 15 Best In Shows.

The latest entrants into the show scene are Ch. Ultima's Stetson V Huffmeister (Ch. Colsidex Nani Reprint–Ch. Ultima's Sadie Hawkins), bred by Ann Johnson and Ann Loop and owned by Tom and Teresa Hill, and Ch. Aria's Allegra of Colsidex (Ch. Colsidex Nani Follow A Dream–Ch. Top Hat's Aria), bred by Chris Buckley and Cheryl Orr and owned by me, together with Joyce Kealoha and Mrs. Elaine Meader. Ch. Ultima's Stetson V Huffmeister is a Futurity and Maturity winner, multiple Specialty and Group winner and 4 time Best In Show winner. He was #2 Weimaraner in 1995. Ch. Aria's Allegra of Colsidex finished her Championship with three five point majors including the National Specialty, won the 1995 Eastern Futurity and is currently the #1 Weimaraner with nine Best In Show wins to her credit.

Although there are many noteworthy dogs that I did not mention, the dogs that I have profiled are those who have had an impact on the breed. These dogs are the history makers and the dogs who, through the years, continue to have a positive influence on the breed. They remain in the pedigrees of the top winners and top producers because they were able to pass on to their offspring their ability to produce. The proof of this observation is in the Top Ten BROM List of Sires and Dams. In the past few years a Weimaraner winning Sporting Groups and Best In Shows is no longer exceptional. Our Weimaraners are now top contenders for these awards. The Sporting Group judges of today now look at the Weimaraner in the Group, thanks to those outstanding dogs of fifteen and twenty years ago who, by virtue of their remarkable quality, paved the way for future Weimaraners.

As a breeder it is important to be able to recognize the faults in your dogs and the virtues in other dogs. To know what a dog is is not as important as knowing what a dog produces. To breed outstanding dogs you have to know what the pedigree produces, what you need to improve, and then make your best educated decision. Above all, being honest and forthright in discussing any problems with your peers, is the key to preserving the quality and integrity of the breed. What the future hold for Weimaraners in America remains to be seen. However, the outstanding accomplishments of the past years, and the sincerity and integrity of the top breeders of today predict a successful future for the breed.

LEADING KENNELS

ARIMARLISA
Jackie Isabell & Lisa McClintock, Tempe, Arizona.
Jackie bred her first litter in 1968 under the Arimar kennel name. In 1983, Lisa McClintock and Jackie pooled their resources under the kennel name of ArimarLisa.

TOP DOGS
Ch. Halann's Schonste Madchen CD, NSD, NRD, V, BROM (Ch. Verdemars Von Bradford – Ch. Halanns Woodland Pixie BROM). 'Madchen', Jackie's foundation bitch, was Best Bitch in the 1967 Western Futurity and was locally famous for her hunting ability, especially her toughness and keen nose. She is the dam of eight Champions sired by Ch. Dougs Dauntless von Dor, and grandam of three Dual Champions.

Madchen's outstanding daughters include **Ch. Maribil's Firebrand von Arimar NSD, NRD, V, BROM** (Ch. Dougs Dauntless von Dor – Ch. Halanns Schonste Madchen): She was the foundation bitch of Maribils kennel, the dam of Dual Ch. Marbils Baron Von Josephus and seven other show Champions all sired by Ch. Archduke Von Brombachtal BROM.
Ch. Arimars Desert Dream SD, NRD, V (Ch. Dougs Dauntless von Dor – Ch. Halanns Schonste Madchen): 'Dream' was second in the 1972 Field Futurity and dam of **Ch. I've A Dream of Arimar**, Best Bitch in the 1976 Western Bench Futurity, who was a stud fee puppy sired by Dual Ch. Arimars Ivan.
Ch. Arimars Desert Diana NSD, BROM (Ch. Dougs Dauntless von Dor – Ch. Halanns Schonste Madchen): 'Diana' was Best Bitch in Futurity, had multiple Group placements and was the breed's first dam of two Dual Champions, both record holders. She was the dam of two other show Champions which included Futurity winner **Arimars Tana V Donar.** All of Diana's Champions were sired by the Dorilio son, Ch. Eichenhofs Ginger Man BROM.
Dual Ch. Arimars Lovely Lyric CD, NSD, VX, BROM (Ch. Eichenhof's Ginger Man – Ch. Arimars Desert Diana): 'Lyric' was the breed's youngest Dual Champion at 34 months of age. She was bred to Dual Ch. Halanns The Judge v Reiteralm and produced Dual Ch. Takusans Sonic Boom.
Dual Ch. Arimars Ivan CD, NSD, VX, BROM (Ch. Eichenhof's Ginger Man – Ch. Arimars Desert Diana): 'Ivan' was a multiple Specialty winner and won several Group placements. He was the first Dual Ch. to qualify for a BROM title. He was the sire of 23 Champions which included three Futurity winners.
Eng/NZ/Aust Ch. Arimars Rolf vd Reiteralm (Dual Ch. Ronamax Rufs vd Reiteralm – Ch. I've a Dream of Arimar): After completing his Championship and winning several Field Trial placements, 'Rolf' went to England en route to Australia. While in England he sired Eng Ch. Reeman Aruac. In Australia, Rolf was a leading sire with 61 Champions which included nine All Breed Best In Show Winners as well as winning field dogs.

Ch. Arimars Prelude to Arokat BROM (Ch. Colsidex Standing Ovation – Ch. I've A Dream of Arimar): 'Patty' was the foundation bitch for the Arokat kennels in Canada. She was an outstanding producer and when bred back to her sire, Ovation, she produced the top producer, Ch. Arokats Legionnaire.

Ch. Arimars Majestic Moriah BROM (Ch. Valmars Graf Schwenden – Eichenhofs Pecan Sandee): 'Moriah' was the foundation bitch of the Wustenwind kennels. She was the dam of the Top Producing BROM bitch, Ch. Valmars Serenade V Wustenwind, and granddam of BIS winners Ch. Valmars Pollyanna (sired by Ch. Sir Eric v Sieben) and Ch. Valmar Smokey City Ultra Easy (sired by Ch. Smokey City Easy Does It).

ArimarLisa's Reiteralm Falco VGP: A longhair who was donated to the German Weimaraner Club. In the 1989 Youth Trials he earned the highest score for Weimaraners and the second highest score of all breeds. He went on to earn Germany's most prestigious performance title – the VGP.

Ch. ArimarLisa's Rona v Reiteralm (Ch. Nani's Rudi Vallee vd Reiteralm – Ch. Reiteralms Hi Octane Emmy): The latest member of the kennel, 'Rona' finished with three five-point majors, including the 1996 National Specialty and was also Best Bitch in Futurity.

Both Jackie and Lisa consistently breed Weimaraners with the qualities of friendly, bold responsive temperaments, sound, healthy physical qualities and last, but by no means least, dogs with natural aptitudes for pointing, retrieving and tracking.

ARNSTADT
Elizabeth Raimen, Chicago, Illinois.
Arnstadt Weimaraners began in 1981. The Arnstadt name was taken from the birthplace of her mother in Germany, in the area which was formerly the Weimar Republic. Arnstadt in Germany is just a short distance from the town of Erfurt, birthplace of the Weimaraner Club of Germany.

Liz has been dedicated to demonstrating the versatility of the breed – 11 Weimaraners from the first three generations have achieved almost 100 titles in breed, obedience, tracking, field and temperament tests. All 11 are Champions and have achieved the Versatile Title awarded by the Weimaraner Club of America. Six of these have also earned the Versatile Excellent Title.

Ch. Arnstadts Wotan von Doblen.
Alex Smith Photography.

Ch. Arnstadts Class Act v Doblen.
Booth Photography.

TOP DOGS
Ch. Arnstadts Wotan von Doblen (Ch. Doblens Arnstadt Siegfried – Ch. Doblens ZZ Top Bad Girl): In addition to his Championship, 'Trooper' has earned a long list of titles: CD, TD, JH, NSD, SD, VX, CGC, TDI and TT.
Ch. Arnstadts Class Act v Doblen (Ch. Doblens Arnstadt Siegfried – Ch. Doblens ZZ Top Bad Girl): 'Girlie' has outdone her brother 'Trooper' earning the following titles: CD, TD, JH, NSD, SD, NRD, VX and CGC.

Liz feels that the strong natural instincts of the breed, if combined with an owner willing to provide sensible and consistent training – and the time and attention the dog demands – will provide an outstanding companion willing to work at any task.

BINGS
Jean White, Austin, Texas.
The first litter bred by Jean to carry the Bings prefix was whelped in 1966. In addition to showing in breed, Jean is also active in the obedience ring as well.

TOP DOGS
Ch. Bings Konsul von Krisdaunt CDX, BROM (Ch. Dougs Dauntless von Dor – Ch. Bings Krista II): 'Konsul' was in the Top Ten Breed and Top Ten Obedience, and also achieved a Highest Scoring Dog In Trial in Obedience. He was a multiple Group winner and was Best Opposite Sex at the National Specialty. He was the sire of 19 Champions.
Ch. Bings Galactica von Konsul CDX, NSD, NRD, BROM (Ch. Bings Konsul von Krisdaunt – Bac's Aurora Elisa): 'Galactica' was a Best of Breed and Group winner from the classes. Like her sire, she was on the Top Ten in both Breed and Obedience. She was the dam of 15 Champions which include two Futurity winners.
Ch. Bings Picante von Konsul CD, BROM (Ch. Bings Konsul von Krisdaunt – Bac's Aurora Elisa): 'Picante', sister of Galactica, is the dam of 10 Champions. The Top Producing Ch. Bings Razzmatazz von Konsul CD, BROM is the result of Picante bred back to her sire.

Ch. Bings Galactica von Konsul.

Ch. Bings Razzamajyk v Arnstadt.

*Ch. Bings
Razzmattazz
von Konsul.*

Ch. Bings Razzmatazz von Konsul CD, BROM (Ch. Bings Konsul von Krisdaunt – Ch. Bings Picante von Konsul): 'Razz' finished his Championship at 10 months of age and is the sire of 62 Champions, which include several Futurity winners. He is the result of a father to daughter breeding.

Ch. Bings Tatiana V Windsong NSD, NRD, V, BROM (Ch. Bings Razzmatazz von Konsul – Ch. Bings Galactica von Konsul): 'Tatiana' finished her Championship with a Best of Breed and Group I from the classes. She is the dam of 10 Champions which include a Best In Show winner.

Ch. Bings Southern Saga Del Oro CD, NSD, NRD, V, BROM (Ch. Bings Razzmatazz von Konsul – Ch. Reichenstadts Summer Magic): 'Saga' was in the Top Ten Breed and is the sire of 28 Champions which include Futurity and Maturity winners and a Best In Show winner.

Ch. Bings Razzberri V Winfield BROM (Ch. Bings Razzmatazz von Konsul – Ch. Bings Galatica von Konsul): Dam of five Champions.

Ch. Bings Southern Reign Von Rex NSD, NRD, V (Ch. Bings Southern Saga Del Oro – Ch. Bings Tatiana V Windsong): Top Ten Breed.

Ch. Bings Southern Sass CD, NSD, NRD, V (Ch. Bings Southern Saga Del Oro – Ch. Bings Tatiana V Windsong): All Breed Best In Show winner.

Ch. Bings Razzmajyk V Arnstadt CD, TD, NSD, NRD, VX, CGC (Ch. Bings Razzmatazz von Konsul – Ch. Doblens ZZ Top Bad Girl): Best In Futurity winner and All Breed High in Trial. She finished her Championship at 10 months.

. Although Jean breeds very sparingly – less than 25 litters since 1966 – over 100 Champions carry the Bings prefix. Jean's dogs have excelled in all areas – show ring, obedience ring, tracking and field and water ratings.

COLSIDEX
Judy Colan, Foster, Rhode Island.

Colsidex Weimaraners had very meagre beginnings in the early 1960s. A big, gray dog followed my brother home from school and I fell in love with him – although I had no idea what kind of dog he was. I called the dog officer who immediately said: "That's George Bailey's Weimaraner, he runs all over town. I'll be over to pick him up and take him home." Twenty minutes after he was picked up, the dog was back on the front porch. He refused to stay home and made the decision to live with people who appreciated him. After two months of his owner locking him up and the dog breaking out and coming to my house, I purchased him for $5 and a vacuum cleaner.

Ziegfried was intelligent but unruly. He had done exactly what he pleased his entire life and so he was enrolled in an obedience class. He went on to earn a CD and CDX obedience title, and kindled my interest in the breed. While attending dog shows and showing in obedience, I started watching Weimaraners in breed competition. I realized that the majority of dogs I liked were sired by Ch. Shadowmar Barthuas Dorilio. I met 'Dori' owner, Dorothy Remensnyder, who was a wealth of knowledge. She discussed pedigrees, anatomy, movement and shared her years of knowledge. Dorothy had a beautiful Dorilio daughter, **Shadowmar Winema von Elken**, who she had acquired at 12 months of age. The bitch had been brought up in a kennel and did not have a lot of self-confidence. Dorothy gave me the bitch, with the understanding that I would try to finish her. Although she was wonderful at home, great with children and loved to hunt, she would not show.

She was bred to her half-brother, sired by Dorilio, Ch. Dougs Dauntless von Dor, and this produced **Ch. Colsidex Dauntless Applause** (Ch. Dougs Dauntless von Dor – Shadowmar Winema von Elken), a multiple Specialty winner, BROM Top Producer and one of the first bitches elected to the Weimaraner Club of America Hall of Fame. 'Pixie' was the dam of 12 Champions, three Futurity winners, six BROM Top Producers and the breed's all-time top producing sire and multiple Best In Show winner, Ch. Colsidex Standing Ovation. Pixie is the #8 All Time Top Producing BROM dam.

TOP DOGS
Ch. Colsidex Standing Ovation (Ch. Seneca's Medicine Man – Ch. Colsidex Dauntless Applause): The product of an outcross of two inbred dogs. His dam, Applause, was the result of a half-brother, half-sister breeding on Ch. Shadowmar Barthaus Dorilio. His sire, Ch. Seneca's Medicine Man was the result of a half-brother, half-sister breeding on Ch. Durmar's Karl. Ovation was the best of both his sire and dam. He had the balanced conformation of his dam, and the showmanship and tail set of his sire. He won 5 Best In Shows (3 US and 2 Canada), was #1 Weimaraner in the US and Canada, and twice won the WCA National Specialty from the Veterans class. 'Joga' was a prepotent producer, the sire of three Best In Show winners, 28 Futurity winners, numerous Group winners and an unprecedented 147 Champions. He is the #1 All Time Top Producing BROM sire. Both Joga and Pixie had the wonderful easy-going, easy-to-live-with temperaments that I bred for when I used Ch. Shadowmar Barthaus Dorilio as the foundation of my breeding program. Joga was the first dog elected to the Weimaraner Club of America's Hall of Fame.

Ch. Colsidex The Farms Act One (Ch. Colsidex Standing Ovation – Ch. Colsidex Dauntless Applause): The result of breeding Ovation back to his dam 'Cinny' was a multiple Specialty and Group winner as well as a Best In Futurity winner. She was on the Top Ten for two years. Although bred only once, with only two puppies resulting, both finished their Championships, and her son, Ch. The Farms Country Aire, was a BROM Top Producer.

Ch. Colsidex Nani Reprint JH (Ch. Colsidex Standing Ovation – Ch. Nani's Cobbie Cuddler): 'Jack', out of Ovation's last litter, was Best Dog in Maturity, a multiple Specialty and Group winner and on the Top Ten for two years. He is the sire of over 50 Champions and 12 Futurity and Maturity winners, and a multiple Best In Show winner in the US. He is the #9 All Time Top Producing BROM sire. In Australia, Jack's frozen semen was used on Aust. Ch. Grauhund It N Abit. This produced five Champions, four multiple Best In Show winners and Australia's #1 Weimaraner, Ch. Grauhund Nite Moves, who was Best in Show at the Sydney Royal over an entry of 5,000.

Ch. Bryrwood The Farms Hotstreak (Ch. Colsidex Nani Reprint – Ch. The Farms Ride Sally Ride): Co-owned with Joyce Kealoha, 'Marie' was the result of half-brother, half-sister breeding on Ovation. She was a multiple Specialty winner and multiple Group winner, and was on the Top Ten for two years.

Ch. Colsidex Blueprint (Ch. Colsidex Nani Reprint – Ch. Nani's Colsidex Crosstalk): 'Carlos' finished his Championship in less than 10 shows with two 5 point majors, a 4 point major and a 3 point major. Shown occasionally as a Special, he is a Specialty winner and multiple Breed winner. His offspring have been doing extremely well, with many Specialty winning and Group winning get to his credit.

Ch. Aria's Allegra of Colsidex (Ch. Colsidex Nani Follow A Dream – Ch. Top Hat's Spitfire): The latest member of Colsidex, 'Fergie' was a stud fee puppy sired by a Joga frozen semen son. She finished her Championship with three 5 point Specialty wins, including the WCA National Specialty. She is a multiple Best In Show winner (13 Best In Shows) Specialty and Group winner and was Best Bitch in the Eastern Futurity. She is currently the #1 Weimaraner and in the Top Ten Sporting Dogs and Top Ten All Breed Dogs.

Although I do not breed often – usually one litter a year – I feel that temperament and type are of the utmost importance, and this is what I strive for in my breeding program.

NANI'S
Christine & Ted Grissell, Fairland, Indiana.

Nani's was established in 1971 with its first litter of 13 puppies out of a bitch Chris and her first husband, Smokey Medeiros, had acquired while in Hawaii. Four Champions resulted from this first litter. One of these, **Ch. Nani's Silver Sparkle**, was bred to Ch. Maxmillian vd Reiteralm and produced **Ch. Nani's Ariana vd Reiteralm BROM**. 'Ariana' was bred to the Dauntless son, Ch. Brandy's Rebel vd Reiteralm, and produced 13 Champions.

TOP DOGS

Ch. Nani's Soul Sensation BROM (Ch. Brandys Rebel vd Reiteralm – Ch. Nani's Ariana vd Reiteralm): 'Bertha' was ranked on the Top Ten for two years. She was bred to Ch. Ann's Magic vd Reiteralm twice and was the dam of 12 Champions, which include a Maturity winner and the Top Producer, Ch. Nani's Cascade vd Reiteralm BROM.

Ch. Nani's Soul Sister BROM (Ch. Brandys Rebel vd Reiteralm – Ch. Nani's Ariana vd Reiteralm): 'Sisi' finished her Championship winning Best Breeds over Specials. She was then bred to Ch. Nani's Silver Slate and produced three Champions out of this breeding. Bred to Ch.

Reiteralms Rio Fonte Saudade BROM, she produced six Champions which include the breed's youngest Best In Show winner, Ch. Nani's Visa vd Reiteralm BROM, Ch. Nani's Master Charge BROM #1 Weimaraner in 1982. Ch. Nani's Cartel who was in the Top Ten, Ch. Nani's Carte Blanche BROM, a multiple Group winner and Specialty winner, Ch. Nani's Ann of Enchantment BROM and Nani's Spirit-O-Moonshine BROM.

Ch. Nani's Cascade vd Reiteralm BROM (Ch. Ann's Magic vd Reiteralm – Ch. Nani's Soul Sensation): 'Cadey' finished her Championship with two 5 point majors at Specialty shows. She was the dam of 12 Champions which included two BROM producers, Ch. Nani's Cobbie Cuddler and Ch. Nanis Ananas of Silvermont. **Ch. Nani's Visa vd Reiteralm BROM** (Ch. Reiteralms Rio Fonte Saudade – Ch. Nani's Soul Sister): Visa was the #1 Weimaraner in 1980 & 1981. She was the youngest to achieve a Best In Show win at nine months of age from the Puppy Class and retired with a total of five Best In Shows to her credit and was also a Futurity winner. She was bred to Ch. Colsidex Standing Ovation and produced nine Champions which included Futurity and Best In Show winner Ch. Nani's Hawaiian Punch BROM, Futurity winner Ch. Nani's Colsidex Hula Cooler NRD, SDX and Maturity winner Ch. Nani's Apple Sass BROM. Visa was one of the first bitches elected to the Weimaraner Club of America Hall of Fame.

Ch. Nani's Cobbie Cuddler BROM (Ch. Nani's Master Charge – Ch. Nani's Cascade vd Reiteralm): 'Cuddles' finished her Championship with two 5 point majors at Specialty Shows. She was bred to Ch. Colsidex Standing Ovation and produced 15 Champions sired by Ovation. These Champions include Futurity winner Ch. Nani's Scirroco of Mattrace BROM, and four Maturity winners – Ch. Nani's Island Breeze, Ch. Nani's Valley Girl, Ch. Nani's Kona Gust BROM and Ch. Colsidex Nani's Reprint BROM. Ch. Nani's Totally Awesome BROM went to New Zealand and has been a very influential sire there. Three of Cuddles' offspring, Scirroco, Kona Gust and Reprint, are the sires of Best In Show Winners. Cuddles was inducted into the Weimaraner Club of America Hall of Fame in 1996.

Ch. Nani's Southern Cross BROM (Ch. Arokats Legionnaire – Ch. Forshadow Nani's Crystal Vision): 'Cross' was the youngest National Specialty Best of Breed winner in 1989. He has been an outstanding producer and has sired over 50 Champions who have distinguished themselves by winning Specialty Shows. He is also the sire of a Best In Show winner.

Nani's has had dogs in the Top Ten consistently since 1973. All the present-day Nani's dogs trace directly back to Chris's foundation bitch, Ariana. Chris has become active in AKC Hunting Tests and has put Junior Hunter titles on many of her dogs.

SILVERSMITH
Alan & Elena Smith, Johns Island, South Carolina.
Allen and Elena got their first Weimaraner in 1976 as a pet. In 1979 they purchased their foundation bitch **Ch. Wismars April Silversmith BROM**. In addition to finishing her Championship, April proved her versatility by earning a CDX degree in obedience, a TD degree in tracking and an RD degree in retrieving and qualified for the Weimaraner Club of America Versatility title. She is the dam of six Champions which include a Futurity winner and a Top Ten Obedience bitch.

TOP DOGS
Ch. Silversmith Omni V Reiteralm BROM (Ch. Reiteralms Rio Fonte Saudade – Ch. Robins Song vd Reiteralm): This dog has produced 14 Champions which include the multiple Best In Show winner, Ch. Silversmith Dawn V Greystoke, and several Futurity and Maturity winners.

'Feebee' has produced two FCI International Champions, one of which is the only American Champion to win All Breed Best In Show in Germany, Int. Ch. Silversmith Harbor Pistol.
Ch. Silversmith Pazlee Greystoke BROM: This is the Smiths' current Top Producing bitch. She has produced seven Champions out of her first two litters, one sired by Ch. Nani's Sanbar Ringside Rumor BROM and the other by Ch. Camelots Matinee Idol BROM.

The Smiths, both AKC Hunting Test Judges, are keenly interested in field work. They owned, trained and campaigned in the field **Field Ch. Weicks Tidewater Silversmith**. This dog has earned 13 titles in field, obedience and retrieving, and was ranked in the Top Ten Field and Top Ten Obedience Weimaraners. 'Tide' has sired a several dogs with Hunting Test titles including two Master Hunters, a title which is very difficult to achieve. The Smiths strive to produce dogs that are sound, friendly, family companions, who are competitive in both the show ring and in the field.
VALMAR
Joan Valdez, Rolling Hills Estates, California.
Valmar originated in Southern California in 1965 when Joan acquired her foundation bitch, Ch. Von Gaibergs Anna Schwenden. Anna was an outstanding bitch and was strongly line bred on the Von Gaiberg line. She was bred to Ch. Dougs Dauntless von Dor and produced six Champions: Elke, Eclipse, Exa, Graf, Greco and Grafin. All the Valmar dogs descend from these dogs.

Ch. Valmars Jazzman CD, NRD, NSD, V, BROM (Ch. Valmars Chancelor V Starbuck – Ch. Valmars Elke Schwenden): 'Jazz' was a National Specialty Winner, Top Ten Breed for three years, and a Top Producer siring 75 Champions including the Dual Champion, Valmars Valiant Knight.
Ch. Valmars Pollyanna BROM (Ch. Sir Eric von Sieben – Ch. Valmars Serenade v Wustenwind): 'Polly' was on the Top Ten for five years, Futurity and Maturity Winner and #1 Weimaraner in 1985. She was the winner of three All Breed Best In Shows and holds the record for a Weimaraner defeating the most dogs in one year – over 16,000. She came out of retirement won the National Specialty. She is the dam of 10 Champions including the Dual Champion, Valmars Valiant Knight.
Dual Ch. Valmars Valiant Knight, CD, NRD, VX, BROM (Ch. Valmars Jazzman – Ch. Valmars Pollyanna): 'Val' was ranked on both the Top Ten Show and Field lists. He is the sire of 25 Champions as well as a Futurity winner.
Ch. Valmars Evening Sonata BROM (Ch. Bama Belles Mountain Man – Ch. Valmars Pollyanna): Sonata was Best Bitch in Futurity and was a multiple Breed winner and Group placer. She is the dam of 11 Champions.
Ch. Valmars Yours Truly BROM (Ch. Valmars Jazzman – Ch. Valmars Serendipity): 'True' was #1 Weimaraner in 1988.
Ch. Valmars Serenade v Wustenwind BROM (Ch. Valmars Jazzman – Ch. Arimars Majestic Moriah) #1 BROM bitch, dam of nine Champions which include two Best In Show winners.
Ch. Valmars Sage V Wustenwind (Ch. Valmars EZ Jazz Time – Ch. Valmars Top Flight): 1995 Futurity Winner, Sporting Group winner.

Valmar has had many great dogs, and Joan is justifiably proud of the outstanding dogs she has produced. They have excelled in all areas; Breed, Futurity, Maturity, Field, WCA Rating, Obedience and BROM producers.

WEIMARANER BREEDERS DIRECTORY

WEST MIDLANDS
RANGATIRA
Mr & Mrs CM Brown
Picton House, Brookside, Myddle, nr Shrewsbury,
Shropshire SY4 3RP
Tel 01939 291191
Puppies occasionally for sale.

LONDON & HOME COUNTIES
PLUSILA
Dr Leon & Mrs Suzanne Walkden
1 Parkside, Hampton Hill, Middlesex TW12 1NU.
Tel 0181 943 3673
Puppies occasionally for sale.

IRELAND
HUNTLY
Morag Hay
Drogheda Road, Togher, Co Louth, Eire.
Tel & Fax 041 52052
Dogs at stud. Puppies occasionally for sale.
Borading facilities available.

SOUTH WEST
GAMEPOINT
Mrs JM Turner
The Old Vicarage, Bishopswood, Chard,
Somerset TA20 3RS
Tel 01460 234336. Fax 01460 234679
Email 100600.3415@compuserve.com
Puppies occasionally for sale.

HOLLIESEAST
Mr & Mrs K Robinson
Mulberry House, Quaker Row, Coates,
Cirencester, Glos. GL7 6JX.
Tel 01285 770070
Puppies occasionally for sale.

NORTH EAST
ARDENSTORM
John & Hazel Abraham
17 Arden Close, Hadrian Park, Wallsend,
Tyne & Wear NE28 9YB.
Tel 0191 295 0498
Puppies occasionally for sale.

CATRUANE
Miss CR & Mrs A Longbottom
9 Beacon Grove, Bradford, W. Yorks BD6 3EB.
Tel 01423 865476
Dogs at stud. Puppies occasionally for sale.

GUNALT
Patsy Hollings, Church House, Carlton Yeadon,
nr Leeds, W. Yorks LS19 7BD.
Tel 011325 05113
Dogs at stud. Puppies occasionally for sale.

NORTH WEST
AMTRAK
Mrs M Brennan
2 Lowood Grove, Lea, Preston, Lancs. PR2 1RL.
Tel 01772 731849
Puppies occasionally for sale.

BANKFIELD
Pat Caine
Bankwood Farm, 98 Long Lane, Charlesworth,
Derbyshire SK14 6ES.
Tel 01457 854903
Dogs at stud. Puppies occasionally for sale.

ORMEROD
Mrs PF Brooks
Sagar Wood, Birdy Brow, Chaigley, nr Clitheroe,
Lancs. BB7 3LR.
Tel 01254 826239
Dogs at stud. Puppies occasionally for sale.